FREE SPIRIT

Growing Up On the Road
and *Off the Grid*

FREE SPIRIT

JOSHUA SAFRAN

HYPERION
NEW YORK

Note to Reader: Some of the names and identifying characteristics of persons written about in this book have been changed due to privacy concerns. Some of the dialogue in this book may have been re-created, as my recollections are not always exact or complete, and may not reflect exact language exchanged at the time. My intent is to allow the reader to understand the circumstances and experience the moments in which those discussions took place. I have done my best to accurately portray my memory of the conversations.

Printed in the United States of America. For information address Hyperion, 1500 Broadway, New York, New York 10036.

Library of Congress Cataloging-in-Publication Data

Safran, Joshua.
Free spirit : growing up on the road and off the grid / Joshua Safran. — First edition.
pages cm
ISBN 978-1-4013-2460-5
1. Safran, Joshua—Childhood and youth. 2. Safran, Joshua—Family. 3. Safran, Joshua—Travel—United States. 4. Coming of age—United States—Case studies. 5. Mothers and sons—United States—Case studies. 6. Children of abused wives—United States—Biography. 7. Family violence—United States—Case studies. 8. Counterculture—United States—Case studies. 9. San Francisco (Calif.)—Biography. I. Title.
CT275.S255A3 2013
979.4'61054092—dc23
[B]
2013008467

Design by Susan Walsh

FIRST EDITION

10 9 8 7 6 5 4 3 2 1

THIS LABEL APPLIES TO TEXT STOCK

We try to produce the most beautiful books possible, and we are also extremely concerned about the impact of our manufacturing process on the forests of the world and the environment as a whole. Accordingly, we've made sure that all of the paper we use has been certified as coming from forests that are managed, to ensure the protection of the people and wildlife dependent upon them.

FOR THE SAFRAN WOMEN

To Leah: I once learned in the Talmud that not even a blade of grass would grow were it not for its own special angel, hovering over it, whispering Grow!—Grow! *You are my own special angel. I aspire to be yours.*

To E, K, and S: Your shining faces make it all worth it. Someday soon you will be old enough to read this book. When you do, you will know me better. And yourselves too.

CONTENTS

FREE SPIRIT

PROLOGUE

Saigon Moses

By the time I was ten I had hitchhiked for thousands of miles and befriended hundreds of remarkably strange people. My mother and I had danced around bonfires and lived in vans, buses, and an ice cream truck. Some nights we slept blissfully under the stars, others I lay awake frightened by the howling of wolves. Fear was commonplace, part of the *will you kidnap me or won't you* calculation inherent in every hitched ride.

I was familiar with fear, but not like this. The repeated doses of terror and the pervasive dread were new forms of craziness, imported into the wilds of Skagit County, Washington, by my mother's latest boyfriend, Leopoldo. He was a former Central American guerrilla fighter and brought with him demons from the Salvadoran civil war and a serious drinking problem. My mother was convinced he was the messianic revolutionary hero she had foretold in clairvoyant visions. I was pretty sure he was going to kill us.

From where I stood, shivering at the gas pump in my frayed thrift store sweater, survival was now a matter of statistics. Even if he didn't murder us outright, how many nights in a row could we race up Cultus Mountain with Leopoldo behind the wheel before our luck ran out? I stamped my feet to keep my toes from going numb and tried to steel myself for the impending drunk drive up the mountain. Home, for now, was up there at the end of a long, muddy trail. A tiny wood-plank cabin with no electricity or running water.

My mother sat cross-legged in the passenger seat of the car. Through the frost on the window, her face looked like a jagged mosaic, one eye refracted into shining shards of silver in the moonlight, the other lost in darkness. I could tell she was meditating, trying to use her imagined third eye to heal her real eyes, blackened for looking at other men. Leopoldo had punched her in the face a few nights back, part of the same jealous rage that left an ugly hole in the back window of our Chevy Citation. I could hear my mother chanting now as she slowly raised her palms into the air to psychically summon blue energy to protect us.

I shook my head and clenched the icy handle of the gas nozzle with both hands. The numbers on the rusting pump spun upward with an antiquated whirr. Leopoldo was supposed to be paying for the gas inside but, since he was savagely drunk, it was just as likely that he was practicing his kung fu on an aisle of snack food. Or lighting something on fire. I kept looking back at the little store, half expecting the building to burst into flames. A moment later Leopoldo's bulky silhouette darkened the doorway, and I watched him walk face-first into the glass door. He rattled himself against the glass like a giant angry moth until he figured out that he had to *pull* the door open.

Leopoldo staggered out into the night, his arms brimming with colorful merchandise. A fat white woman followed him out. "Hey, you gotta pay for those," she called after him halfheartedly. She was dutifully fulfilling some step on her theft prevention checklist. The last thing she wanted was further contact with the raggedy reincarnation of Che Guevara who had just spent the last five minutes screaming at her from under his red headband about her complicity in American war crimes.

"Josh!" Leopoldo yelled at me as he stumbled forward, lighters and plastic ice scrapers tumbling out of his arms. "Get the fuck in the car!" He liked to shoplift the shiny little things they stocked up front by the cash register. It was impulse theft. From past experience, I knew the crime was technically called petty larceny. And I knew that once he hit five hundred dollars it was called grand larceny. As I scrambled into the backseat, I wondered why he never larcened any candy. That, at least, I could forgive.

"Josh, get fucking in!" Leopoldo yelled.

"I'm already in," I said between chattering teeth. I couldn't tell whether I was shaking from the cold or from fear, or both.

We churned through the gravel parking lot and launched onto Highway 9 North. Around the next corner, Leopoldo began weaving between lanes. "That woman, she calling to the *policía*!" he shouted, killing the headlights so the cops wouldn't be able to see him. "She dirty fucking *pinche* whore!"

"She was *just* doing her *job*, Leopoldo." My mother spoke at him with the slow intensity of an animal trainer trying to reason with a gorilla who had just ripped the door off his cage. "Leopoldo, *way* too fast." She braced herself with one hand on the dashboard. "You've *gotta* slow down!"

He sped up.

The flicker of some distant light in the rearview mirror unleashed a powerful wave of paranoia, and Leopoldo began screaming: "*¡La policía!* They following us!" The engine revved into an unhealthy roar, and we were thrown back into our seats as Leopoldo tried to break land speed records in our rundown Chevy. He was still ranting about the CIA and secret cameras in the woods when we reached the straightaway before Clear Lake. With no curves to worry about, the needle of the speedometer disappeared in the shadows, and the car began to tremble and buck.

Blind drunk as he was, Leopoldo still spotted the Old Day Creek turnoff. He yanked the wheel hard, and we went spinning across the road, over the graveled shoulder, and through a small grassy field. As we pulled out of our nauseating spin, I clawed at the seat, trying to regain control over my roiling innards. The car whined, and the wheels tore desperately at grass and mud, and then we found traction and charged back onto the roadway.

This was the part of the ride I had been dreading. At the mouth of the forest, the road narrowed and wound its way up the side of the dark mountain for three long, fragile miles. The roadway was slick with rain and slush, and the curves leaping out of the darkness were sudden and sharp. All it took was one errant little tug at the wheel, and we would be plummeting down the precipice to the unforgiving rocks below.

Leopoldo had forgotten about the CIA and was now screaming at my mother: "You cheating on me! You fuck José! You fuck the other mens!" As his paranoia blossomed into fury, he wrenched the car back and forth across both lanes. Each time he dipped the wheel a little further into the narrow shoulder at the edge of the cliff, flirting with the promise of sudden death.

My mother had completely abandoned any pretense of control. Now she was shielding her face with her arms as we hurtled around each curve and shrieking: "Pull over! Stop, stop! Please!"

I had been on Mr. Leopoldo's Wild Ride before, and I knew there was no use in yelling at him. Panic and chaos only excited him, and each new danger propelled him faster forward toward some inevitable climax of fire and death. I took deep breaths and struggled to control the hysteria building up inside of me; I had to accept that there was no safe way out of this. He wasn't going to slow down, and the car was moving too fast to jump out.

The seat-belt buckle was missing in the backseat, so I knotted the two lengths of belt together as best I could and closed my eyes. It was time to pray, but I didn't know which higher power to call upon. My mother's Spirits and Mother Earth and Gaia reeked too much of moss and marijuana. The hell-obsessed Jesus that the trailer park kids taunted me with was too scary. And the elephant-headed Ganesha that my Mexican-American "Uncle" Tony worshiped was too silly. Yet I sensed that there was something out there. An omnipotent being who ruled the entire universe and also, somehow, cared about me personally. I had taken to calling him Edward because the name sounded so regal and exotic.

I knew revelation waited around the next corner, and it was to Edward that I now directed my prayers for an easy landing. The Janicki Road cutoff would require a hard right and, at the speed we were going, only a miracle would keep us from flying off the road. This left two possible outcomes: hurtling off the cliff or hitting a muddy ditch at 45 m.p.h.

I gripped my surrogate seat belt and braced for impact. A moment later Leopoldo stomped on the brake pedal with both feet, and a hideous screeching tore at my ears. My head snapped to the left, and a terrible force spun the world around me. An alien scream involuntarily poured out of my mouth.

When I opened my eyes, I saw that someone had answered my prayers. Against all odds, we were still on the road, sliding slowly forward. Leopoldo was cursing wildly in Spanish, slapping at the gear shift. My mother was looking back at me, screaming something. My head was still spinning, and I couldn't make out the words. The engine revved, and we began to surge forward again.

"Get out of the car, Joshey! Jump!" my mother was screaming. "Jump, Joshey, jump!"

This was the most sense she had made in months. Nothing could be worse than another minute with Comandante Leopoldo at the wheel. I pulled the seat belt apart in one tug, popped the door handle, and leapt into a rush of cold, wet air. The bushes came at me sideways, cracking and crunching. I plunged into an endless thicket, every branch in the forest whipping past my head. And then I came to a stop in a clump of slimy ferns. The forest floor smelled like old bread.

I pulled myself up and climbed back onto the roadway slowly, flexing my limbs as I went, checking myself for damage. One pant leg was torn up to the knee, and my skin burned and stung here and there, but nothing was broken.

The darkness was punctuated by the red glare of taillights ahead of me. My mother was standing in the middle of the road, yelling back into the idling car: "No! Then, you let *me* drive! No!"

Leopoldo finally gave up on her, and the car lurched forward, fishtailing down the road and out of sight.

"Are you OK?" my mother asked me as I limped up to her. She looked like she was going to cry.

"Yeah, I'm fine," I said. And I meant it. Things could have been so much worse.

My mother ran her fingers over a dozen little scratches on my face and nodded. "You're OK," she said, and then she shrugged. "Leopoldo gets like this sometimes when he drinks." We walked down the road together, the frozen mud crunching under our feet. Dark walls of forest framed our narrow horizon. After a time it started snowing. Soft little flakes that blanketed the ground before us, muffling our footfalls. We walked together in complete silence like the only people left on Earth.

Every journey seemed to end this way—the two of us wandering through the silent forest out beyond the perimeter of human civilization. When I was younger, our sojourns in the woods had been mysterious expeditions, carrying the promise of adventure. But now I knew there were alternate realities, and I wanted what most other ten-year-old kids in America already had: a cozy house, school, running water, television, candy. Instead, I was limping through the snow with nothing but a couple of carob chips in my pocket.

Whenever I peeled away the layers of cause and effect that brought me into the wilderness, I always came back to Saigon. That faraway, long ago city stood at the center of the strange circumstances that conspired to deprive me of everything normal.

I was nothing more than a fetus gestating inside my mother's womb on April 30, 1975, but that day would determine the course of my entire life. My mother told me she stood pregnant and crying on the back porch of the commune in the Haight-Ashbury. In the distance she recognized howls of celebration, the resonant throbbing of drums, and the wail of police sirens. The breeze carried hints of tear gas and hashish and rustled the newspaper laid out before her. The headlines cried out: SAIGON GIAI PHONG! SAIGON HAS FALLEN!

The war was over. It was *really* over. The end of dreams and nightmares all at once. My mother cried tears of joy for the People of Vietnam. The warrior poets, the peasant soldiers, the mothers nursing their babies in one arm

Claudia, circa 1968. Revolution was in the air.

and cradling their AK-47s in the other. They had done it! They had defeated the American army—the greatest killing machine that capitalist greed had ever assembled. But she also cried tears of bitterness because the Revolution had failed. What, she wondered, would become of New America now? The post-Revolution America where barter would replace money, where cooperation would trump competition, where love would cure hatred. Did it still have a chance?

My mother had seen the writing on the wall early on and dropped out of college in 1963, before she finished her freshman year. In New America, she believed, a university degree would be meaningless. In New America, it would be experiences that mattered. And she experienced it all. She lived without money or possessions. She transformed sex into the making of love. She focused with marijuana and visioned with peyote. She expanded her consciousness with LSD, experiencing the brilliant purple revelation that we are all part of a river of flowing electrons.

Imbibing the brilliant flares of energy emanating from his saxophone one night, my mother met Frankie. He was a black revolutionary jazz musician, and she joined his struggle in the Struggle. They were married, and she passed for mulatto in the ghettos of New Haven. They set the night on fire, and when the FBI and the Draft caught up with them, they fled north to Canada. When the marriage fell apart, my mother returned alone to fight. Vietnam was but one battlefield in the Revolution, and she served zealously on the Home Front.

She took to the streets, she organized, and she marched. She built barricades, commanding men twice her size: "You! With the headband, get the front bumper! And you with the feathers, get around back! Let's move this VW into the street to block the cops!" She grappled with the police, seeing blood spray from the flowered heads of brothers and sisters, and she screamed: "What are you *doing*!? *What are you doing!?*" She was clubbed and tear-gassed. She was chased and arrested and made free again. She gladly tasted blood in her mouth, confident that blood must flow in the birth of a nation.

Out West, the Revolution was already manifest. "Sister, we ain't no more the counter-culture; we is . . . the Culture." My mother was part of the rising tide that flowed out to San Francisco in the Summer of Love. Walking down Haight Street, she saw that New America was already born, waving the flag of a thousand tapestries. Her citizens gathered and whirled and danced to a rainbow harmony. Sandalwood and patchouli wafted through the air. The street corners called out poetry. Arm bangles jangled to the bleating of tablas and the lowing of *djimbes*. In the park, the Dream Weaver sat on a blanket next to the man bartering bolts of cloth from the Orient next to the man in the dashiki dispensing fucks.

In San Francisco, the Revolution was being actualized. It was the tip of the spear, and from here they would pierce the heart of the Establishment. The liberation army started with ragtag groups of skittish draft-dodgers. As they took to the streets they became draft-resisters—full of fight, but untrained. Then *they* came: the veterans. The Vietnam Veterans Against the War came back with combat skills and discipline. They electrified the crowds. "Ten hut! Company, march!" Fists in the air. My mother told me bedtime stories about the jolt that ran through the protestors the first time the sudden cadence of the march locked them into great, roaring unison: *"¡El pueblo unido, jamás será vencido!"* The crowds swelled and grew and grew until their words finally appeared true: The people united would never be defeated.

But that all depended on the Draft. Selective Service brought the brutality of American imperialism to every doorstep in America. With each son or brother sentenced to kill and die on some unnamed jungled track in Southeast Asia, another American family was forced to rise from its slumber and choose sides. Faced with imminent death and exploitation in the Old America, who wouldn't choose New America?

But with the fall of Saigon, my mother knew the American people would lose their endurance for the Struggle. They wouldn't fight if they could watch TV. After Vietnam, the government would be striking back harder than ever. My mother had already seen the paramilitary crackdowns in the streets of New Haven. She had witnessed the decimation of the ghettos by the CIA, introducing heroin like poisoned candy. Some stranger nobody knew, smiling: "Hey, Brother, this first one's free, on me." Now it was happening in San Francisco, too. My mother told me the CIA was bringing in hard stuff: cocaine, PCP, heroin. At the same time, the cops were busting the counter-culturals for possession of marijuana. The landlords were raising the rents. The downtown shops were selling "tie-dye" shirts retail, and "revolution" was starting to be used by the advertising firms. The hippie-dippies were trickling back to work. My mother could feel the tide ebbing beneath her feet.

On the back porch of the San Francisco commune, she accepted the fact that New America wasn't happening any time soon. The writing on the wall wasn't prophecy, it was just graffiti.

Now she had to decide. Would she crawl back to mainstream society on her hands and knees? Or would she take to the hills to keep the Struggle alive? It was an easy decision—one was perfidious surrender, the other was dignified retreat. She looked to the hills, thinking not only of herself, but of me, her unborn child. No child of hers would grow up on a diet of artificial ingredients and capitalist lies. If the baby were born a boy, my mother knew that it would be only a matter of time until the Man came to take him away from her to serve in the next Draft, to die for a lie in the next war. As the sun set on the end of the world, my mother began to envision a new beginning somewhere under the North Star. A promised land where the System wouldn't find us. We would be the guardians of the resistance, ready and waiting to lead the People when they rose up in the next Revolution.

With the death of the old dream, a new dream was born. My mother stood on that redwood porch at the commune like Moses on the far side of the Red Sea, realizing that the destruction of Pharaoh's army wasn't going to lead to a New Egypt. No, it was time to wander through the wilderness in search of a new home.

I wasn't there the day Saigon fell but—like the Israelite children born in the Sinai—my entire childhood was a reaction to a formative day I couldn't remember. I sojourned from place to place, lamenting the loss of a New America that had never been, running from a society I had never known, and searching for a promised land I would never recognize. Along the way, our journey would keep us on the road, off the grid, and far from normal.

As my mother and I trudged through the woods on Cultus Mountain, a chorus of yips and yelps cut through the night. I smiled to myself. When I was younger, I would have mistaken the howling for wolves. But I could tell from the high staccato voices that they were only coyotes. You could scare off a whole pack of coyotes with a big stick.

Another mile or so up the mountain, the snow began to come down thick and heavy. I started mumbling a Bob Marley song to give myself strength: "The sun shall not smite I by day, nor the moon by night . . ."

If he hadn't driven off a cliff already, Leopoldo was probably home by now, waiting for us. But I wasn't worried about him just yet. My focus now was on getting home without freezing to death. We still had a few more miles to go, and my thrift store sweater was already stiffened with frost. My left shin was swollen and throbbing, and I was limping.

From atop the next ridge, a new set of howls went up, deeper and longer, like a gathering storm. Now *those,* I said to myself, were wolves.

ONE

Parental Truths

"At your birth . . ." my mother would sing to me, "the room was lit only by candles."

It was always: *at your birth*. It was never: *when you were born*, because everyone went around getting born. That was routine, just the normal prerequisite for admission into our world. But *at your birth* meant that the beginning of my life was an event. Something unique. Something unlike anything the world had ever seen before.

We lived in San Francisco when I was three and four years old, and every day ended with my mother leaning over me, gesticulating slowly with gentle sweeps of her hands and soothing me to sleep with a wondrous tale. She chanted with reverence and awe, speaking to me of my own birth as Paul must have conjured up the Nativity for his rapt listeners.

"At your birth, the room was lit only by candles. We were in the commune on Ashbury Street. The room was soft and warm." Her hands descended, fingers extending, to illustrate warmth. "You were born into a pool of warm water. From the waters within me you flowed into the waters without. The witches"—there was always a coven of witches in my birth story—"they saw that you were wearing a caul, the bag of waters, as a hat. And they knew right away that you were strong with magic. And they did your chart right there." It was always important that they did my astrological chart exactly at that moment, so they could capture the precise positioning of the celestial deities. "And they said that your sun sign was Sagittarius. And then they saw that your *moon* sign was Sagittarius. And then they saw . . . they saw that your *rising* sign was Sagittarius! Triple Sagittarius!" I had no idea what this meant, but three of something was clearly better than one. My mother gave a long pause, allowing the witches time to decipher the mystery of the constellations. "And then they made a prophecy that you would grow up to be a warlock! A holy man surrounded by followers."

The story always went more or less like this. Usually Uncle Tony, our housemate from the commune, made an appearance. Sometimes I was serenaded into the world by a *shakuhachi* flute player sitting cross-legged in the corner. Other times a birth coach and a midwife featured prominently. One version of my birth story included a dramatic flourish where one of the witches held me up for all to see. My fervent, forceful cries punctuated the silent room. That was when my mother knew that I would be called Joshua. Like my namesake, she told me, I would use the power of my voice to break down the walls.

My mother enjoyed reciting the story as much as I loved hearing it. She carried it with her wherever we went, telling it to me in the line at the Welfare office or while waiting to hitch a ride by the side of the road. But mostly she told it to me at bedtime. I heard the story so many times that I began "remembering" my own birth, as if I had been one of the spectators, wedged in somewhere between the coven of witches and the flute player. Under drowsy eyelids, I imagined myself emerging golden and glowing into the candlelit chamber of expectant priestesses.

And then, one Sunday in Golden Gate Park, Uncle Tony ruined my tale of sacred beginnings. We were feeding the buffalo, which Tony told me were really American bison, and Tony mused: "I'm glad you were born a boy."

"Why?" I asked, shoveling more alfalfa through the chain-link fence.

"You were supposed to be a girl."

"I was?"

"Yeah, the witches did their magic and they went around telling everyone you were going to be a little witchling. When you were born, one of the witches held you up and said: 'Oh, it's a . . . well, she's a boy.'

"All the witches started yelling: 'What!? How can you tell?'

"And the head witch said: 'She's got a penis.'

"And they said: 'Are you sure? Check again.' "

When I got home, the canon crumbled. My mother admitted that I was supposed to be a girl. She told me that if I had followed the plan, she would have named me Rivka Paloma Tabei. *Rivka* for my great-great-grandmother, a folk healer in the Old Country. *Paloma*, the Spanish word for dove, the bird of peace. And *Tabei* for the first woman who climbed Mount Everest. When I defied expectations and emerged in the form of a man-child, she pulled biblical names like Benjamin and Joshua out of the air. In the end she went with Joshua because I was loud.

I went to bed that night without wanting to hear my birth story, pouting into the darkness at the unfairness of it all. I had no namesake, no middle name, no illustrious backstories. I should have been born a girl. But then a hopeful thought came to me. Even though I was a boy, maybe I could still grow up to be a woman.

My dreams of being a woman were partly the product of my feminist schooling. My mother's circle of lesbian witches believed that *wymyn* were created in the image of the Goddess, while the human male was cast down the evolutionary ladder to a lowly rung somewhere between apes and amorphous, predatory lumps of meat. But my womanly aspirations were also influenced by the faces I saw around me. So many women crowded my view that I hardly even knew what a man looked like. And the one man whose face should have been most familiar lived only in my imagination. My father was just another character in my mother's stories, a minor part of my creation myth.

My mother, Claudia, met my father, Claude, in a San Francisco poetry workshop in 1974. They shared the same name, like some strange spell that was destined to bring them together, but were otherwise total opposites. Claudia walked through the door hoarse from heckling the North Beach poets for being a bunch of sexists. She looked like a thin, Semitic Janis Joplin. Torn purple bell-bottoms, sandals from the free box, a shirt she had made out of a bedspread. Across the room was Claude, radiating the blond-haired, blue-eyed dynamism of a surfer just toweled off from a day spent riding the waves.

As soon as they met, the two of them began matching each other poem for poem. The themes, feelings, and images from their poems meshed perfectly as they volleyed back and forth in a poetical duet. Night after night, the Claude and Claudia show became a fixture of the poetry workshop. During that time, my mother wrote of my father:

Claude is a very beautiful man/angel
brought up on California
sunshine acid - turned on
his entire family and continues
his search as i less and
less drug but high always

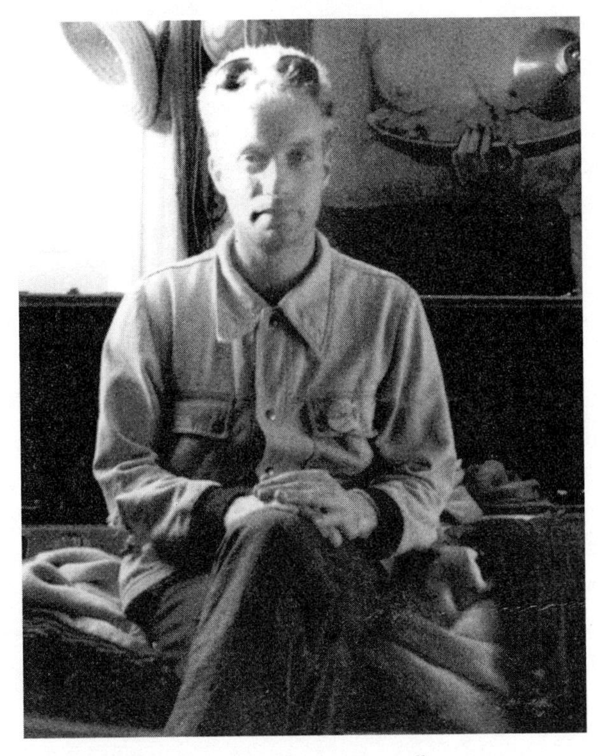

My father, Claude, in one of the photos he occasionally sent my way.

One full-moon night as the poetry workshop let out, Claude said: "Let's walk together for a little while." Immersed in moon-goddess light, they walked over the hill, talking Pablo Neruda and Victor Jara. My mother gesticulated animatedly as she spoke of the coming Revolution; my father, seven years her junior, spoke in deep poetic abstractions about changing the world through his music and the meditative highs he reached on his surfboard.

Their meandering path brought them to Claudia's apartment in the Noe Valley. Inside they sat on the mattress on the floor, smoking a little of the herb. And then, in what might have been one of the least romantic conversations of all time, she told him she had come to the point in her life where she was ready to have a child. He thought about this and, between puffs of the joint, said: "I know I'm not ready to be a father. I don't know if I ever will be." And, with that, they lay together and had sex for the first and last time and unwittingly (or perhaps half-wittingly) conceived me.

After that one night together, Claude grew aloof and distanced himself from my mother, even as she began to feel me growing inside of her. She stopped attending the poetry workshop and began looking for a safe commune where she could raise a child. Some months later, the two of them ran into each other on the street.

They stopped to talk, and Claude said: "I understand something interesting is happening with your body. Is that true?"

"Yes," said Claudia. "I'm going to have a baby."

"Do you know who the father is?"

"Yes."

"Does *he* know who the father is?"

"*He* can figure it out if *he* wants to," Claudia replied.

Claude nodded and from this my mother knew that he knew. He wished her good luck, and they went their separate ways.

It wasn't that Claudia didn't want Claude involved as a father, she later explained to me. To the contrary, she dreamed about it. She thought if she visualized it intensely enough, maybe it would become reality. But she wasn't going to ask him. She was too much of a feminist for that. She wanted him to want it. But if he didn't, she would raise the baby all by herself.

Over the years, my father aspired to be a lot of things: a poet, a musician, a guru. But he never wanted to be my father. Luckily someone else did. A dark, giant stranger who went by Tony because *Antonio* had too many vowels for the Anglo ear.

My mother met Tony in 1975, before I was born. He was chairing the interview panel for the commune on Ashbury Street. My mother was nervous on the day of the interview because openings in a good commune were rare, and the admissions process could be fiercely competitive. She relaxed a little as she shared sourdough bread and kale with commune members around the long communal table in the kitchen. My mother was pleased to see that the interview panel included a black man and his Chinese wife. The place had the right diversity and a real earthy vibe. Leading the panel was a tall bearded Latino or Native American man named Tony. He stood against one wall, arms crossed, rocking back and forth a little, asking questions. He looked like he could have been the head of a revolutionary cadre. A freedom fighter from Central America, maybe.

But what he wanted to know was strictly Capitalist. How would she afford the rent?

"Well, I've always lived my life in such a way that if you are in the right place at the right time, with the right *attitude*, you can find anything you want—even money."

Tony frowned at this. "What about a job?"

"Yes, jobs are good too. I've been nude modeling for art schools. And I do my own artwork. Sometimes modeling and painting at the same time!"

Tony was still skeptical. "That doesn't sound like making a living." They were all staring at her.

"Well, you should know, I will be eligible for Welfare soon."

"Welfare? How?"

"I'm pregnant."

A child!? She wouldn't have garnered more surprise if she had said she was a CIA agent.

"You're pregnant!?" Tony took a step back and dropped his gaze to the floor.

Someone else said: "Are we ready to live with a baby?"

Tony nodded. "We all need to talk." And the whole group of them adjourned into the next room to deliberate. When they came back in, my mother was prepared for more questions. But Tony was smiling. "We decided," he said. "You're in."

My mother's room at the commune was next to Tony's. She discovered not the guerrilla leader she had imagined, but a soft, dreamy intellectual. A student of philosophy and history. He was the only one in the commune with a real job, though she was shocked to find out he was a janitor. "A *janitor*, Tony!? You went to college, for chrissake."

His round face trembled. "I had to drop out. I had a nervous breakdown. I couldn't finish."

Tony had no memories of his real family. He had been kidnapped from his Mexican-American parents at a young age by an abusive and hateful Cuban woman who told him she was his "grandmother." She claimed to be pure-blooded Spanish, and Tony was raised with the shame that he was nothing but a "dirty half-breed." Tony's childhood was a catalog of abuse and neglect visited upon him by his grandmother, her predatory boyfriends, and frightening Catholic schools.

In this total darkness, Tony sought redemption in his schoolwork and tested his way into the selective Lowell High School. There the light began to shine in. He started high school as the brown, dumpy, depressed "grandson" of an erratic, abusive Cuban maid. But he left feeling like a refined intellectual, his spirit on fire with philosophy and Hindu theology. Stepping out of high school full of academic promise, he went on scholarship to San Francisco State University, where he promised himself that his studies would replace his past. He grew his hair out to become someone new and tried to toss himself into the ferment of the '60s, to embrace freedom. But his traumatic childhood haunted him relentlessly. He was barely able to keep a lid on the nightmares, the flashbacks, and the phobias that crippled him. He had panic attacks in enclosed spaces and disabling fears of heights, flying, driving, and public speaking.

Before he could graduate, he was drawn back to his grandmother's side as she lay dying in the hospital.

"Antonio, this is your fault," she hissed. "You abandoned me. After all I did for you. I saved you from growing up like a dirty *Mexican*."

"I'm sorry," Tony said, feeling a void of darkness rushing in at him.

"You left me alone," she whispered. "It's all your fault." Her wrinkled face froze into a scowl and then turned to wax. She was dead.

Tony was choking up as he confessed all of this to my mother, and then he told her about his nervous breakdown and his suicide attempts. "Now I'm a janitor," he concluded. "And I'm all alone."

My mother leaned in and hugged Tony over her expanding belly. They were both lonely. Both wanted to be held. After a long hug, Tony pulled back, his eyes alive again.

"What did you eat today?" he asked, brightening.

"I had some broccoli and tofu."

"That's not enough!"

"I'm not hungry, Tony."

"No, I told you before, it's not for you. It's for the baby! We have to feed the little guy."

Tony returned shortly, bearing a plate loaded down with a massive cheese omelet. He began feeding my mother forkfuls of his latest culinary creation. "We're going to have the strongest, healthiest baby. Eat!"

My mother put his hand to her belly. "Feel, Tony, feel! The baby's kicking!"

Tony felt me moving inside of her. *"¡Ay, mi angelita!" Oh, my little angel!* Tony swore he couldn't remember any Spanish but reverted to it whenever he became emotional. *"Angelita*, he likes my omelets!"

When I was born, Tony threw himself into the role of father with abandon. After cleaning the State Building all evening, Tony would come home to the sound of my colicky cry, and dutifully scoop me up from my foam pad on the floor. He would bounce, burp, and change me, and then sing me to

Uncle Tony with me on the steps of UC Berkeley in 1976. "You'll go here someday, Joshey."

sleep with a mixture of Spanish lullabies and the Rolling Stones. Night after night Tony paced back and forth with me until the first rays of sunlight filtered in through the leaves of the commune's raised marijuana garden.

Once I could sleep through the night, my mother decided it was time to leave the commune—and Tony. With all the cooking and the child care, he was starting to act like a father and a husband. My mother wrote in her diary:

> *Afraid that I am becoming his wife . . . to allow him to care for me . . . what do I owe him? Others are there for the drama, he's there for the grind—the dirty diapers and the night feedings. Have I sold myself to him for payment of debt?*

The bottom line for my mother was: Tony was not the hero of the Revolution he appeared to be at first glance. He lacked the requisite toughness, guts. He was too prone to fall back into a pattern of self-destruction. He just wasn't her type.

Taking a bath in the commune at 431 Ashbury Street.

My mother broke the news to Tony one night after I'd fallen asleep.

"Why?" he pleaded.

"Tony, my room is too small. Josh is starting to crawl. Steve, from the basement, almost stepped on him the other day. Marian's got hepatitis. Did you see the open sores on her face? And how am I supposed to bathe him in the sink with George's coffee grinds clogging it up? I have to find a place Josh can move around safely."

"Can I come with you?" Tony asked the question she was dreading.

"No, Tony. You're acting like we're a married couple, and we're not. You've got this shabby outer world, this *job*. That's hard for me to relate to. And I know that you've got this magnificent inner world where you're having ecstatic visions of the *Virgin de Guadalupe* and experiencing parallel universes, and I enjoy sharing that aspect with you. But you're asking me to help you deal with your emotional problems and the ghost of your grandmother, and I can't spend all day long reading your energy." My mother took a swig of rosehips tea. "I want to have a real boyfriend, Tony. Someone committed to the Struggle. When we go out, I see guys who look interesting in cafés and restaurants, but they all assume we're together. I've got to get away, Tony. Besides, think about it. The longer we wait, the harder it will be on Josh to leave you."

Tony had tears in his eyes, but he accepted her decision. "Claudey, you know, after you leave, can I still visit you and the Babu?" He called me Babu, which was short for *Baboso—the Slobbery One.*

"Of course, Tony," she reassured him. "You can always visit us."

My mother and I moved around the city four more times, and throughout it all, Tony was my loyal and regular visitor. Wherever we were, I could count on his weekly visits. He came every Sunday, bearing some little gift, and each time he took us out to dinner.

At first my mother resisted the weekly dinner: "Tony. I'm a feminist. I'm not going to let a man pay for our dinner. I'll pay my own way."

"Claudey, if you have to pay for your own dinner, will you still go out to dinner with me every Sunday?"

"No."

"OK, so I want to eat dinner with you every Sunday. So let me pay for it on the days you wouldn't have come out on your own."

"Fine."

He paid for dinner every week.

At one of those dinners, I asked Tony whether he was my father. Tony looked at Claudia for a long time and received only silence in return. Tony finally shook his heavy head, *No.*

"But he's like my brother," Claudia offered as a compromise, "so he can be your uncle."

Uncle Tony. I liked the sound of that. It was like a father, only better. Uncles were real.

Claude did not appear on my birth certificate. My father's first name was listed as Joshua, but the rest of the *Father of Child* section was a sea of "Unknown"s. In my vital records, Claudia described my father as a "poet moving to South America." My father would have remained Joshua Sr., the unknown South American poet, had it not been for an accidental meeting and declaration of paternity in a peasant food restaurant in the Haight-Ashbury. I was two years old and, as I spooned up my organic barley, Claudia began telling me about the CIA overthrow of the Árbenz government in

Guatemala. Behind her a strange man entered the restaurant and walked past our table. He glanced our way, turned away, and then spun his head back in a dramatic double take. The man sauntered over to the table pensively, looked to my mother, and then looked down at me.

"Can I join you?" he asked.

My mother nodded, and he sat down next to me, his face working with emotion as he tried to avoid my inquisitive eyes. I could sense that there was something important about the moment and sat up on my knees, facing him. We were both wearing Sherpa hats and turquoise down jackets. Our big blue eyes stared across a generation at one another.

"How are you?" he asked me, his voice shaking.

"I'm good," I whispered.

"What's your name?" he asked me.

"Josh."

"I'm Claude," he introduced himself, putting his hand over his heart.

Something about Claude resonated deeply with me. I stood up on my chair and leaned toward him, staring into his face, locking blue eyes. He cloaked me in a deep embrace and called me Son.

This first time that we met was to be my only perfect moment with my father. But I don't remember any of it. I recall only my mother's memory of the event. She told me the story over the years, and I enjoyed the hope in her voice and the dramatic outpouring of paternal love she reenacted. There, watching our Sherpa-hatted heads come together in an embrace, my mother felt the Spirits working their magic. Once Claude had seen me—the delightful little spitting image of himself—how could he not step up to become my father?

But, despite Claudia's newfound expectations, he didn't step up. One of my earliest memories is not of my father, but of waiting for him. Pacing back and forth over the black floorboards in our apartment, standing on Claudia's foam mattress on the floor to stick my head out the window. I stared at the unyielding sidewalk below, my hopes rising and falling as each new figure coming into view failed to become my father.

"When is Claude coming? When?"

"Five more minutes."

"Is it five minutes yet?"

"No," my mother called back from the little kitchen. "You just asked me, it's only been a minute."

"Is he coming now?"

"I called him to remind him. He'll be here soon."

Time slithered languidly by. Eventually my mother sighed: "Well, I guess he's not going to make it, Josh."

"But he promised."

"I know," she said. "Damn it! He didn't make it last time, either."

I began crying and worked myself into an inconsolable fit. Only sleep soothed my sobbing.

The day after one of these no-shows, my mother and I came across Claude on the street. She tightened her grip on my hand. Claude avoided making eye contact with me.

"I'm sorry," he said. "My mom made dinner for me last night and insisted I eat with her."

"You don't owe us anything," Claudia said. I could hear an unfamiliar angry register in her voice, escalating with every word. "If you don't want to come over and be with your son, then don't! But for chrissake, don't promise a little kid you're going to come visit him and then bail on him."

Claude nodded thoughtfully: "Well, I guess I could see how that might make you feel helpless."

My mother let go of me, stepped in toward Claude, and slapped him across the face.

She shouted: "I'm not helpless and neither are you! If you could manage to give your child half the attention you give to your mother, you might be a man."

His stunned, stubbled cheek turned away from me. His eyes were moist with the sting of the slap that kept reverberating in my ears. Claude walked away silently, his head down.

My father didn't come to my fourth birthday. At the end of the party, a scattering of wrapping paper lay before me on the floor. My mother told me that I should be happy. "You had a nice little party. Uncle Tony came. Look, Josh, you got a toy piano and a truck."

"Claude was supposed to come," I protested. "Why doesn't he want to see me?"

My mother knelt down in front of me and focused all her attention at my eyes. "Your father will never come through for you. He never will. He'll say he's going to do something and maybe, sometimes, he'll actually do it, and that'll be nice. But don't expect it. He'll never keep his promises. That's just the way he is. Do you understand?"

I did. Something about the certainty in her words convinced me that I wasn't to blame. If he didn't want to see me, then something was seriously wrong with *him*, not me. And, like that, Claude was transformed from an aloof and intriguing role model into an unreliable liar.

A few months after my birthday, a girl with pigtails in Dolores Park asked me: "Who's your mommy?"

"Her name is Claudia," I said, "but I'm not supposed to call her Mom because that name is too limiting. She's more than a mother. She's a full person named Claudia."

The girl nodded knowingly and then asked: "Who's your daddy?"

The question caught me off guard and I had to think about it for a few seconds. "Oh, I don't really have a father."

"You don't have a daddy?" The girl frowned.

"No," I reassured her, "but I at least have an Uncle Tony."

While Uncle Tony's weekly visits gave me a hint of what it might mean to be a man, the rest of my time was spent immersed in an estrogen-rich environment. Claudia and her friends and lovers remained my role models and, naturally, I wanted to be just like them.

One day when I was three, Claudia and her lover, Linda, cuddled on the bed as I ran around the apartment with a little green pillow under my shirt. "Look, Claudia, I'm pregnant now. Look, I have a baby in my womb." I threw a blanket down to serve as my bed and squatted down to give birth to my baby.

Linda couldn't keep from laughing. "It's time you told him, Claudia."

My mother nodded and decided to break the news to me: "Joshey, you're a boy. Boys can't give birth to babies."

"But when I grow up I will?"

"No, Joshey, you'll never be able to have a baby."

"Never!?"

"No, not ever. You don't have a womb or a vagina." She brightened. "But you have a penis! Someday a woman could put your penis inside her and you could shoot semen into her to make a baby in *her* womb."

I was so disappointed. Who wanted a boy's semen-shooting penis when you could be a life-giving woman?

I wasn't the only one who was disappointed by my lack of a womb and vagina. My mother's coven remained scandalized by my sex. How could they tolerate a future rapist and batterer in their midst? Perhaps even more shocking to them was the realization that raising a child, of any sex, was hard. I was the first child born to the coven, and when the witches were asked to stop changing the world and start changing diapers, they were quick to distance themselves from my mother. Claudia felt abandoned by these Sisters who had promised to support her, and she moved on in search of a community that allowed children to be part of the Revolution.

For a while she was able to afford the help of the Candy from Strangers Collective. The Collective was made up of gay male babysitters who would watch the children of activist feminist mothers so they could take part in political protests. My mother's favorite Stranger, Taj, would come to the apartment to take care of me while she was out fomenting the Revolution. He would arrive promptly, giving her enough time to change into her cobalt moon-goddess outfit and make it to the rally before the police broke it up. While she was out, Taj would clean the entire house, reorganize the refrigerator, and dust the altar. When she made it home, still buzzing with the energy of the streets, she would find me tucked into a professionally made bed, bathed and hair-styled so I looked like a sleeping model from a children's magazine. As he let himself out, Taj would stroke his waxed handlebar moustache and tell her: "Sometimes I go out with the mommies too," letting her know he was bisexual and might be up for more than just babysitting.

When I got a little older, my mother enrolled me in the Feminist Center Playgroup. The parents were all radical single mothers. I shared nonviolent wooden toys with the likes of Jody Gai (named for a merciless woman officer of the Vietcong), and Katanya, the half-black daughter of a prisoners' rights activist who had been assassinated by the FBI upon his release from prison.

But even with the gay babysitters and the feminist playgroup, my mother still wasn't getting enough time to herself. The never-ending demands of single motherhood were more than she could handle, and she began sneaking out in the evening after I had gone to sleep. One night I awoke in a panic, somehow sensing that she was gone. I ran around our little apartment screaming for what felt like hours. When Claudia returned she found me climbing out onto the fire escape to search for her.

"Where were you!?" I demanded.

"I'm sorry, Joshey. I went to a women's bar down the street. I was just going stir crazy." I stared at her, my face quivering. "Josh, my days used to start at eight o'clock at night. I'd wander around to all-night poetry clubs and hear music. Now when you go to sleep I get so bored." I shook my head, refusing to accept these answers. "I was feeling lonely, Josh. You were sleeping. I just ducked out for a minute."

Claudia in her cobalt moon-goddess outfit, which was often mistaken for a burqa.

"Don't . . . you . . . ever . . . do that again!" My voice was breaking and seething.

"I won't."

I slept in her bed that night. As the dream world came rushing up at me, I looked over to see that Claudia was still awake, staring up at the ceiling. I put my hand on her arm to keep her with me and fell asleep.

We spent the next few nights at her girlfriend Linda's house so my mother would have someone to talk to after I fell asleep. My mother openly identified herself as a lesbian, and she tried hard to be a "woman's woman." But, despite her best efforts, she couldn't stop herself from being attracted to men. In the end she had to admit that she was only gay for political reasons. One of her girlfriends, a Southerner named Jody, cried as they broke up: "I want you to love me for who I am, not who I represent. I wish ya'll breeders would just fuckin' go home!"

The radical women's movement had become too anti-man for Claudia, and we began spending time with more moderate lesbian couples who were part of the Compost Reunion Coven. The name was a sort of euphemism for "witches getting their shit together." They weren't just lesbians playing at being spiritual, they were serious, honest to Goddess Wiccans. To my mother's delight, these witches worshiped the Goddess, but they also thought there was room in the world for warlocks.

Through the Compost Reunion Coven, my mother was invited up to a witchcraft colony in Ukiah called Greenfield Ranch. She left me with Uncle Tony for the weekend, packed her magic staff, and headed north to celebrate the fertility rites of Beltane. She came back crackling with blue energy: "Joshey! Oh my Goddess, it was beautiful! I want a community like that for us. It's got *everything*: it's feminist, it's spiritual, and they honor Mother Earth. I'm hungering to get back to the land. Wait till you hear about it." Despite my mother's enthusiasm, I was happy to have missed out on the transcendental adventures at Greenfield Ranch. Something didn't sit quite right with me about losing control of yourself to a drug called "acid" so you could dance naked on a hilltop all night while the Goddess exploded your head into an energy fountain and showed you your past lives. I preferred listening to Tony expound on Kierkegaard while I rode the carousel in Golden Gate Park.

The more my mother began to experience Wicca, though, the more it began to feel like an organized religion to her. One full-moon night, she joined Starhawk, the anarchist high priestess, and four thousand other witches in the park at Fort Mason. As the service to the Goddess commenced, my mother stood at the water's edge, looking down at the moonlight rippling in the waves. Starhawk grabbed her suddenly from behind and forced her down to her knees to worship the Goddess properly. She came home dejected. "Joshey, there's as much hierarchy in Wicca as anywhere else. You may be tripping out of your mind, but it's still a church."

After so many false starts, Claudia was beginning to doubt that a real revolutionary community existed for us in San Francisco. When she meditated on it, this didn't come as a surprise. After all, her plan had always been to leave the city and head for the hills once I was old enough to make the journey. Maybe that day would come, but the Spirits were telling her *not yet*. She decided to give San Francisco one last try.

Claudia quickly found new promise in the avant-garde radical neo-paganist lesbian music scene where she became a regular dancer for an all-women band called Alive! Composed exclusively of drummers, their shows began with silence. Then each drummer would begin with small chirping sounds. The audience would respond in kind. Then the animal sounds from the drummers would get louder and crazier, and the audience would call back. Then the drums would explode. The room would fill with women shrieking like banshees, and the drums would rumble like a herd of zebras. No woman could resist this primal invitation to dance. My mother spun round and round, whirling as Miriam must have danced with her timbrels at the Red Sea, until her side hurt so badly she thought she might throw up.

One night, she staggered out of the steaming jungle cacophony into a little courtyard, gasping for air. There she met Anahid, an Iranian artist. The two of them, drenched with sweat, talked into the night about metaphysics and revolution. The next morning my mother raved to me about Anahid, this sophisticated artist visionary who was part of Project Artaud, a live-work art studio and theater of the absurd. Anahid was changing the world with her paintbrush. She and Claudia could share chakra readings just as easily as others could share a meal.

My mother was deeply impressed by the artists she met through Anahid and began to feel that perhaps the Revolution could be achieved through art. They didn't need rifles and ammunition. They had canvas and paint.

When the People's Cultural Center on Valencia Street put out a call for revolutionary artists to install a massive mural capable of transforming reality, my mother volunteered for the mission. She became part of an anarchist collective of five artists that would spend a year of their lives painting the side of a building for zero dollars. Because the political statement made by the mural had to be profound, and because their decisions had to be made by consensus, the collective of artists tended to meet more than they painted. My mother volunteered our apartment as the venue for their evening planning sessions, but was told that the meetings had to rotate to each artist's house.

"But, if we meet at my place every time," she said, "my kid can stay sleeping in the other room so I don't have to get a babysitter."

"Sister! Don't you get it? The basis of an anarcho-Communist society is equality in small-group decision-making. If we have a meeting more than once in a row at any one artist's house, then that artist will have too much power. It has to be equal."

"But I'll have to hire a babysitter every night, and I'm on Welfare."

"Sister, if we compromise our ideals in the planning process, how can we bring about a revolution through our finished work?"

Claudia (lower left) *displaying her art with feminist comrades in San Francisco, 1978.*

The mural was too important. My mother called the gay babysitters from the Candy from Strangers Collective, and rotated from house to house for meetings. A year later, they finally unveiled the mural that was to spark revolution in all who saw it. From the right sprang images of oppression: factories spewing pollution, people in gas masks, war. The middle of the mural conveyed the concept of revolution: people surging forward, rising up to overthrow oppression in joy, rainbows, peacocks, love, energy, and a woman holding up her little boy. On the left the public was treated to the post-revolutionary peace of the future. The world to come was full of farming, windmills, and diverse people passing each other trays of fruit and vegetables and feeding one another.

Much to my mother's surprise, the day after the mural was completed, people continued walking past the painted wall on Valencia Street as they had before. They weren't ripping off their neckties and taking to the ramparts. They were still going to work. While the mural didn't spark the flames of revolution its creators intended, it did inspire my mother, who was moved by her own illustration of Utopia. That was what *she* wanted—an agrarian collective of peacemakers. It had become clear to her that the process-oriented urban anarchists were not her community.

She moved on to a group of revolutionary artists known as the Haight-Ashbury Humanist Artists, known as HA HA! With HA HA! she felt that she could really express herself without having to seek anyone else's approval. Her visions flowed through the swirls of oil paints and drenched the canvases with climaxes of color. Painting day after day she felt truly alive. HA HA! put together an art show at Fort Mason, and my mother installed her pieces with the trembling hands of a girl emerging from the darkness into the light. But the critics didn't like her oil paintings. Devastated, she wanted to hurl herself back into the darkness. Another artist pulled her aside and told her that her passion was real, but that she needed more formal training. He suggested that my mother go to City College for art school.

The idea of going back to school overshadowed all else in her mind that night. Was she good enough for art school? Why not? She had every right to trade the model's platform for the student's stool. But between her boy and school, she wouldn't have time for the Revolution. Was she selling out? *No,* she told herself. Her strength as a revolutionary artist fundamentally rested on her skill. The better the artist she could be, the more effective her message. She would drop out of the Revolution now to invest in its future. Besides, how could she not paint? When I was a baby, she couldn't even pause to breastfeed me. She had held me at her chest with her left hand and painted with her right.

"I'm going back to school, Joshey. I'm tired of all these political types who think they're making a statement by mixing their menstrual blood into the paint. I'm going to art school, to be a real artist."

"What's minstrel blood?"

"I never showed you before? Menstruation is a woman's monthly bleeding. Every month the lining of a woman's womb basically dies and it flows out of her vagina in a thick, meaty stream of blood. It takes about a week for it all to come out." Then she showed me the amber-colored sea sponge she used to soak up her flow.

I was suddenly and profoundly relieved not to have a womb. If my mother could give up on the Revolution, I could give up on being a woman.

TWO

The Day Before the Apocalypse

After her first day of art school, Claudia returned home awash in artistic inspiration. She had plunged into her classes with abandon, soaking up every second of painting, sculpting, print-making, ceramics, and life drawing with a live nude model. In the studios, she told me, she was completely immersed in the creative world of her fellow artists. "Joshey, they're the freest people I've ever met, just wildly expressing themselves in every medium. For once I don't have to be political. It doesn't matter to them. All I have to do is create with every fiber of my spirit!" And create she did. Our apartment was soon adorned with her new paintings: the atomic angel of death; the dead body moldering in the grass in El Salvador; the massive portrait of Victor Jara, the Chilean revolutionary musician, framed by people stabbing an anaconda to death with sharpened sticks, representing the struggle against the Anaconda Copper Company; and the larger-than-life portrait of a redheaded woman—half her body naked flesh, the other half skeleton.

While Claudia was crafting these disturbing manifestos on canvas, I was fretting about the nuclear apocalypse she kept telling me about and attempting to learn Tagalog at the City College preschool. Through some unexplained socio-educational phenomenon, 75 percent of the kids in my preschool were from the Philippines. They tended to stick together, and none of them came to my feminist-themed birthday party.

Most of my time in preschool was spent playing with a girl I called Karina Katherine Cheese. She had a single mom too, and we both played mother to the tattered stuffed animals from the blue toy bin.

"Karina, did you know that President Carter has a button that can blow up the whole world with nuclear bombs?"

"Yes. The Russians have one too."

"The Russians are just an excuse, I think, for the nuclear power company to use."

"Here, Josh, the turtle wants you to nurse her."

The Filipino kids around us were laughing, playing games, and riding back and forth on the Big Wheels as if nothing were wrong, as if the world would last forever. They didn't seem concerned about the coming nuclear war or the nuclear winter. Maybe their parents weren't telling them the whole truth.

The worries were still on my mind when Uncle Tony took me out to a Chinese restaurant later that week. I tried his patience quickly—sweetening my bitter tea with ten packets of sugar and dropping my chopsticks on the floor twice before needing him to take me to the bathroom.

"Oh, Josh," said Uncle Tony. "You have to put the toilet seat back down when you're done taking a wizz. What if a feminist came into the bathroom after us? Claudia will kill me if she finds out you're leaving the toilet seat up."

Heavy thoughts weighed on me as we walked back to our booth. When we reached the table, Tony looked down at me and his eyebrows jumped up in astonishment. With a comical stage whisper, he said: "Oh, Mr. Josh, don't look now but your pants are undone. You have to button them up."

"I don't like buttons." I pulled myself back up into the red booth, still unbuttoned.

"Why not?"

"They're scary."

"Why?"

"Buttons are scary because they don't just hold up your pants, Tony. They can also blow up the whole world. Did you even know there's a red button in the White House and if the president is mad at the Soviet Union or even just in a bad mood, he can push it, and everyone will die from nuclear power? It used to be that if you wanted to kill someone, you had to look at them and shoot them or stab them with a sword. But one day it changed. It was in a town called Hiroshima, which is in Japan. People were at work, and women were painting with Japanese paintbrushes, and in the park kids like me were playing. Then there was a nuclear bomb from America. It exploded the sky and melted the buildings and the trees. People's skin burnt off. The nuclear light was so hot it burnt kids' shadows into the sidewalk. The survivors, the people who were left over, they're called the *hibakusha*. They're still losing their hair and throwing up their guts from it."

"You're too young to worry about all this stuff."

"I know that already."

At night my eyelids could not shield me from the images of the fiery mushroom clouds erupting along Market Street. Through the choking smoke, I could hear the strained animalistic shrieks of my fellow passengers on the Muni crawling out the shattered windows of the streetcar.

But what was even worse than nuclear war was the nuclear winter to follow. Once the fires had died down and the masses had succumbed to nuclear radiation, the unfortunate remnants of humanity would be left to wander the gray, snowy forests in search of food. The hazy skies would forever smudge out the sun in a perpetual winter of deprivation. Lying on my foam mattress on the floor, I projected myself up into the filigreed canyons of the chalky crown molding above me. These were the snowy tracks through the forest. It would be cold. The frozen air would lash at our faces. We would be trudging, Claudia and I, through knee-high snowbanks. I would hold on to her gloved fingers with my right hand and caress an old crust of bread with my left. Hunger would claw at my insides, and we would wander endlessly, propelled forward by fear.

In the light of day I'd shake the image of the nuclear winter and remind myself that Hiroshima was far away in Japan. And a long time ago—back when people were still black and white, and wore straw sandals and pagoda hats. This was enough to reassure me.

At least it was until March 1979, when Hiroshima came to America. Claudia was cooking bok choy for dinner and telling me about the CIA's overthrow of Allende in Chile when the phone rang. I ran to answer it. It was Elizabeth, one of Claudia's closest friends.

"*¡Hola!*" I said, trying out the revolutionary Spanish Elizabeth had taught me. "*¡Viva La Revolución!*"

She wasn't playing: "Josh, put Claudia on please."

"*¡Hola, hermana!*" Claudia greeted her. "*¿Qué . . .*" my mother's voice trailed off and she listened intensely. She nodded her head a few times. Then she became very still, pushing the receiver into the side of her head until it looked like it hurt. "Oh my God," she said. I knew it was serious or she would have corrected herself to say "Oh my Goddess." When the call ended, Claudia's hands were shaking and her eyes were red. She turned to me, trying to keep her voice steady:

"Joshey, something horrible has happened. That was Elizabeth . . ."

"I know."

"Well, her mother, Elizabeth's mother, lives near Harrisburg, Pennsylvania. No one really knows this yet but there's been a meltdown at the nuclear reactor at Three Mile Island. No one is being let into the area. They're evacuating the children and pregnant women. We don't know how many have died."

We rushed to the bookshelf together and began flipping through the pulpy pages of the road atlas. There was Harrisburg, a knot of yellow roads lodged in the bottom-right of the map. My mother traced her finger in concentric circles of impact. York, Lancaster, Reading. Expanding out into Baltimore, Philadelphia, and edging in on DC and New York. The death of so many people was sickening, but we both took selfish comfort in how far away Harrisburg was from California.

"Is it going to be OK?" I asked.

"We don't know yet," my mother answered.

"Here's what's next, Joshey, look." The atlas was now open to California. My mother put her finger on an indentation in the coast line. "Diablo Canyon nuclear power plant. It's about to go operational." She traced her finger up the coast. "Here we are. Joshey, we've got to stop it." Her jaw was tight and her lips curled up. She looked so tough. But tough enough to stop nuclear power? I wasn't sure.

That night the twin specters of Three Mile Island and Diablo Canyon haunted me. Particularly Diablo Canyon. It was right on the same map we were, and the word *canyon* seemed so sinister. A few months later, I met some kids who told me they were going on vacation to the Grand Canyon. I took a step back from them and shook my head in sorrow. Those poor bastards. Those poor irradiated mutant bastards.

For Claudia, Three Mile Island was the summons that dragged her out of the good life of an artist. She had been naive, she concluded, to think she could ignore the Revolution. The stakes were too high and she was too valuable to the cause. She joined a group called No Nukes Is Not Enough and began to reengage herself as a political activist.

Claudia didn't quit City College, not yet. But she was having increasing difficulty fitting motherhood into her commitments to art school and the Revolution. From the moment I woke with an exuberant burst in the morning to the moment I collapsed with exhaustion late at night, I was constantly demanding my mother's undivided attention.

The preschool took me off her hands just long enough for her to get new assignments in class, and then I was back with renewed energy. With me around she couldn't paint, she couldn't study, she couldn't think. She would become stony silent, refusing to make eye contact with me. She'd cup her mouth in the palm of her hand and rub her upper lip with the flap of skin between her thumb and forefinger, trying to control herself. She told me she felt like her mother in those moments—a suffocating, frustrated artist about to lash out at her consanguineous distraction.

One night, in desperation, my mother opened the phone book to the listing for psychotherapists. She slid her finger down the page until the Spirits led her to the name Amanda Light. She called the number. "I'm so angry at my kid," she told therapist Light. "It's rougher than I thought. I don't want to hurt him. I don't want to pass this rage on to him. But I'm trying to go to art school and I'm trying to fight nuclear power. I have no money or insurance, but can you help me?"

Therapist Light told her: "Come see me. Someone did free therapy for me once on the condition that I pass it on. So now I'll counsel you for free." At their sessions together, therapist Light gave my mother a pillow. "This pillow is your mother. Tell the pillow what you would tell your mother."

My mother was soon screaming at the unfortunate pillow. She cried and screamed and began punching and then strangling the pillow. "You never loved me!" After a time she was quiet.

"Is that all you have to say, Claudia?"

"No!" And she started screaming and punching the pillow again.

My mother came home from these sessions limp but placid. She cried when she told me about punching the pillow embodying the mother of her lost childhood.

With therapy—on top of taking care of me, classes, studio time, and plotting the Revolution—Claudia was overextended. For a few months she made it work, living off of bagels and coffee and little or no sleep, but one day she collapsed while climbing the steps to the preschool to pick me up. Every deep breath felt like a stab to her chest. She had no energy. She sat there crying until some passing parent agreed to bring me down to her. We hobbled home together, with my mother needing to rest every few steps. I waited at her side, holding her hand while she wheezed and grimaced. When we finally got back home, she called a nurse in one of the feminist support groups, who told her to check herself into the hospital.

Claudia came back with a diagnosis of pneumonia and stayed home with me for two weeks until she regained her health. I tried to entertain her, staging plays and arranging elaborate puppet shows, but she was depressed and bitter.

"Where's my community to help take care of you, Joshey? This is the feminist promise? Not one of the Sisters will even call me back. Oh, Josh, I'm so isolated and lonely. I should be out *there*," she said, pointing at the window.

"They need me. Fighting nuclear power, stopping Diablo Canyon, and here I am flat on my back. The whole world is on the brink. And school!? How am I supposed to keep up in school, Joshey? What's the point?"

I didn't know what the point was.

My mother had new clarity when she got back on her feet. At the next No Nukes meeting, she interrupted an argument over a point of order and took the floor:

"What do you think you're all accomplishing by protesting at San Francisco City Hall? The same six people get arrested every time, and then we protest their imprisonment until they get released and arrested again. Nothing changes. Spilling blood on City Hall steps doesn't change anything. City Hall doesn't give a shit. What we need is a parade that manifests all of our best creative energy: drama, art, poetry. And we take that parade not to City Hall but to the Black community, to the Chinese community, to the neighborhoods that really matter. We'll get the *people* involved. It'll go national, and then we'll be unstoppable. The politicians will be shamed into shutting down the nuclear power industry once and for all, and then we can all go home and go to sleep at night knowing that the nuclear arms race is over."

She received a standing ovation and was unanimously selected as the organizer and spokeswoman for what would become the Three Mile Island Memorial Parade held on the first anniversary of the disaster. Art school was over.

When informed, I accepted my mother's chosenness as the anti-nuclear messiah with stoic pride. I knew it was an honor, but why did it have to be *my* mother? The Struggle took so much of her time. For months it felt like I was competing with the entire world for her attention. The city wanted her because they needed to give her parade permits. The Sisters of Perpetual Indulgence wanted her because they were transvestite nuns who wished to be taken seriously. The American Indian Movement wanted her because the government was taking away their land for the uranium rocks that lay beneath it. The veterans wanted her because they had been forced to watch the nuclear bomb blasts at Enewetak and Bikini. They all wanted to be in her parade. And when it wasn't the meetings with the groups, it was the meetings in the warehouses with the artists to build the floats: the giant papier-mâché nuclear cooling tower; the Trident nuclear submarine; the skeletal nuclear grim reapers.

When she was home with me, my mother spent endless hours on the phone, strategizing, negotiating, wheedling, and pleading. If she wasn't on the phone she was so deeply absorbed in thought that I could have peed my pants or endorsed Governor Reagan for president without her noticing.

Claudia's flyer for the 1980 Three Mile Island Memorial Parade.

Three Mile Island ruined my preschool graduation. While Claudia actually got me to my ceremony on time, she promptly wandered off, mulling over the logistics needed to shift seamlessly from the Plutonium Players' performance to the dance by the Gays for Nicaragua. By the time she wandered back, she'd missed the entire ceremony, including my solo in the lyrical tribute to our Filipino ancestors who came through Angel Island, the Ellis Island of the West.

As the Three Mile Island memorial came closer to fruition, my mother was organizing the parade every waking hour and envisioning the parade-to-be in her dreams, mumbling in her sleep: "Freedom Socialists to the left, bring up the Abalone Alliance." With no time left for me, she asked Uncle Tony to take time off of work, and even asked Claude to take time off of unemployment to care for me in her absence. Tony ultimately had to take three weeks of vacation and sick leave, and Claude brought me along to some New Wave gigs where I was officially introduced as the band's go-go dancer.

The one-year anniversary of Three Mile Island dawned clear and full of promise. This was the day my mother had been working toward for so long.

My mother wrote of the parade in a long letter to Elizabeth:

> *[I] jumped on a flatbed truck containing the nuclear altar. . . . People made a beeline for me: the float people wanted to know why we couldn't relocate the control panel; Susan S. wanted to know where the children's truck was; and, somebody else wanted a parade outline, a script for a theatre part, and some tape . . . Josh and Tony arrived needing immediate hugs. Josh had been traded off between daddy 1 and daddy 2 for the three days preceding.*

Claudia was surrounded by a frenzied swarm of raggedy activists. She called out orders like a line officer, huddling and unhuddling, pointing and guiding with hand gestures. I was proud of her but disappointed that no one knew I was the captain's son. On the ground near her crew were an untidy heap of protest signs and a disassembled Trident submarine monster composed of a massive harness the length of a football field and studded with black flags. I knew that each flag represented one bomb, and each bomb was equivalent to five Hiroshima blasts. That much fire power made me nervous.

Claudia's letter continued:

> *A monitor runs up and tells me Wavy Gravy is here and looking for the children. Where the hell is Allan with the kids' truck? I run to find Wavy and he's already found the pole marked "Children." No problem except trying to make eye contact through the clown costume. Andy Hawkinson of the atomic vets arrives and is excited by the crowd which is now undeniably large. We hug and Starhawk goes off to be interviewed by the press for the second time this morning.*

Uncle Tony looked at his watch. "OK, Josh. I have to go to work for a change. Tell Claudia I'm not bailing her out if she gets arrested. I'm leaving you with Wavy Gravy and these other children."

Wavy Gravy was a nearly toothless, balding, fat, tie-dyed political clown who was universally beloved as an icon of the Left.

"OK, little freaks! What are we here to do today!?"

We kids stared back at Wavy Gravy in stunned silence.

"Fight nuclear power! Who needs nuclear power when you can do this?" Wavy Gravy jumped up like a whale gasping for air, and hit himself on the head with the butt of a red and yellow horn that squeaked on impact. We stared back in horror. "Jeez, tough crowd. Hey, kids! Here's Allan with the kids' truck, finally. About time, Allan. What happened, you smoke out with your dog again?"

The kids' truck was a little orange Toyota pickup. We were stuffed into the bed of the truck like crates of organic broccoli. Allan, the sweaty, bearded driver, slammed the gate shut and waved a finger at us: "No one fall out!"

"Hear that, kids!" cackled Wavy Gravy. "No falling out."

The truck lurched forward with a deep groan, and a belch of diesel exhaust slithered over us.

Claudia wrote:

> *A woman in fatigues with buttons and literature from the People's Workers Proletarian Whoosis Whatsis Vanguard stares hard at her "question authority" button and refuses eye contact. Finally she walks right past me. I don't exist. I can't stand it. I say: "Hey, I'm also a person." She looks like she might cry. Oh well. John has arrived with his spectacular solar microphone and Jason the professional whistler who is wearing a Guatemalan sunburst shirt . . . I use [the solar microphone] to get things underway: . . .*
>
> *"Um, yummy. This is a solar microphone," I say. "Nobody has to die of radiation."*
>
> *Somebody sees authority and shouts: "I hope you have all the answers."*
>
> *I say: "Somebody just said he hoped I had all the answers. I don't have answers. It's got to be all of us together providing answers. There's just too damn much at stake." It's quarter to noon. Some women near me are smiling at me, and I'm all turned on. "OK. Let's get this thing on the street! Nothing's happening in the park anymore. Let's get it into the streets!"*

We children found ourselves packed tight against one another in the back of the idling kids' truck. The unrelenting sun and smell of diesel were making me nauseated.

"Why are *you* here?" I asked the boy sitting on my foot, hoping that he would ask me the same question.

"My mom made me come," he said. Silence.

"My mother is Claudia. She's the organizer of the parade," I said proudly.

"My mom's a dyke," said the boy.

The truck lurched forward violently, and I cracked skulls with the son of a dyke. We both winced but showed each other we were too tough to cry.

"We're up," Wavy Gravy shouted back through the sliding window in the cab. "Hang on, little freakies."

The truck stopped suddenly. A flatbed truck passed in front of us with a huge gray papier-mâché nuclear cooling tower tethered to its back. It belched forth smoke.

"I made that," I told the boy. He stared at the faux reactor in silence. A rumble of drums filled the air. A massive black jumble of platforms floated by, bearing the drummers. They were Japanese people in dark robes. Their faces were painted white and set like stone. As the drums began to die down, a truck passed bearing nuclear grim reapers wearing frightening masks and waving scythes.

"I'm scared," he confided in me. I nodded. I was scared too.

The truck lurched forward again, and this time we let out a collective shriek.

The kids' truck bucked sharply when it hit the base of a hill. Suddenly I was pitched forward, and a crushing mass of heads and elbows and feet hammered against my back. We all slid along the bed of the truck, shrieking in terror. I struggled to right myself, but the truck seemed to be climbing vertically. Gravity was beckoning us over the tailgate, and we tried to press ourselves against the bed of the truck. But there were too many of us to lie flat. We clung to the sides of the truck, to each other, clawing at any little handhold we could find. As the truck fought its way up the incline, we heard the grinding of gears and the straining howl of the engine. The truck lurched backward a couple of times, as Allan tried to find a gear low enough to keep us from careening backward down the hill and into a flatbed truck full of transvestite nuns. With each lurch it felt like the bottom of the Earth was falling away beneath me. This was the first time I discovered prayer. I was bargaining in my mind: "If you let this truck get to the end of the parade without me falling out and dying, I won't even complain once if a nuclear winter comes."

Claudia continued:

I look back. The parade is stretched out all the way down the hill and half way up the next one. Blocks and blocks. Banners sparkling in the sun. The next day's TV said 1,000 people. The Examiner *estimates 2,500.* The Chronicle *says 4,000. Add a thousand or two, considering who owns the press.*

I'm crying now. Watch faces of the spectators. We're in the Fillmore now. A small group of women is reading the sign about irreversible genetic damage, jaws tight. The parade passes and passes. One man is about to enter his car but freezes on the spot. He listens to the entire altar script, is extremely moved. (Too much a "man" to cry.) Suddenly shakes himself out of it, jumps into his car in a hurry.

The Union of Concerned Comics are dressed as soldiers and chanting: "Look up, bend down, get pushed around!" . . . The new day banner. A peal of pleasant bells and song. We are alive. Let it begin now, a world of plenty. Let it begin now, a world of love. Let it begin now!

The water dragon hugs me. Don't know who you are but you're beautiful. Turns out to be a guy I slept with New Year's Eve. The Goddess float—a woman wearing a huge Goddess mask, the face of a black woman. The costume includes enormous breasts. No one laughs. The women start chanting: "No Nukes, More Dykes!" On and on to the end of the parade . . . Stop for a while to take a turn pulling a heavy white coffin. The letters on the side say "Capitalism" in bright red. The kids want to know who's in there.

"Rich people!" I say.

After the sickening, lurching series of free-falls up and down a dozen hills, the kids' truck finally pulled into the panhandle part of Golden Gate Park, its transmission smoldering under the hood. Wavy Gravy unloaded us, and we kids panted in a group, catching our breaths and dismissing as silly the various vows and oaths we swore to our gods to get us through the ordeal. A sudden break in the crowd revealed a frenzied mob screaming and descending on the nuclear cooling tower I helped build. They smashed it apart with sticks and ripped at its papier-mâché skin with their hands. It was the most violence I'd ever witnessed. I turned my face away and looked around hopefully for my mother.

Claudia's letter concluded:

I announce there is a closing ritual. Closing ritual a tug of war—two groups pull at the altar in opposite directions. It rips apart. A huge roar . . . "We are alive, let it begin now!" over and over. I stop trying to make it take any sort of form, stop organizing. Feel that I'm holding hands with Morning Glory—a witch from Greenfield Ranch. Morning Glory can't hold another hand. She's carrying a scepter, a long stick with the skull of a small animal at the top of it. One of the transvestite nuns bowed to her as she passed. We sing and sing and finally the parade is over. Joshey says: "And now there's no nuclear power anywhere on Earth!"

With the parade over, I was confident nuclear war had been averted and the specter of nuclear winter would now dissipate like the Pacific fog on a sunny San Francisco morning.

Over the next few days, I was shocked to learn that it would not. Apparently, the masses had not been moved to dismantle the military industrial complex. We were still on a collision course for nuclear war because some horrible man named Reagan was set to win the presidency. To add insult to injury, Starhawk, the anarchist Wiccan high priestess, took all the credit for organizing the Three Mile Island parade. In one of her many news interviews, she was asked: "How long did it take you to organize the parade?"

"Oh, you can't really organize something like that," she responded flippantly. "It just happens." Starhawk's name vaulted onto Claudia's shit list, right below Governor Reagan.

"*If* he gets elected?" I overheard my mother saying on the telephone. "You mean *when* he gets elected. Of course they'll target San Francisco. It's a major population center." When she put down the receiver, Claudia announced she was leaving for a month to Mexico. She was going to stay with her friend Elizabeth to help her birth her baby in a village in Michoacán. Elizabeth wanted her newborn to have Mexican citizenship so he could avoid the Draft when the next Vietnam came. And, politically, it was a whole lot better to be a Mexican than an American. Claudia thought rural Mexico might provide the community we'd been looking for. What better place to take refuge when nuclear war with Russia came storming out of the skies?

My mother left me with Uncle Tony and Claude for the month and, when she returned, she was full of wondrous stories about the poor but poetic and beautiful people of Mexico. In Mexico the children didn't cry. Boys my age were herding bulls. In Mexico, you said *¡Buenos días!* to everyone, even the burro and the drunkard. In Mexico, the people couldn't understand why we were about to elect Ronald Reagan.

We visited Uncle Tony after Reagan was officially nominated at the Republican Convention, and Tony and my mother debated who to vote for in the fall. Tony was a diehard Peace and Freedom Party man and had never voted for a mainstream candidate before.

"Tony, you *have* to vote for Carter."

"But, Claudey, I don't think he's a good president. I like Maureen Smith. She's a dedicated Socialist."

"Tony, it's not about *Carter*. It's about *Reagan*. If Carter doesn't win, Reagan will. I don't have to tell you how much worse than Maureen Smith *he* is."

"But, Claudey, I don't want to vote for the least worst candidate. I want to vote for the person I think would do the best job."

"The button, Tony. He will have his finger on that button." My mother jerked her head in my direction as if to say: "Do it for the kid."

Tony sighed and shook his head. But he agreed: "Alright, I'll vote for Carter. But it's not going to help. Reagan is winning whether we like it or not."

Reagan. The name made me shiver.

That night I packed carob chips and extra socks into a plastic bag by my bed. If we weren't wiped out in the first strike, at least I'd be ready for the nuclear winter.

THREE

Life as a Verb

With rent and crime climbing every month, and nuclear war on the horizon, my mother decided that we needed to embark on our exodus from San Francisco now—and a man named Bob DiNardo was the one who would lead us out. We had met Bob in an industrial warehouse building floats for the Three Mile Island parade. He had come for the free food but stayed late to help Claudia and me slather the giant papier-mâché nuclear cooling tower with gray paint. Bob didn't seem to notice me, but he noticed my mother. They scurried around the base of the nuclear cooling tower, chattering at each other like radical leftist squirrels.

Claudia told Bob of her belief that public schools were propaganda centers for conscienceless Capitalism. He agreed with her. He was, he said, a schoolteacher, and he was totally disillusioned with the so-called *Educational* System. She told him of her aching thirst for a rural intentional community. He had the same thirst. He was already living in a commune in Berkeley called the Frog House—but it was too urban. She told him she was ready to head for the hills to keep the Revolution alive. She'd build the community herself if she had to. Bob told her he was ready now too. He was also a builder, and who better to build a community with. He knew some people already living off the land up on Mount Lassen. All they needed were a couple more folks to join them. Bob and Claudia entered the warehouse that night as strangers with two separate visions. They walked out realizing they shared the same one.

On our walk home from the warehouse, Claudia told me she'd felt a deep physical and emotional connection with Bob.

"Why do you like him, Claudia?"

"He has the same vision we do."

"He does?"

"Yes. He knows schools are no place for kids. He knows we have to go back to the land to keep the Struggle alive. That kind of thing. And Bob has this very yin-yang thing going on, don't you think? He's strong, good with his hands, a builder. But he's also sensitive, a teacher, and, unlike other guys, he isn't turned off by the fact I have a kid. And he's fine that I'm on Welfare. In fact, he wanted to know everything about it—what I had to do to qualify for it, how much it is, how often the checks come. I like how responsible he was. When I told him it was time for me to go, he went—without me even asking—and found you talking to the belly dancers. He scooped you up onto his shoulders and brought you to me before I was even finished washing out the paintbrushes. I think he's a real man of action."

In his own way, Bob did turn out to be a man of action. He didn't believe any good came from standing around talking about things. He believed in doing. When he ran out of grass to smoke, he'd sneak right into the nearest room in the commune and raid someone else's stash. When he ran out of clean sheets and towels, he'd faux-hobble right into the nearest hospital and take some. When he ran out of gas, he'd saunter right over to the nearest unattended vehicle and siphon some by mouth through a hose into his red gas can.

Once the Three Mile Island Memorial Parade was over, Bob came to visit my mother regularly. He'd pop his shiny head into the living room, say hello, and then sequester himself in the bedroom with Claudia for an hour or so before sneaking out the front door, silent and sweaty.

After Claudia returned from Mexico in the summer of 1980, we picked up and moved across the Bay to the Frog House, where we shared Bob's little ground-floor room. I slept on a foam pad on the floor, sandwiched between Bob's clothing pile and the jumble of milk crates that served as shelves. The adults claimed the rickety wooden bed that Bob had designed and constructed. Claudia was deeply impressed by the ingenuity and workmanship. "Joshey, Bob *built* this bed . . . himself," she said, running her hand admiringly along the CONTENTS MAY SHIFT stamp on the rough-hewn salvaged lumber. Our little room opened directly onto a heavily trafficked communal living room. The evening discourse between the drunk and stoned housemates kept me awake at night. But this noise was often a welcome distraction from my mother's unspeakably disturbing moans as she and Bob grappled in the bed above me.

I was the only child in the Frog House, but I did my best to make friends with the adults, who weren't very enthusiastic playmates. James, the emaciated musician, begrudgingly let me play his drum set in the basement, but no one appreciated the volume and arrhythmic cadence I beat out for them. Kevin, the smiley, long-haired white guy and his girlfriend, Cheri, the taciturn dreadlocked black woman, were so young I couldn't tell whether they were adults or still children. My mother was stirred to her core by the bravery of their biracial love. I forced them to play Go Fish with me after dinner every day, but their alleged bedtime seemed to get earlier and earlier each night. The woman street artist who made the feather jewelry strictly forbade me from playing with her glue, and the tall skinny magician wouldn't let me touch his magical silver rings. Everyone hated it when I eavesdropped on their conversations and then leapt out from behind the couch to ask questions like "What's a 'big boner'?" The only Frog Houser who tolerated me was the perpetually drunk fifty-year-old biker guy who let me watch *The Incredible Hulk* with him on his little black-and-white TV. But his snoring was so loud I couldn't concentrate on the show.

The one thing the residents of Frog House did seem to appreciate about me was that my mother was paying half of Bob's share of the rent, which was more than the $0.00 a month that Bob had been kicking in. Apparently this no-rent routine had been going on for some time. And it was wearing thin. Bob's name was spoken like a swear word around the Frog House: "Bahb!" Or sometimes in combinations: "Fuckin' Bahb!" or, upon discovery of something missing, "What the . . . Bahb!?" I took to saying his name this way under my breath when I dropped my banana on the floor or missed the toilet bowl. "Bahb!"

For a man whose name was synonymous with exasperation, Bob was remarkably sanguine about his housemates' discontent. "I don't know what they're yappin' about. I built them that hot tub." No one could dispute this. The gigantic concrete hot tub took up much of the backyard. True, the water didn't technically get hot. And, yes, the hot tub reeked of the same toxic odor as the half-melted, sun-baked garden hose that delivered its water. But the hot tub was most definitely there. Bob had built that marvel of aquatic engineering and thought that should count for something. And, if it didn't, the whole pack of ungrateful bozos could go stuff themselves.

Before the Frog House People's Democratic Subcommittee on How to Kick Bob Out could reconvene, Bob announced that he'd found a subletter for his room—some dude he knew who was getting out of treatment. The housemates needn't worry because the lucky bum was getting a steady flow of rent money from his parents until he got back on his feet. As for us, we were taking to the open road.

Our home for the next few months was Bob's box-shaped blue van. It had once belonged to a bakery whose ghostlike name was almost discernible through the layers of blue house paint. Although metal was its base component, the van relied on all manner of tape to maintain its integrity: duct tape over dents, packing tape on the headlights, masking tape over the split in the steering wheel, and scotch tape holding on the rearview mirror. The van had everything we needed to make ourselves at home: a full-size bed in back for the three of us, hanging mesh baskets to store our fruit, a propane camping stove, and a small wooden marimba to play when the need for music arose.

We began our wanderings up the coast, following Highway 1 north and parking overnight in fallow fields or empty parking lots. I spent a lot of time staring out the dusty back windows, watching the crooked highway flow out from under us. Claudia was invariably perched in the passenger seat, passionately preaching about the Struggle against Capitalism and gesturing like a sign language interpreter while Bob scanned the roadway for found objects or diners. We stopped at every road sign that said *free* on it. Free samples, free tours, free boat launch.

Somewhere between Bob's victorious whoops upon finding a perfectly good cooking pot on the riverbank and Claudia's three-part indictment of the United Fruit Company for war crimes in Guatemala, the two of them made a pact for the future. They were going to found Utopia. Bob was going to build and teach at our new community school, and Claudia was going to grow the food and help raise the children. The question of location came down to the twin criteria of politically sophisticated people and land-based living. Mexico and Canada were out because they had no rural intellectuals and, like the Bay Area, their urban intellectuals were too divorced from the land. Claudia didn't know where to begin but, after all his travels, Bob could think of one place that met both criteria: Mount Lassen. Good people were working the land there already.

"Are we going to visit Mount Lassen before we move there?" I asked.

"No, bud," said Bob. "But if we are going to take on a project like this we'll have to head over to Sacto and see Mr. James." The next day Bob's funky blue van pulled off the freeway into an industrial area of Sacramento. The van bucked and rattled as the streets deteriorated into a minefield of potholes. We bottomed out over a dozen train tracks before finally pulling up to a walled compound festooned with scraps of sheet metal and topped with razor wire.

"This," announced Bob with proud giddiness, "is Mr. James' place."

A small flock of children opened the massive metal gates for us, and we rolled into an industrial, post-apocalyptic Third World village. Blackened hulks of machinery and a fleet of vehicles in varying states of disrepair stood out like islands amid a domestic lake of wandering animals and playing children.

Mr. James was a sixty-year-old African-American man who wore a leather golf cap above his impossibly thick glasses and white fuzzy sideburns. They'd known each other for a long time, maybe from Bob's train-hopping days. Mr. James was Bob's mentor and guru, someone who'd mastered the art of living off of society's discarded, or almost discarded, waste. Bob introduced us as his woman and her boy. Mr. James wanted to know how old I was.

"Four and a half. But I'm almost five."

"Almost five? I got me an almost fiver too. Bradford!? Where Bradford at!?"

Bradford stepped out from the semicircle of children curiously watching us. He was holding some sort of deformed cat in his arms.

"What is that?" I asked.

"He a piglet," Bradford educated me. "That a baby pig." He grinned: "We gawn eat him!"

"For real?" I asked in disbelief.

"For reals," said Bradford. "Ain't you never had bacon before?" I shook my head. "You a poor little boy." I laughed because Bradford was shorter than I was.

We ate beans and rice at a table saw in a makeshift barn with Mr. James and some of his family. His wife was about my mother's age. She was very dark-skinned and was nursing a plump baby at her breast.

"Don't she look like she from Africa, Bob?" asked Mr. James.

"I don't know," said Bob diplomatically.

"Well she does. Like she just came off the boat," said Mr. James. "I got me a good one, Bob. She love me something fierce."

Mr. James had apparently found several good ones because, from what I could tell, everyone else in the compound—from the fat baby up to the balding guy with the limp—was one of Mr. James' children.

"Why do you live in a junkyard?" I asked Bradford.

"That the way it is." He shrugged. "Where you live?"

"Right now, in that blue van."

"Why you live in the van?"

"I don't know."

"That called: *That the way it is.*"

We played with the piglet, and Bradford told me about all the times he'd seen naked ladies. I'd seen lots of naked women too, but I felt more embarrassed than proud of it, so I didn't compete with his tallies. After lunch it was time to get down to business, and Mr. James took us on a tour of the inventory.

"Now, Bob, when you is starting out a new place, what's the one thing you need most? Shelter. And if you is planning on up and building your shelter, especially on the side of some mountain, you is going to get cold and rained on and stuff. So what you need is to bring your shelter with you. Follow me?"

"Well, we've got the van, Mr. James. We're living in it now."

"That little thing? Bob, you know what a caboodle is? No. No one know. Right now you going round in a caboodle. What you need is a kit *and* a caboodle. And this baby right here is the *whole* kit and caboodle."

We'd arrived at a big green bus. It looked like it might have been used as a military transport, shuttling soldiers on and off a base somewhere. Inside it had a fold-down sleeping platform, shelves on the walls, curtains on the windows, an old rocking chair, and a rug.

"Wow," said Bob. "Mr. James, this is amazing."

"That ain't the half of it," said Mr. James. "Listen to this." He slid into the driver's seat and started the engine. "You hear? It purr like a kitten."

"It really does sound like a cat purring," confirmed Claudia.

"Sure it does," said Mr. James.

"Are you selling it?" asked Bob.

Mr. James turned off the engine. "Bob, this here is a four-thousand-dollar bus. I got a two-thousand-dollar bus over there, but I ain't even gonna show it to you. You a friend a mine. And being that you a friend a mine, I could give this here bus to you for three grand."

"That sounds fair," said Bob.

"And that includes a full tank a gas."

They shook on it and, all business being concluded, we filed back outside. Mr. James peered down through his magnifying glass lenses at Bradford and me.

"You know what I likes, boys? I likes me a race." Mr. James straightened up and squinted into the distance. "You see that caterpillar tread all folded up by where the chickens is fighting? First one there and back is a winner."

Bradford solemnly transferred custody of the piglet to Mr. James, stretched his legs, and went into a runner's crouch. I tried to imitate Bradford's athletic movements, but I didn't want to put my hands down in the dirt.

"On your mark, git set, go!"

Bradford tore off ahead of me like a proud gazelle. I churned the dust after him and almost caught up, slapping the rusty steel of the caterpillar tread just as he was turning back. I turned to follow but felt my strength draining away. My side hurt and I couldn't get enough air through the dust. My handmade

Mexican sandals were sliding all over my feet, and my floppy hair was in my eyes. I slowed to a jog and watched Bradford cross the finish line ahead of me and heard Mr. James' congratulatory "Alright!" I walked the last few steps and came to a halt in front of Mr. James and Claudia. Mr. James was misty-eyed, shaking his head. "Ain't that a sight. To see a little black boy outrun a white boy like that." I looked up to see that my mother was misty-eyed too. She was nodding. The racial healing accomplished by me losing that race was apparently quite moving.

On the van ride to nowhere in particular that evening, Bob and Claudia discussed the green bus.

"But you heard Mr. James. We need it for shelter. Plus how else are we gonna move all our stuff up? You gonna hire movers?"

"Bob, I agree with you about the bus. I just don't see how we're going to pay for it."

"Mr. James told me he'd give us a couple of months. Do you think we could ask your mother?"

"To give us three thousand dollars!?" Claudia snorted.

"To *lend* you the money so you, her daughter, and her grandson can have a proper roof over their heads."

"Bob, I have so much negative energy with her. So much rage. I'm not asking her for anything."

"She's in Arizona, right? How about we just go explore the Southwest for a while? Stop by to pay her a visit. Let her see her grandson. And if the spirit moves me, I'll ask her for you. No. Big. Deal. It's for the Cause, right?"

Only the blue van made noise for a while. Claudia stared out at the swamp passing by the window.

"OK, Bob. Fine."

"Great! We'll head back toward Berkeley, pick up your Welfare check. That should be in by Monday, right? Then we'll follow the winds into the Southwest and *maybe* borrow us some money for the bus."

As we drove, the undulating ridges of the Nevada desert lay hidden in the darkness. Little patches of tan sand bloomed and bubbled at the edge of the headlight beams before withering away back into blackness when we changed lanes.

I stared out the cracked passenger-side window of Bob DiNardo's funky blue van. Claudia was crashed out in the back. Bob was behind the wheel, whistling old-time hobo songs. When he was younger, Bob told me, he'd hopped a lot of trains and befriended some of the legendary train-hopping tramps of yesteryear. Men like Catfish Russell and Jerky Ray. These were real men of character who managed to crisscross this great land of ours without working a day of their lives. When Bob meditated, he told me, he projected himself back into those halcyon days when dangling your legs from the side of a boxcar and roasting up some roadkill for grub were your only order of business.

"Bob, when will we get there?" I asked without turning my head to look at him.

"Get where?"

"Somewhere."

"We are somewhere." He was annoyed with me for asking so many questions, but I was too bored to stop. "Bob, why do we have to live in the van?"

"Can't beat the rent!" I could hear the earnest smile in his voice.

"Where are we, Bob?"

He took a hissing sip from his can of beer, burped, and said: "We passed Battle Mountain a while ago, buddy. We're comin' up on the Utah line probably pretty soon, OK?" We traveled on in silence for a while before I felt the van slowing. "I'm gonna pull into this truck stop, buddy. Looks like they've got a diner. You wanna come in with me?"

The van smelled of gasoline and brewer's yeast and a thousand farts. "Yeah," I said.

"Put on that hat I gotcha, buddy."

The hat in question was an old tattered baseball cap with a grease stain snaking down the brim. Bob found it for me in a field behind a service station in Sacramento and, when I complained that it was too itchy, he washed it out for me in a marsh north of Arcata. Claudia said it made me look like an urchin. Bob loved the look.

We parked in the darkened perimeter of the truck stop, and I followed Bob into the light. Massive arc lamps floated in the ether above like a constellation of suns. In the gritty, artificial brightness, semi-trailer trucks lumbered about like grumbling dinosaurs, and tanks, wires, and hoses intertwined overhead to form a mechanical jungle.

Bob summoned me out of my disorientation: "Buddy, in here." He held a door open into a fluorescent hallway. "You always wanna enter a restaurant by the side door," Bob schooled me. "That way it looks like you're just comin' back from the bathroom." At the end of the hall the bustling little diner opened up before us. Bob stopped and stooped. He stood poised like an eagle surveying a field of mice. "Follow me, bud." Bob stepped forward with casual confidence and wove his way through the forest of rumpled and weary diners. I trailed behind, following the tan stripe of Bob's bald head as it proceeded toward the far corner. I could tell from the bobbing of his baldness that he was smiling and nodding as he went. Bob closed in on the booth in the corner, where a leathery old couple were unfurling their gnarled frames from the strictures of the table.

As the couple hobbled forward, Bob spun gently, slid into their booth just behind them, and brought the old man's coffee mug to his lips. Bob gestured to me with his left hand and then slid the old couple's stack of dollars seamlessly off the table and into his lap. I knew restaurant rituals well—Uncle Tony had schooled me in everything from ordering to tipping—and Bob had clearly violated every commandment of patronage. I pulled myself into the booth next to Bob warily lest his antisocial behavior escalate into eating the sugar packets or peeing on the table.

The table in question was littered with the remains of a mostly eaten hamburger and a tangle of vestigial fried eggs and ketchup. They were orbited by a side salad, two triangles of toast—one of them bearing a perfectly semicircular bite mark—and a debris of soiled glasses, silverware, and napkins.

"Here, buddy, you want some toast?" Bob slid the untouched triangle of toast my way.

"But, it's somebody else's," I protested.

"It's yours now, buddy. They didn't want it anymore. Woulda just gone to waste, right in the trash. Look, it's perfectly good toast. You want me to put some jam on it? The jam's free. You can take as many of these packets as you want. Put some in your pocket."

I didn't want to put the little white tubs of jam into my pocket. They might leak. And I didn't want to eat the old people's old toast. It just wasn't done. It would be like walking around naked, which Bob was also fond of.

"Can I get you folks anything else?" The waitress was standing over us, swinging a battered coffeepot in one hand. "You want some more . . ." The coffeepot ceased its mindless rotations through the air. The waitress was staring at us. She squinted suspiciously, like a mother sparrow scrutinizing the cuckoo eggs sleeping in her nest. ". . . coffee?"

"Miss, I would love a refill," Bob said, offering up the old man's coffee mug as his own. Bob leaned toward her as the waitress began to pour and confided in her, "I've gotta stay awake. I've gotta hit Frisco by morning so I can get little bud here back home for the funeral." And then he mouthed a few more words silently to the waitress.

What was he talking about?

The waitress's clenched face softened, and she nodded as she poured Bob's coffee.

"Oh, and you can bring the check for the hamburger and whatnot. We're ready for it." Bob added: "Oh, and do you mind bringing buddy here some more toast? He dropped his on the floor."

The waitress nodded again: "Sure thing." And she walked away.

"Josh," Bob said, "I gotta go make a *numero dos* like you wouldn't believe. When the waitress comes back, order us some pie." Bob got up and tiptoed toward the bathroom, clenching his buttocks.

I watched the diner's cast of characters come and go. The truckers with their netted hats and flannel shirts, the white family that held hands and prayed before they ate, the state trooper brooding alone. We weren't in San Francisco anymore.

The waitress came back with the check and the fresh toast for me. I thanked her and asked her for pie as Bob had instructed.

"Sure thing," she said. She lingered over me as I figured out how to work the jam packet. "Where's your mommy at?" she asked. I peeked at her from underneath my tattered hat. The waitress was old, but she looked younger at first glance because her face was slathered with makeup. I'd seen this kind of face-painting on the transvestites in the Castro before, but never on a woman. "Did your mommy pass on?" she asked.

"She's sleeping," I said, turning my attention back to the jam.

"With the angels, baby. With them angels now," she said softly and turned and walked away.

Bob returned invigorated after his *numero dos*, and started in on the hand-me-down salad. "Josh, did I ever tell you the time I got put up in a hotel for free?" He hadn't, so he proceeded to tell me about this one time he'd gone into a hotel just to use the bathroom, but they'd assumed he was there for some conference. The next thing Bob knew, they'd given him a name tag and a packet of papers about insurance. "In hotels, buddy, they've got something called room service. It's super duper. They bring the restaurant to you."

The waitress returned bearing a dish of chocolate pie.

"What's this now?" Bob wanted to know.

"Your little friend wanted some pie."

Bob turned to me: "Joshua! I told you we don't have money for dessert no more!"

What the hell!? He'd told me to order it!

"But . . ." I protested.

The waitress rescued me: "It's OK, it's on me."

Bob brightened. "Are you sure? You won't get into trouble?"

"Nah, no trouble. It's the least I can do."

"Bless your heart, dear," Bob called after her. And then to me: "Good job, buddy. Dig in."

I reluctantly sunk a fork into the gelatinous flesh of the pie and drew it back to my mouth.

"Good, isn't it, buddy?"

Damn! It was good. Even the ice cream Uncle Tony sometimes bought for me when Claudia wasn't around couldn't compare to this delightful confection. I went in for bite after bite, happy for the first time that my mother wasn't awake and with us. She would have never allowed me to have something so full of sugar. Whatever Bob's annoying eccentricities, I had to admit that he could deliver when it came to the dessert department.

Bob checked the bill and laid down a couple of bills and a small pile of coins. "Look at that, buddy. It's a win-win. She still gets ten percent tip."

"Uncle Tony says with tips you're supposed to triple the tax."

Bob conjured a toothpick from inside his jacket and began picking his teeth. "You know, Josh. There's a lotta things you don't know. Did you know that different states have different taxes?" I didn't know that. "We're in Nevada now, buddy. That's totally different from California. So if I went around pulling California tricks in Nevada, we'd be in a lotta trouble. Your Uncle Tony probably never thought of that."

We reemerged into the eerie, grainy brightness of the truck stop and skirted a wall back toward the blue van. I could feel the sugar gnawing at my teeth.

"We did pretty good in there, buddy," Bob declared. "We got coffee, water, a salad, fresh toast for you, and pie, for guess how much? Guess, Josh."

"I don't know."

"Negative ten cents. We got all that and we *made* ten cents, buddy. Food for free and we're a dime richer. Now that's what I call a good deal. And look at this." Bob opened his jacket to show me a mass of whiteness. "I scored a whole bunch of toilet paper from the bathroom."

We spent the next few days in the mountains, and when Bob had pilfered all he could from off-season ski resorts, we slipped back into the desert like a rowboat pushing off into the high seas. We were just a funky blue speck of metal and tape floating in an ocean of sand and scrub. Under the limitless heavens, I realized I'd never really looked at the sky before. By day I was awestruck by the vastness of the blue expanse. And at night I watched with wonder as the horizon's riots of color retreated before the fullness of the cosmos. The Milky Way and a billion stars reminded me I was just a small part of some colossal greatness.

Claudia liked the stars too, but didn't like the oppressive heat. Bob's appreciation of the stars seemed to rise and fall based on how many paper towels we'd managed to pilfer from the gas station restroom or how many forgotten odds and ends we'd collected from the last rest stop. But his favorite activity remained the restaurant leftovers trick. Sliding into the right table at just the right moment, Bob believed, was a proud art, not only rendering free food, but making an important politico-spiritual statement.

"Claudia, this salad's for you. And, buddy, *mm-mm*, look at these scrambled eggs. Not even touched."

"But, it's like stealing."

"No, bud, it's not like stealing. In fact, it's the opposite of stealing. We are taking something that *nobody* wants and wanting it. Society is all about consumption—just buy, buy, buy. And then throw away, throw away, throw away, so they can buy some more. We've gotta be like the Indians. You know what they used to do when they killed a buffalo?"

"American bison," I corrected him.

"No, when they killed a buffalo they ate all of it. Not just the steaks. The whole thing. The heart, the eyes, the nose. And then they used the skin for clothes and they even made the hoofs into glue. We're like the Indians. And, like them, I believe in karma. You know what that is, buddy?"

"It's when you're reincarnated . . ."

"No, it's if you open yourself up to the Universe and you've got an open heart and you say: 'OK, Universe, I'm ready to receive.' Then you'll be given everything you need."

Claudia looked up from her Ursula Le Guin novel and nodded. "You have to open your heart, Joshey."

Walking out of the restaurant, Bob picked his teeth triumphantly and announced: "I'm stuffed. All that for a buck twenty-five." He was always keeping score: "Free picnic cooler! Second one this trip." "That meal came to a

Playing a fife in the New Mexico desert.

grand total of zero dollars!" I came to think that he was keeping a tally so that he could have his lifetime freeloading statistics etched onto his tombstone. It would read: HERE LIES BOB DINARDO. HE SCORED: 425 PAIRS OF USED SHOES; 1 BILLION LINEAR FEET OF TOILET PAPER; AND, 7,000 PIECES OF PIE. Bob truly, honestly thought we were pulling one over on society by bathing in the filthy sinks of stinking truck stop bathrooms, scavenging through the garbage, and sleeping in a van parked in abandoned rock quarries and KMart parking lots.

From Utah over to Colorado, down to New Mexico, and through Arizona back to Utah, Bob DiNardo's van spun great freeloading circles around the Southwest. But we were never truly aimless. Bob was keeping his eye on that $3,000 potentially waiting for us in my grandmother's bank account. One morning, when the energy seemed just right, we suddenly swooped south toward Tucson. As we pulled up to Grandma Harriette's little house, I noticed that Bob was not only wearing a shirt—which was in and of itself a big deal—but that he was wearing a button-down shirt. And it was tucked in. Claudia was anxiously rubbing her upper lip. Based on my mother's descriptions of her, I fully expected my grandmother to start punching people in the face once she'd figured out how to get her complicated screen door open. But she was totally nonviolent, wearing a tight little smile on her made-up face.

"Well hello, Claudey." She gave Claudia a hug. "And Joshua, how much you've grown." She gave me a hug too. "And you must be Bob."

Bob took a step back, opened his arms like a bald eagle preparing to leap from its arboreal perch, and dived forward into a hug, emitting a loud sigh of "Mom!" He wrapped his arms around Grandma Harriette and rocked her gently from side to side, groaning with pleasure. When my grandmother extricated herself from the hug she was still smiling.

"As we say in the Old Country," she said, *"ve iz mir!"*

"Vase beer!" Bob greeted her back with an ethnic hand flourish.

I'd met my grandmother once before when she'd come to visit us in San Francisco. She was as I remembered her. Her long, woolly, black-and-white hair pulled back tightly from her face. Her porcelain features and Levantine angles—like her otherworldly Yiddish-Boston accent and her tiny, immaculate house full of antiques—were a throwback to some other time and place. Her potential energy was palpable to me, polite demeanor papering over a frothing forcefulness.

"Look here, I've made beds for you in the living room," Grandma Harriette instructed.

"Oh, Mom," said Bob, "we can stay in the van. It's not *too* bad, and we're used to it."

"Nonsense! You'll stay here."

"Really? Thank you, Mom! We'd like to take you out to dinner. What's your favorite place?"

Bob took us all out to Grandma Harriette's favorite Chinese restaurant, but they didn't accept checks, so Grandma had to pay since she was the only one with enough cash. Then we walked down to a Denny's restaurant to have pie.

"Did you have pie back when you were growing up, Mom?" asked Bob.

"Did we have pie?" She turned to me with the smile still on her face. "He wants to know if we had pie. We had all kinds of pie. Meat pie, vegetable pie, fruit pie, noodle pie, Boston cream pie."

Bob looked dreamily off into space. "That's a lotta pie, Mom."

"Well, pie is anything you put in a pie shell."

"Ha! That's a good one. You know what I think, Mom? I've been listening to how you speak and the ideas you come up with, and I think you're a very well-educated mother."

My grandmother's face contorted into a contemptuous snarl for a nanosecond, and I expected her to start strangling Bob at any moment. But she restrained herself admirably. Bob went on being obsequiously unbearable, and she kept up the same strained little smile that failed to extend to her eyes.

The next day Claudia was excited to explore some of the Native American heritage sites. Bob thought he might be able to finagle free admission, since he was friends with a real Indian chief. I had no desire to watch Bob say "How!" to stunned Natives all day so I stayed behind with Grandma Harriette. We played Chinese checkers and I Spy. She showed me family photographs and told me about the Spanish Civil War and the Battle of Stalingrad.

"What am I supposed to do?" she asked me once Zhukov had finished encircling the German Sixth Army.

"With what?"

She lit a cigarette. "With this. She comes home with this Baab character." She spit the name out again: "Baab!" This was a new epithetic version of his name, connoting "contempt," which I liked almost as much as "Bahb!" connoting "exasperation." "What's he after, kissing my ass all the time?"

I sat very still, eyes wide open trying not to see that image in my mind.

"What does this Baab character want? Money, I guess. At first I thought he was a straight *goniff*. But with his song and dance, he must be a *shyster*, waiting to pitch something. What do you think he is, Joshua?"

"I like that first thing you called him yesterday. A Hendrix?"

"What? Oh, a *schmendrick*?"

"Yeah."

"Oh, don't worry, he's still a *schmendrick*. The question is whether he's a *schmendrick* of a *shyster* or just a *schmendrick* of a *nebbish* with shit for brains." She was silent. Then she spit out "Baab!" again. "That's not even a name, Bob."

"It's not?"

"No. Bob's not a name at all. It's a verb."

"What's a verb?"

"It's supposed to be an action word. To bob is to float up and down with the waves. Something that has no direction of its own. No weight, no intensity. It just bobs up and down in the water, subject to the whims of the elements."

"Do you like him, Grandma?"

"Do I like him? There's nobody there to like or not like."

The following day was overcast but punishingly hot, and the grunting of some large animal rubbing itself against the back of the air conditioner pulled me from my dreams. The summer rains had withheld their blessings, and the javelinas were left to lick up the evaporating discharge from leaking air conditioners. The arroyos conveyed nothing but dust.

We holed up inside and, toward evening, Bob declared that he was taking us all out for a proper dinner. The diner was too crowded, so he took us to a sandwich place. In the middle of the meal, Bob became unusually serious and leaned across the table toward my grandmother.

"Mom. Your daughter and I have a new business opportunity, and we want to ask you to invest in us. As you know, I'm a certified schoolteacher, and we have an opportunity to start a new school and a new *community,* really, up in Tehama County, California. Now, to make that happen, we need to move both of our homes up there and get a new place, together. I don't have to tell you how expensive getting a place can be. But we've come up with a way of both moving and living with one investment. An associate of mine named Mr. James has made a mobile home available to us for the very reasonable price of three thousand dollars. That's all we need. Now, I know it's a lot, Mom, but this is the loan we need to get settled down and to get started on *our* future."

Bob concluded with a proud paternal nod toward me.

Although I could tell her jaw was clenched while Bob made his pitch, Grandma Harriette never lost her little smile.

"Well, that's a *very* interesting proposal, Bob. Why don't you let me think on it."

The next morning my grandmother handed Claudia a check for $3,000. "This is what you want, yes?" said Grandma Harriette. "It's a *loan*, not a gift. And it's for *you,* to use as *you* see fit. *Shumesh gezunt.*" Claudia pocketed the check sheepishly. My grandmother turned and gave Bob her polite smile. "Well, Bob, it was very nice to meet you." She extended her hand.

Bob shook his head in amused adoration. "Mom!" he laughed. "Come here!" Bob wrapped her in a long, deep embrace and kissed her on the top of her head. "Good times, Mom!" he said.

With Grandma Harriette when she visited me in San Francisco.

Grandma Harriette bent down and held my head to hers. "Now we know," she whispered into my ear: "*Shyster!*" She nodded at me knowingly and winked. The doorway of the van narrowed into darkness.

As we cruised down Speedway Boulevard out of Tucson, Bob punched the ceiling of the van. "We got it! Claudia! Three large!" If stealing toilet paper was a major score for him, the $3,000 from Grandma must have been the score of a lifetime. Bob carried this ebullience with him for the rest of our wanderings in the desert.

When we reached open desert again, the steel sky finally broke and the long awaited rains plunged salvation into the broken Sonoran. The saguaros shivered and stood straight again. The javelinas grunted with delight, wallowing in the soothing mud. And the arroyos rumbled with the brown waters of new life.

Bob ran outside to dance in the rain. He loved the rain and got naked in it as often as possible. When the drops would start pasting the windshield, Bob would swerve the van into the open desert, strip his clothes off, and run out into the fresh sandy mud with a bar of soap and a bottle of shampoo. "It's a free shower!" he'd whoop. Claudia loved these spontaneous celebrations of nature and would join him as fast as she could, stumbling in the back of the van to undress without losing her glasses. They'd call at me like cheerleaders: "Come on, Josh! Come join the free shower! You can do it!" I would sullenly and reluctantly strip down, hoping that the free shower would shut off before I got out. But once I was out, I prayed that the celestial management would keep the free shower water pressure high so that I wouldn't get caught with soap in my eyes or shampoo in my hair.

The outdoor bathing concept became so popular with Bob and Claudia that we started screeching the van to a halt at the first signs of standing water. We were soon bathing in lakes, streams, and pools of brackish effluent. Watching them frolic in the water before me, I detected something familiar in their playfulness.

They were acting like children. Which was weird because *I* felt like an adult.

When we weren't bathing, we were scouring the desert for obscene rock formations. "There's one, Bob. Out there. Pull over!" We walked out to the rounded rock cleft in twain.

"It's a butt!" snorted Bob. "Look, buddy. Butt Rock!"

We discovered and photographed Butt Rock, Vagina Rock, Cock Rock, and Toilet Rock. And then we discovered newer and better butts and vaginas in other parts of the desert until it seemed that geology itself had a dirty mind. A billion years of sedimentation and erosion culminated in a perverted series of rock art.

In the eastern Mojave Desert, the earth started sprouting cacti—a hundred varietals, each more alien than the last. The van swerved into the desert at once, and Bob and Claudia emerged like mostly naked astronauts eager for first contact. "Come on, buddy!" Bob called after me.

"No. It's too dangerous," I said to the empty van.

The appearance and variety of the cacti were impressive: teddy bear, prickly pear, hedgehog, foxtail, barrel. But I refused to leave the safety of the van, based on my personal belief that sharp spikes were nature's way of saying Do Not Touch. Bob and Claudia did not subscribe to this theory of evolution and were soon all over the cacti.

"Look at this one, Bob. The barbs look like fish hooks."

"Ouch. This one has long dusty prickers that look like bones."

"This one's like a hairbrush. *Ow!* A really sharp hairbrush."

"We should try to grow those in our new bus and sell 'em," he said. They looked at each other and then raced to the back of the van and began rummaging through the milk crates. A moment later they were skipping back toward the perilous cactus with a bread knife and an empty plastic yogurt container. They returned triumphantly with the stubby severed arm of a cactus protruding from the container.

"You have to water it," said Bob. Claudia dumped some water into the container and placed it on the broad black dashboard in front of her.

"That's not a good idea," I said.

The van jerked forward and the cactus tumbled onto my mother's lap.

"Aaah!" she yelled.

I watched with detached curiosity as Bob worked his grungy pocketknife tweezers to pull the crescent slivers out of my mother's thighs. Having seen the inevitable unfold, I felt a puzzling and ironic sense of satisfaction. It was perhaps my first *I told you so* moment.

When Bob was finished, Claudia put what was left of the cactus back on the dashboard. Bob scotch-taped the container in place and declared: "There!"

A few miles later we came upon an even more resplendent patch of cactus. They were out of the van again in a flash, cavorting through the cacti like children at a petting zoo. "Hey, buddy! We found one that shoots its prickers at you before you even touch it." To my continued surprise, they began hacking at the dart-shooting cactus with the breadknife and replanted a hunk of it inside an empty tahini jar. They soon landscaped a little cactus garden on the dashboard, relying on the power of scotch tape for protection. "That's not a good idea," I said again.

Later that day, we stopped for lunch at a truck stop. After Bob had fished some perfectly good day-old or days-old bread out of the dumpster, we took off again. The van lurched forward out of the parking lot and the entire cactus garden jumped onto my mother's lap, and another piercing scream rang out.

Bob helped Claudia hobble around the van and laid her down next to me on the bed for the cactus needle extraction of a lifetime. "Come on, buddy. There's too many. I need your help. Don't be squeamish. They don't bleed too bad."

It wasn't the cactus needles I was recoiling from. It was the image of my mother's unkempt pubic hair pouring out from under her hiked-up, faded yellow short shorts. I felt deeply that this somehow violated the social contract every bit as much as Bob's food theft and stingy tipping.

We wisely left the mangled remains of the cactus garden by the side of the road and drove on in silence. We passed several more patches of cactus without any reaction from the adults. I relaxed my shoulders, confident that they could take care of themselves for the rest of the day.

In the afternoon, we passed an Army convoy going in the other direction. Hundreds of military vehicles snaked back into the horizon. We watched in tense silence. Here was the military industrial complex on full, naked display.

"How sad," Bob finally said. "Being trained to destroy."

"And to kill," added my mother, who pulled out her pocket instamatic camera to document the state monopoly on violence. "Oh my Goddess, look," she said. "They're waving at me."

"Why are they waving?" I asked.

"Because they think I'm taking their picture because I think they're heroes."

We all chuckled about how clueless the soldiers were. They looked young, the soldiers. I felt sorry for them. These young guys who had to go kill strange peasants in strange lands. But watching the convoy unfurl with its parade of the machines of war, I felt something else too. Twinges of jealousy. How exhilarating it must be to wear a uniform and fire guns, I thought. And to drive these wondrous tanks, half-tracks, and big trucks. And more. To be a part of something larger than yourself. Part of a powerful team of warriors. These were the modern-day knights. I thought about that convoy often, wishing at times that I could have been a part of it rather than the lonely boy in the blue van rambling down the empty highway.

We stumbled back into Berkeley, unwashed and sunburnt, in time to hear the phone ringing in the Frog House. It was for my mother.

"Oh my God!" she exclaimed. Her eyes were wild with fear. "He's a madman. He'll kill us all." Just as she feared, Ronald Reagan had been elected president.

This added extra urgency to our planned move back to the land, and we drove directly to Sacramento to see Mr. James. Bradford's piglet was now an ugly, bristly pig, but Bradford was nowhere to be found. The green bus, however, was right where we left it. As Claudia was digging in her Mexican shoulder bag for a pen to sign the pink slip, Bob grabbed her arm.

"Claudia! I just thought of something. If you put the bus in your name, I bet it'll mess up your Welfare benefits. You know how the government is." Bob had a panicked look on his face.

Claudia thought about this. "You know, you're probably right. I hadn't thought of that. What should we do?"

Bob appeared to be puzzled by the problem, taking a moment to work it through in his head. Finally, a solution emerged from his mouth. "Why don't we put the bus in my name for now. That way they won't be able to trace it back to you. Then, later, if we can figure out how to get by the Welfare rules, we can put it back in your name."

"Good idea."

Mr. James sold the bus to Bob for my grandmother's $3,000. Then Bob sold his funky blue van to Mr. James for $100, and we headed back to the Bay Area for the last time.

Before we left, I celebrated my fifth birthday with Uncle Tony, and he put me to sleep by chanting the Gayatri Mantra by my bedside. He pronounced the Vedic Sanskrit with a soft Spanish accent that made the mantra sound like gently bubbling water. I could feel myself beginning to drift into the dream world, gliding on the currents of his prayers.

"Why do you say that mantra over me?" I mumbled.

"I have to say it every night to keep you safe, to make your dreams come true."

"But what if I don't see you again?"

"I'll say the mantra for you every night whether we're together or not. Wherever you are in the world, you'll be able to hear my voice when you go to sleep."

A few days later, someone ran through the halls screeching the news. John Lennon had been assassinated by the CIA. The killing sent the Frog House into a panic, and our packing went into overdrive. A chill, dark fog enveloped us as we shuttled the last of our worldly possessions into the green bus. The last things to go were our feminist cat, Ms.Ms., and a cage filled with the two white roosters one of the housemates had found terrorizing picnickers in Golden Gate Park. We were taking them back to the land with us. All of the Frog House turned out to see us off.

"See ya, Baahb!" They called out, his name finally synonymous with relief and absurdity.

The green bus coughed to life and rumbled forward, creaking under the weight of the two visions it carried back to the land. The roosters crowed, the cat hid, and I perched up front in the rocking chair. I was happy that our trip was beginning, but was very much looking forward to the moment the trip would be over. After so much talk and preparation, we were finally on our way to settle down and build a new community, to start a school for me, and to meet new friends. Bob's buddies, Stan and Maureen, were waiting for us up in the town of Manton on the side of Mount Lassen, and they would introduce us around when we arrived. We'd be there just in time for Christmas.

FOUR

Back to the Land

Our green bus set a course due north on I-5, and we crawled through endless expanses of withered farmland. When we reached Red Bluff, we turned east on State Route 36, and the road began to climb and curve as we navigated our way into the mountains. Around a bend, the sky darkened, and then the air was filled with fluttering white moths.

"Snow!" Bob announced.

It was snowing! I'd never seen snow before, and I ran up and down the bus singing, "It's snowing, it's snowing!" The roosters eyed me menacingly, and I returned to the rocking chair, panting and a little motion sick. Around the next bend, the whole Earth had turned to snow. Ahead of us, only the thin black ribbon of the roadway stood out from the amorphous sea of whiteness. The gentle flakes soon brewed up into a blizzard. The green bus crept forward. Bob was silent and tense, hunched over the wheel. After what seemed like hours of crawling along in this manner, Claudia spotted the sign for Manton. The snow flurries eased as we pulled through the cow-skull-capped gates of Stan and Maureen's farm at nightfall. Instead of turning left toward the big glowing farmhouse, we turned right and bumped along parallel to a snow-rimed fence for some time until we came to a low outbuilding. A doorway of light opened, and a silhouette waved us in.

We crunched through a thick field of sparkling snow and entered a Dorothea Lange photograph. Maureen was a long, leathery woman of indeterminate age with greasy dark hair that clung to the contours of her skull before jangling limply about her ears. "Come on in folks and git warmed," said Maureen, welcoming us into her dilapidated home. The house was populated by a large black-and-white television, in front of which four gaunt children were gathered, and an old couch bleeding springs and stuffing.

Maureen's husband, Stan, lay on the couch. "You gotta forgive Stan," she said. "He's real full ah arthritis."

Stan waved from the couch. "Merry Christmas," he coughed. He was thin and ashen with sunken eyes. He was missing every other tooth in his mouth so his head looked like it closed with a zipper whenever he smiled.

In one corner lurked an unadorned little Christmas tree. Beneath it was a small pile of presents wrapped in newspaper comics. I took a place on the shag rug with the other children and watched the fuzzy car chase on television. Stan and Maureen's children didn't notice me. The place had the subtle but distinctively pungent odor of urine.

"Come on, kids. Come on up here an' git some chow."

The adults had prepared some card tables and covered them with an old sheet for the holiday feast. I was given a stool to sit on. A hodgepodge of miscellaneous cutlery was distributed, and small servings of meat and potatoes were doled out in order of age. Their sallow faces revealed no emotion, but the children eyed the competing portions jealously. Much to everyone's surprise, Claudia and I passed on the meat. Claudia offered up the tray of tofu she'd prepared for the occasion. The fermented bean curd was passed around suspiciously, sniffed, and passed on. Stan said a blessing that seemed to be directed at some guy named Jesus, and then the children dug into their food like wolverines.

"Ma," grunted one of the big boys. "We git seconds?"

"Sure ya do. It's Christmas. Wait ya turn though," Maureen called back.

"So, Maureen," began Claudia. "How big is your farm?"

"Oh, I reckon about six hundred acres."

My mother nodded appreciatively. "And how is it held?"

"What now?"

"How do you own the land? In trust, as a cooperative, or some sort of nonprofit collective?"

"Oh, Mr. Worthington owns the farm."

"And you rent it from him as a cooperative?"

"Nah. Only thing we rent is this house. We got two bedrooms. One for the kids with a couple a bunk beds and one for Stan and me. It does us OK."

"So you don't farm the land?"

"Oh, Stan does nothing but farming. Or at least *did* nothing but till recent. He used to farm it all for Mr. Worthington. Now he's more like fixing tractors and the like on account of the arthritis. I clean the Worthingtons' house for 'em. But right now we done hit a rough patch. Stan's laid up pretty good. Some days he just curls up in the fecal position the whole day."

"You mean the *fetal* position?"

"Nah, you know, *fecal*, like a baby. Stan got rear-ended a while back, though, and we finally got us some settlement money. That's the good news. We went and bought us . . ."

"Some land?" Claudia interjected hopefully.

"No. A cow. So now we're getting us fresh milk. At least most days."

"But are you saving up to buy your own land?"

"Saving? I wish. We're in debt to Mr. Worthington already. And he just raised our rent."

Claudia's class consciousness flared up into an incensed roar. "What!? In case this Mr. Worthington didn't get the message, the feudal system was abolished in the Middle Ages. He's a wealthy landowner, Maureen, and he's treating you like serfs."

Maureen was a little taken aback and hurried to clear up the misunderstanding. "No, ma'am, I don't know what middle-age system you're talking about. We ain't never been to the ocean, much less surfing."

"No, Maureen." Claudia put her face in her hands and then looked up with controlled patience. "What I'm trying to tell you is he's probably a millionaire. What interest does he have in raising your rent other than to control you?"

Maureen came to Mr. Worthington's defense. "Well, now for a person like that, he don't think he's rich. So, he's probably thinkin' he needs more money yet to be happy."

After a few more failed attempts to enlighten Maureen, Claudia retreated into silence and chewed at her tofu like it was meat.

We froze that night in the green bus. I pulled my watch cap down over my ears and zipped my patchwork jacket up over my chin. I rooted down into the depths of my sleeping bag, but still couldn't get warm, my breath crystallizing in the air above me. The roosters woke us before dawn, and we scrambled back into Maureen and Stan's shack, where the woodstove pumped out some warmth. We watched our hosts open their meager presents: cheap little toys from Taiwan for the children, chewing tobacco for Stan, and wool socks for Maureen.

"Boy are my feet gonna be warm this winter!" Maureen was genuinely excited about her socks.

Bob and Claudia and I adjourned to the bus after the present-opening. I stamped my feet and clapped my hands to stay warm.

"Baab!" my mother blasphemed in my grandmother's dialect. "These

Pretending to drive the green bus.

people are complete peasants, what my father would have called the Great Unwashed."

"They're good people, Claudia."

"That's not the point, Baab. I'm not concerned with whether they're good or not. The point is they're like Okies straight out of the Dust Bowl. They're indentured servants to the master on the hill. And they are most certainly *not* counter-cultural activists ready to start a conscious intentional community."

"They're good people," Bob mumbled in the general direction of the half-frozen roosters huddling in the back of the bus.

"Do something, Bob!" my mother threatened, as she led me off the bus by the shivering icicle that doubled as my hand.

Two things became clear to me as we alighted into a snow drift: 1) Utopia wasn't happening here; and 2) We'd freeze to death if we had to spend another night in the bus.

Bob fired up the green bus, executed a fourteen-point turn in the snowy driveway, and rumbled off toward town to check in with his other "contacts." Claudia and I fled back into the malodorous shack to thaw out our extremities. Toward evening, we heard the bus snorting its way back up the driveway. Bob returned in a merry mood. He smelled of beer and announced he'd hooked us up with a house to stay in. He'd been to see Carole and Jim, who also lived in Manton. And they'd reminded him about his friend Susan. How could he have forgotten about Susan? He'd called Susan down at her house in San Francisco, from Carole and Jim's place, and she said we could stay in her vacation cabin. In fact, she was *happy* to have us stay in her cabin. It was out of town, further up the mountain, way back in the woods. I fell asleep huddled on the floor of the green bus with the promise of warmth chanted into my ears by the staccato mumbling of the diesel engine and the growling of gears.

I awoke to the gentle rumbling of Ms.Ms. as she purred with warm satisfaction on my belly. We were laid out on a dusty couch in a tiny log-walled room. Blinding sunlight, inspired by the glare of the snow outside, poured enthusiastically through the window above. I could hear Bob and Claudia talking in the next room, their conversation punctuated by the clatter and clink of metal and glass.

"Bob, you don't stir it. It's rice, for crying out loud. You just let the water boil off."

"How am I supposed to know? I'm not from Chinatown."

"Are you sure we have permission to stay here?"

"Yes, I told you. Sharon *invited* us to stay here while we make connections with community."

"I thought you said her name was Susan."

"She goes by both. Look, Susie wants us here, OK? This is a summer cabin for that lake that's all frozen over right now. No one will be here for months. She's not just doin' us a favor. *We're* doin' *her* a favor."

"What are we doing for her?"

"We're looking after the house to make sure no one breaks in."

"Why would anyone want to break into this place?"

"I don't know. Crazy people."

"And she's not going to mind that we tore into her fifty-pound sack of rice?"

"No way. She said 'Help yourself.' Let's put this on it."

"Bob, that's really fancy stuff. It's imported Worcestershire sauce."

"Sue said she didn't mind. Jeez! I'm gonna put more wood on the fire."

Ms.Ms. and I closed our eyes again as the waves of heat radiated off of the woodstove. We loved the warmth, and we loved Susan or Sharon or whatever her name was for letting us hibernate in her cabin.

The more suspicious Claudia became that Bob's friend Susan didn't exist, the more generous Susan became. She was almost saintly in her disembodied benevolence.

Bob and me in front of the green bus on Mount Lassen.

"I called her from town, Claudia. Don't worry. She said she doesn't mind if we eat all the rice. She said *mia casa is sua casa.*"

"How come the lock on the front door is broken, Bob?"

"She doesn't believe in locks. She's very Zen."

Claudia's concerns were quickly muted because we ran out of money. And then the roads to town were snowed in. Under Bob's gracious trusteeship, Susan's generosity knew no bounds. As the weeks wore on, we ate up all the dry goods, including her fancy sauces and hand-canned preserves. Susan then authorized us to crack open her emergency supplies which, through rationing, got us through the rest of winter. She was so generous she didn't even mind when Ms.Ms. clawed at the furniture or peed in the corner.

"Don't worry, buddy," Bob waved his hand dismissively. "She *loves* cats."

One day the snow began to melt under a new, hotter sun. The white siegeworks barricading Susan's cabin retreated, leaving a morass of mud and mangled greenery in their wake. Susan's generosity had ended.

"We gotta go," announced Bob.

The next day Claudia picked up her accumulated Welfare checks waiting at the Manton post office and rented a new place for us further up the mountain. It was a half-built cabin perched on the ridge above a little creek. The green bus clawed its way up the twisting driveway of volcanic rock. Claudia twirled her hands like a real estate agent.

"Look at those pine trees. And the manzanita. You can eat their berries. And here's the cabin. See how the refrigerator is outside? Ingenious. It gives us more room inside, and in the winter you just unplug it. We'll save so much on electricity. And look . . . we've got *land*!"

"And poison oak," said Bob.

Trapped inside over the winter, I had longed to be back in the relative warmth and comfort of the city, but I had to admit that spring on Mount Lassen was something amazing. Our little dirt road was hidden from the world by a canopy of sugar pines and lined with *Ceanothus*, gooseberry, and a brilliant mosaic of wildflowers. The bright colors and sweet scents gave the world an unreal gleam.

This sense of wonder was enhanced the next day when we visited an old lady down the mountain to buy ourselves some chickens. She lived in a secret hollow tucked into the side of the mountain, and looked like she must have been a thousand years old. The skin of her face was ancient parchment, and her thick white hair was swept back until it melted into her billowing white smock. Her spotted, gnarled hands flitted about her, serving as perches for a steady rotation of parakeets and canaries and endlessly doling out pellets, seeds, and treats to the eclectic flock flowing around her. Wherever she went, the Noahide crone was surrounded by a cloud of dogs, cats, goats, sheep, geese, ducks, chickens, and a potbellied pig. As we approached, this diverse herd broke in two, half of the animals surging forward to greet us and the other half seeking shelter behind their fairy godmother. I negotiated the leaps and licks of a border collie and the gentle head butts of a pygmy billy goat while Claudia was schooled in the relative merits of Rhode Island Reds versus Leghorns.

"You want Reds," the old lady decided. "You ain't gonna eat 'em, so that means you want layers, and when it comes to layers, you can't beat a Red. Reds are friendly, good pets for kids. They'll come when they're called. They'll lay you an egg a day. And they'll forage for themselves if you're running low on feed. No, if I were you, I'd go with Reds every day of the week and twice on Sunday."

My first disappointment with the old lady was her voice. It didn't sound appropriately magical. She should have spoken in an archaic British accent that reverberated in the ears when she came to a dramatic conclusion: "It is the Rhode Island Red that you seek!" Instead, she sounded like a local. My second disappointment came when she began introducing me to her menagerie. "This is Ricky the rooster, and Peggy the pig, and Billy the billy goat." What kind of nomenclature was this? Her animals should have been named Cornelius and Ambrosia and Ramakrishnan. Instead, I shook paws with Dave, the dog.

"Well, come back with your man, Bob, and a car, and we can load up the Reds. Say, what're you folks doin' for milk?" the Old Lady wanted to know, as she pulled a canary out of the air to tickle its head. Claudia hadn't given the subject much thought. "You're gonna need a goat. Goats're no trouble to take care of, and when you're pullin' fresh milk every day for your boy, you'll feel like a super mother. Goat milk's the closest thing to human milk. That's why I talk to my goats like people. Come with me."

We followed the Old Lady over to a dilapidated wire-and-wood enclosure. "Hey, Mammy! Hey, Mammy!" she called. A big black goat with comically bulging eyes trotted up and accepted a stalk of celery that suddenly protruded from the Old Lady's sleeve. Glued to Mammy's side was a slightly smaller goat with an auburn coat and russet eyes. Her clinginess seemed to annoy Mammy, who kept butting the smaller goat's head away. "See this here nanny goat? This is Nancy. She's already almost a year old and she still won't leave her mommy alone. I want you folks to have Nancy."

"Oh, we don't have the money to . . ."

"Nope, don't worry, I won't hear of it. Nancy's gonna be my gift to you folks, so I can know your boy's gonna be gettin' fresh milk. Nancy's gettin' in the way of Mammy freshenin' again, anyhow. In a couple a months, she'll be ready to breed and she'll start makin' you some milk. In the meantime, take her in and let her get to know you so she'll be comfortable with you when the milkin's to be done."

We walked back out of the secret hollow leading Nancy by a rope around her neck. The nanny goat kept looking back dolefully and bleating softly. As we paraded up the mountain across a bed of pine needles, I told her: "Leaving home is really hard, Nancy, but you'll get used to it."

With spring in full bloom, Claudia unleashed her supercharged creative energies into cultivating our little patch of Earth into a flowering Utopian model for what New America should be all about. We would grow vegetables!

With Nancy, my best friend on the Mountain.

We had Nancy the goat for milk, and the three Rhode Island Red hens for eggs. If the two white roosters (who had somehow survived the winter) had their way, we'd soon have even more chickens for even more eggs.

Bob was put off by the frenzy of activity and sequestered himself in the green bus for long stretches of the day.

"Bob, come help us hoe the garden!"

"Come on! It's springtime. This is the season to relax. I deserve to take it easy, maybe drink a beer."

"Bob, the henhouse is leaking. You said you'd patch up the roof."

"Stop bothering me! You always want things from me. You're never content with anything."

Bob stomped off to the animal enclosure and threw some scrap pieces of corrugated metal onto the chicken coop.

"There! It's fixed. By the way, the roosters are gay. They won't come near the hens."

"Bob, when are you going to get moving on the school? Do you have parents on board, kids lined up? Are they going to pay you?"

"You know what your problem is, Claudia? You're always thinkin' about money."

"Well, Bob, I'm thinking about money right now because we're really stretching my Welfare checks. You have to at least pay for your own food. If you're not going to teach, can't you at least get a job in town?"

"You're just like everyone else. You just want to exploit me."

"OK, Bob. How about this? The Old Lady who gave us the goat needs someone to chop her firewood for her. Why don't you do that? She'll pay you."

Bob stared at my mother in disbelief, gathered up the lunch she'd made for him, and locked himself in the green bus for the rest of the day. And the next day. And the next. Eventually, another Welfare mother from down the road chopped the Old Lady's firewood, while Claudia and I planted Swiss chard, bok choy, and kale. The hens laid eggs, and the roosters eyed the hens suspiciously. And Nancy the goat cried for her mother. The sun rose and traveled across the sky again. Bob emerged from the bus at last, full of his old vigor.

"I got it," he said. "We don't need two of everything. I'll sell my stuff."

So began a series of treks down to the flea market in Red Bluff. Bob took me along to help with sales. The flea market was an open-air warren of card tables and blankets, littered with junk. Poor and desperate people sold homemade corncob pipes, homemade liquor, homemade ammunition, Ozark mouth fiddles, rebuilt toasters, and used motor oil. Bob fit right in and became the social leader of a little group of merchants on day one.

"Buddy, this is Skinny Willy. He used to play one mean banjo before the accident. This is Cubby. He doesn't remember why he's called Cubby. This is Marsha. She came up with her cornbread recipe all on her own."

On market days, we got started at the crack of noon. I helped Bob spread out his blue blanket, and we arrayed his wares: balls of socks (clean), a record player, a bag of marbles, rolls of industrial-strength toilet paper, a backgammon set, a mirror (slightly cracked), and more. The sun pounded down on us as we squinted up into the faces of passing would-be buyers.

"Looking for some help raisin' my boy, here," Bob would call out. "Look at these cooking pots. Hardly used. I'm sellin' 'em for my friend Susan."

When I got a headache from sitting in the sun for too long, Bob traded a ball of yarn (newish) for a tattered straw hat. This kept the sun out of my eyes pretty well, and Bob said my look helped with sales. Bob was happy and talkative on market days. He was back in his element.

After a good day of sales, we stopped off at the nearby diner to celebrate with secondhand coffee and banana cream pie. Bob slid a little silver pitcher across the table at me. "You see this stuff, buddy? This is your best friend when you're on the road. It's called 'half and half,' which means it's half milk and half cream. Which means it's chock-full of protein. And here's the best part. It's *always* free. I mean always. It's the cheapest source of protein in the whole world."

Bob had said the same thing to me about his own semen in the past, and the association nauseated me. Bob didn't notice that I was boycotting the half-and-half. He was looking forward to the next market day, when we could sit out in the sun, swapping stories with Black Gregory, and selling worthless junk to hapless suckers.

In this manner, Bob got rid of most of his possessions. And when he'd finished selling everything he owned, he began selling off our stuff.

"Bob, did you take my frying pan?" Claudia asked.

"You weren't using it. You said frying's not healthy."

"Where is it?"

"I sold it."

"Fuck! You're buying me a new one, Bob. Do you hear me!? Oh, and Josh said you sold his teddy bear."

"Sheesh. Big deal. The thing only had one eye. Josh still has the goat to play with."

I tried to play with Nancy but she was not as easy to befriend as I had hoped. She was skittish and easily spooked. When Bob fired up the green bus, she bucked wildly and tried to ram herself into the wall of her shed. When Champ, the neighbors' mammoth St. Bernard, came bounding by for a visit, Nancy would emit a panicked moan and her body would ripple with an involuntary spasm of fear. She was even scared of me sometimes. When I approached her unannounced or made sudden movements she would shiver and retreat into the corner of her shed. But for all the scariness of the bus and the dog and boy, nothing was scarier to Nancy than darkness.

On her first night with us, my head had hardly graced the pillow before a devastating wail filled the air. The cry was so eerily human, yet so totally alien that I couldn't imagine what manner of cruelty was being inflicted on what manner of creature. Claudia stood above me in the silence, projecting her spirit out into the darkness to investigate. When that didn't work, we went out corporeally and cautiously, armed with a flashlight. We found Nancy folded into the corner of her little shed, bleating her terrors out into the night. Seeing her so alone and distressed made me cry.

"The old lady said she would miss her mother," said Claudia. "I think she's just lonely."

I cuddled up next to Nancy, stroking the coarse fur of her head and neck. "It's OK, it's OK, it's OK." Nancy submitted to my petting and eventually put her head down and closed her marbly eyes. But when Claudia beckoned to me, and I began to shift my weight away from her, Nancy opened her eyes, full of terror again. We spent that night, and several subsequent nights, hunkered down in the goat pen, covered in a green army blanket made from scratchy wool. Claudia thought the feel and lanolin smell of the blanket might remind Nancy of her mother. Claudia found a windup clock Bob had salvaged from the dump and brought that into the shed with us. The ticking of the clock was supposed to remind Nancy of her mother's heartbeat.

There was something deep and primal and satisfying about lying up against that goat. The side of her warm, coarse belly pushed me up and brought me down with each sleeping breath. I was awash in the overwhelming smell of goat, which was at once awful and inexplicably familiar. Humans must be born accustomed to the smell, I thought—some affinity for the goat that began thousands of years ago. And there I was, like my unknown shepherd ancestors before me, comforting my little flock under the stars. My very presence assured her that she was safe. A night breeze rose up from the little creek in the vale below, fresh and cool. The goat at my back slumbered peacefully. The clock ticked its reassuring heartbeats. I slept as the shepherd boys must have slept—lightly but swollen with pride in my own heroism.

We slowly weaned Nancy off of human company, until eventually the army blanket and the ticking of the clock were all she needed to get through the night. Nancy now recognized me as family and she would come when I called and eat food from my hand. "I love you, little goat," I told her. Nancy nudged my chest for more lettuce, which was her way of reciprocating the sentiment.

One night, late, the silence was ripped apart with nightmarish screaming. It was Nancy, but her cries were louder and more horrifying than before. She was screaming with every fiber of her being, as though she were screaming for her life. The sound grew fainter and fainter until it died out completely. I lunged out of bed and found Bob standing at the front door, looking down at Champ, who was pacing around excitedly. We ran out toward the goat shed.

"What are you trying to tell us, boy?" Bob was talking to Champ in a halting, encouraging tone. "What is it, boy? Did something happen to Nancy?"

The wood-and-wire door to the animal pen was open, and Nancy's shed was empty. The army blanket lay crumpled on the ground. The clock was hanging from a nail, ticking away to nobody. Champ ran around, smelling everything.

"Look," Bob said to me. "Look at Champ." He was pointing. In the moonlight we could see that the white band of fur on his chest was streaked with red. "Champ! Champ, boy. Where's the goat? Where's the goat, boy!?"

Champ looked alert and seemed to understand. He streaked out of the shed, and we followed him out of the animal pen. He led us down the rocky hillside. I slipped and tumbled in the darkness. Bob picked me up and half-dragged, half-carried me down toward the creek. Champ was waiting for us, pawing at the ground and nodding his head at the body before him. On the graveled bank, next to the little creek that sparkled in the moonlight, Nancy lay flat on her side, unmoving. Bob stopped and let me go. I circled around Nancy's motionless form and saw that her side was not rising and falling with breath. Her eye was inert and glassy. Her throat was dark and shiny and a shiny blackness pooled beneath it.

"Is Nancy dead, Bob?"

"I'm afraid so, buddy," said Bob.

We knelt down together and felt Nancy's side. There was but a little warmth left on her skin, but even that seemed to evaporate under our fingers.

We walked slowly back to the cabin, picking our way among the rocks and tree roots. When we reached the porch, Champ bounded up behind us, panting. I turned around: "Go home, Champ! Go home!" I didn't cry until I saw Claudia. Then deep convulsions rocked my body. My throat constricted, and the heaving of my chest threatened to break my ribs apart. I felt like the lifetime of heartbeats stolen from Nancy were pounding through me all at once. Between thunderous sobs, I gasped out: "She was just a little goat and she missed her mother. She didn't do anything wrong."

My mother hugged me and patted the back of my head and said: "It's OK, it's OK, it's OK," the way I used to comfort Nancy.

Eventually Bob ran out of things to sell at the flea market, and he became taciturn and withdrawn again. He locked himself in the green bus for a couple of days and then emerged, bright eyed with new clarity.

"I got it. Come on, buddy!"

We pulled up to the lip of a vast ocean of garbage. As far as the eye could see, the landscape was a decomposing collage of rotting food, mangled odds and ends, broken appliances, and pieces of furniture. Everything in the world had come here to die. The skeletal remains of a burnt bunk bed caught my eye. As did the puffy black bags oozing soiled diapers. Flocks of birds circled overhead, diving into the garbage to pick off mice. In the distance, bulldozers climbed atop a sea of filth like ants on a carcass. Bob thought he'd discovered the richest racket in history.

"Check it out, buddy. The dump! Everything you see here is free. And so much good stuff. All you can carry away for the low, low price of zero dollars. That means every penny we make for it at the flea market will be pure profit."

The smell was distressing, even from the protection of the bus. But once we emerged into the gaseous air of the dump, the stench was overpowering. I doubled over, gagging on the sweet-and-sour hallmarks of decay, as a swarm of flies sucked the moisture off my face. Little slimy gray rats scurried past my feet.

Bob waved his hand under his nose: "Whoo-wee! Boy, that's stinky. But that's the price of doing business in a place like this, I guess." And he leapt neatly down onto a stained old mattress and began picking through the garbage. "Looks like there was a fire. Look at this, buddy. Perfectly good," he said, offering up a blackened flowerpot.

I gingerly picked my way into the sea of garbage after Bob. I found that if I held my shirt over my nose with one hand, batted at the flies with the other, and focused my vision on one object at a time, I could avoid both vomiting and my atavistic urge to run away screaming. Over the course of our days at the dump, I found a few things that I would have liked to keep: an action figure missing only an arm, an egg timer, a squirt gun with a superficial scratch. But I couldn't bring myself to put them in my pockets. Sure, they were perfectly good on their face, but they posed the same problem for me that plagued Bob's secondhand diner food: once designated garbage by their initial owners, they were forever tainted with an insurmountable stigma.

"Take it, buddy. Take it, it's a perfectly good music box."

"It's garbage, though."

"Why? Who says? Society?"

"No, the person who threw it out."

"But your mother buys you stuff from the thrift store all the time. Someone threw that stuff out, too."

"They *gave* away that stuff. Someone *threw* away the music box."

"So, lemme get this straight. You think if there were two of the same music box, and one was given away and the other one was thrown out, one of them is magically OK and the other one is magically total garbage?"

"Yes."

I believed in the magic of *used* versus *garbage*. And, to Bob's surprise, the buyers at the flea market did too. Somehow they could tell when something had come from the dump. Bob's great plan sputtered out, and he locked himself up in the green bus again.

When he reemerged, Bob was sullen and mean. When I asked him to help me learn how to ride a bicycle, he pushed me down the driveway and let me crash on the sharp lava rocks. He looked down at my bleeding knee and declared: "That's life for ya, buddy." When Sky, the more aggressive of the gay white roosters, would chase me around the yard, Bob would ignore my calls for help and continue nursing his can of beer, deep in thought.

One day we went into town to buy supplies and run errands. Outside of the post office, I climbed up onto a bench.

"Bob, catch me!" I said.

"OK," Bob reluctantly agreed. I leapt into his arms again and again. "OK, one more time," said Bob.

I jumped the last time, but Bob stepped away from me. Time slowed as I clawed at the empty air, watching his impassive face recede into the distance. I crashed to the ground in a tangle of bruised extremities and tears.

"What's wrong with you!?" Claudia rushed to my aid.

Bob looked at the ground: "I don't know."

That night, at dinner, Claudia brought out pencil and paper and began doing math. "Bob, you haven't been paying your half of the rent. You now owe me a thousand dollars. What's your plan?"

"I knew you were going to do this." He began yelling: "You're so damn greedy! And materialistic! All you care about is money!"

My mother's jaw was set like her mother's before her. "Bob, this has been going on for months, and it's just not working out. You need to leave."

"With pleasure! I'm having dinner with Stan and Maureen, *my* friends. They invited *me* over."

Bob turned the ignition switch of the bus and, after three or four false starts, the engine fired up. The bus coughed and sputtered into the distance, and the house was quiet. Claudia locked the front door and slid a chair under the doorknob. Late that night, the bus coughed its way back up the driveway and then fell silent. Bob tried the door to no avail, and then started banging on it.

"Claudia! Open the door!" he yelled. "This is bullshit! Bullshit! I don't care. You think I care!?"

Claudia sat at the edge of my bed. She placed one hand on my chest to keep me down and the other across her lips, indicating silence.

Bob kept yelling. His speech was slurred like he was speaking through a wall of water. "I'm goin' onna trip anyways! I'm goin' down to Berkeley for a few. To visit my buddies in the Frog House. To see my *real* friends! This is bullshit!"

The bus coughed back into the night.

The next day, Claudia and I sat down at the table and wrote a letter to Bob, care of the Frog House. We composed the letter together, honing in on the right message and carefully selecting the right words. Claudia demanded repayment of her $3,000 for the bus and the back rent. On the envelope, she helped me spell out *Don't come back*. We hitchhiked into town, and Claudia held me up to the mailbox so I could take credit for mailing the letter.

"We're done with living with Bob," I said.

The next morning, Sky ambushed me on the front porch and stole my toast. I yelled after him: "We're done living with you too, Sky!"

The next day, Sky glared at me from behind the bars of his cage as we sold him to the toothless old man in town. "Why ya'll wanna sell 'im?" the old man wanted to know.

"We wanted him to impregnate our hens," Claudia explained. "But he won't go near them."

"And he's mean to me," I added.

"But why don't ya'll jus' eat 'im?" he asked.

"We're vegetarians," said my mother.

The old man shook his head in disbelief and said: "Well, jus' so'in ya'll know. I'm gonna eat 'im."

We left the old man to his dinner without so much as waving good-bye.

A few days later, Moon, Sky's gay rooster partner, disappeared and was presumed dead. Whether from a broken heart—as Claudia suspected—or from the neighbors' dog—as I suspected—I was glad to see him gone too.

A month or so later, the green bus wheezed up the driveway one last time. Bob traipsed into the house and began digging through the pantry. My mother burst out of the bathtub naked, screaming: "Get out of here!"

Bob was hunched over and apologetic. "Jeez. I was just lookin' for something I left behind."

"Get out," said Claudia, her naked arm dripping with water as it pointed out the door.

The bus rambled down the driveway for the last time, and Claudia called after it sarcastically: "Be sure to mail me the money so I can pay my mother back."

We never saw Bob again. At least not in the flesh. Many years later, Claudia threw the *Seattle Times* down in front of me.

"Look at that," she said.

The paper was folded open to a holiday solicitation from a men's homeless shelter. It said: HELP US. Beneath the lettering were two scruffy homeless men with their hands out for alms. One of them was an older, chubbier, even balder image of Bob DiNardo, a slight smile on his face.

"I almost feel sorry for him," Claudia said.

I didn't. He probably thought he was pulling off the biggest scam in history.

FIVE

Two Eyes Are Better Than Three

With Bob DiNardo finally gone, Claudia and I had Mount Lassen all to ourselves. One evening in late summer, my mother ended our walk through the woods with a story about the reincarnation of the Dalai Lama.

I didn't quite grasp all the nuances of the Tibetan Buddhist cycle of death and rebirth, so I asked: "Claudia, how did the monks know the new baby had the same spirit as the old man who died?"

"Because his first word was the old man's name."

This made good sense to me, and I asked hopefully: "What was *my* first word?" Maybe *I* had spoken words of prophecy. Maybe I too was the reincarnation of some great spirit.

"Your first spoken word was *juice*."

Bummer.

"But you first spoke to me *telepathically* when you were just a tiny fetus in my womb."

"I did?"

"Yes. I could hear you twinkling at me."

"What did I say?"

Claudia kept walking in silence as though she hadn't heard me.

"What did I say, Claudia?"

She stopped and looked down at me with glistening eyes. Her lips twisted around, wrestling with what not to say. She smiled suddenly and then sniffled, and we resumed our silent march up the driveway of volcanic gravel. It was a secret. I could see that, and something about the crunching of delicate lava rocks beneath our feet and the cool twilight unfolding around us convinced me not to disturb the perfection of that secret. Maybe what I had told her as a fetus was too powerful to repeat. Or maybe she wanted me to figure it out telepathically.

We'd had a lot of time to practice our telepathy since Bob left. Maybe too much time. That night I sat cross-legged on the shag carpet in our little half-built cabin at the edge of the magical pine forest. Claudia sat across from me, holding a card in her lap. Our eyes were closed.

"Is it the crescent?" I asked.

"Good, Joshey! Good!" Her eyes opened, smiling. "That's three in a row. We're really connecting now. OK, here's the next one."

The back of the new card was the same as the rest. Opaque. A dark blue with a tan border. My mother was leaning forward, her eyes closed. She raised the card up to the level of her forehead, to her third eye.

"Close your eyes and concentrate," she coached me.

I closed my eyes and tried to push all the distractions out of my mind. A flurry of images stubbornly flitted though my head, like old photos tumbling out of a shoebox: Ms.Ms. curled up on the corner of the bed; raindrops sliding down the darkened window; the bowl of currants on the peeling linoleum countertop.

I tried envisioning the spinning sword of fire clearing my mind of images, wiping my third eye clean. But I didn't have the patience for it. Nor the discipline. It was too boring. I made a calculation and guessed.

"Is it the river?" I asked hopefully. We called the two parallel squiggly lines the *river* because they looked like the cartographic symbol for rivers in our 1956 world atlas.

It wasn't the river. Her slowness in answering said as much.

"No. Try again. Try to concentrate just a little harder. You can push through it."

"Is it the circle?" I asked again, less hopefully.

Claudia opened her eyes. She shook her head *no*, her lips clamping together. She turned the card around for me to see. It was the upside-down Y. I'd gotten it wrong.

But then her face lit up: "Oh! Did you just see a flash of blue light?"

"Yes," I said, hoping to please.

Claudia beamed. "We are *really* connecting tonight." But she didn't want to wear me out. "Should we take a break, Joshey?"

"I think we should," I said thoughtfully, not wanting to seem too eager.

This was my school. Other kids had kindergarten teachers teaching them how to pledge allegiance to a flag and recite the alphabet. I had my mother, and she was teaching me about my chakras, the I Ching, and Kundalini yoga. But most importantly, she was teaching me about extrasensory perception. My psychic powers. How to harness my sixth sense. How to clear the film away from my third eye, the one that Society didn't want me to use (or know about).

Back in San Francisco, Claudia had trained as a psychic at HeartSong, the expanded perception center where she learned telepathic communication and astral projection. At HeartSong, they would hold healing sessions where seriously ill patients would come to be treated. The psychics would sit in a circle around the afflicted and project deep healing energy into their bodies, sometimes for hours at a time, and the patients would be cured. At least for a day or so.

Claudia would place herself into trances at bus stops, in the park, and in restaurants, reading everyone's energy around her. She once saw two men approach each other in a café. They were friends. They leapt at each other, embracing. They were two gay men passionately in love. But when she opened her eyes she saw that the two men were just standing at arm's length talking. It had been their spirits embracing.

There was nothing mystical about any of this. Claudia believed it was pure science. It just hadn't been recognized by mainstream society yet.

"Joshey, the mind is like a radio receiver. The broadcasts are already out there. You just have to know how to tune in. Someday scientists will discover auras and chakras and ESP and all the things we already know about, and they'll say: 'Oh, my God! Here is a new way of looking at the world!' But we'll be one step ahead of them."

One day I was surprised to learn that psychic power could cure not only the human body, but cars as well. Claudia believed that with enough concentration you could do absolutely anything with your mind. You could bend spoons, lift objects, and even jump-start our rusty Plymouth Valiant stalled out in the middle of the intersection.

The green light turned to red again. "Move your ass!" someone yelled. The honking was growing more incessant. I couldn't let these distractions pull me from my trance as I attempted to meditate in the passenger seat.

Claudia coached me: "Sit still, channel your mind, focus your energy. Start!" Nothing.

The pressure was on. We lived ten winding, mountainous miles from town, and that car was our lifeline for food and supplies. With the pittance that the government gave us for Welfare we could never afford a car that worked for long. The guy who'd sold us the rusty Plymouth Valiant for a hundred dollars had told us: "She looks like she's been through hell, but if you pull out the choke and rev her up for twenty minutes, she'll get you there. Also, the brakes don't work too well, but if you just keep pumping 'em, they'll come through for you." This was an improvement from the seventy-five-dollar Chevy Nova that came without a back window or bumpers and only occasionally started if we popped it into gear on a downward slope.

The line of traffic honking behind us was growing, and the pressure was immense.

"Come on, Joshey! Concentrate! Let's focus. Come on! We've got to concentrate harder." *Rrrr, rrrr, rrrr,* the engine sounded like it could go either way. It just needed that extra psychic push from us. But our telepathic jumper cables didn't cut it, and we had to bail out into traffic and flag down strangers to help us push the car off the road.

It was a familiar experience. We often found ourselves stalled out on the side of the road after dark in some remote mountain pass. But Claudia never lost confidence in her mental powers.

"OK, Joshey, focus your mind. Envision blue light filling up the engine with starter energy. OK, concentrate. Now on three, let's make that engine turn over."

Sometimes our powers worked, and we whooped and revved the engine in celebration. Other times we had an off night, and we shivered by the side of the road, waiting to hitch a ride to the nearest pay phone, so we could spend the last of our savings on a tow to the mechanic's shop. Sometimes the tow truck drivers would take pity on us and give us a ride up the mountain for free. Other times we spent the night hustling for a ride outside of the twenty-four-hour diner. Standing on the shoulder of the road with our thumbs out, Claudia would say: "Next time, we have to try to focus our minds even harder."

"Yeah, we will," I agreed wearily. But I wasn't sure it would matter. I was beginning to believe that cars didn't respond to psychic energy.

If Claudia's ability to conduct clairvoyant car repair work was in doubt, her other psychic skills were unimpeachable. She treated Uncle Tony's bouts of depression with chakra healings over the telephone and was particularly good at energy readings. She could hold an object in her left hand while measuring its emanations with her right. Bric-a-brac in the thrift store, a rusty key I found on the winding gravel road, an old fountain pen. She could read the spiritual auras for all of them.

With her eyes closed, and her third eye open, she would fall into a kind of trance: "This key opened a padlock on an old wooden shed. Gray shed. The door, partly off its hinges. An old man with a full white head of hair and blue-jean overalls. He would come with this key every day to the shed to work on something. A project—a train set maybe, or something with little pieces on a big table. I see the key waiting patiently for the old man, on a hook by the door of the house. And then, after a time, the old man doesn't return. The key is thrown into a box one day and loaded into a truck. At a curve in the road, the box topples over, the key bounces out of the back of the truck. And then one day you come along and pick the key up out of the dust."

"What happened to the old man?" I asked. "Is he dead?"

"Yes," she said, "but now the key has you as a friend. A gift from the old man to you."

This was my favorite of my mother's psychic powers. I never tired of bringing her found objects, of hearing their stories and mysteries revealed. I would carefully select rocks down by Narnia Creek, the little ribbon of water that slid past our cabin. I would run back with my finds rolled up in my T-shirt.

"What about this one, Claudia, what does this one say?" The fresh shiny river rock had a very low energy reading. Her right hand came down to within an inch of its surface. It didn't have much of a story to tell. It liked the water and was young.

"What about this one?" The porous red igneous rock displayed an energy reading of six inches or so. She was born out of eruption and fire from the volcano that had once been Mount Lassen. She was an ancient rock, tired and fading.

The hunk of obsidian generated a startling amount of energy for such a little guy. My mother's right hand hovered dramatically two feet above it in the air. This had been a sacred rock, used by Native Americans. It was kept in a little leather bag by a woman shaman, a crone, who used it for healing. A great fire had burned her village and consumed the bag. The various magical stones had become scattered, leaving this little piece of obsidian all alone until I stumbled upon it.

Any rock that had been used by Native Americans was sure to generate a heightened valence of energy. And I didn't have to go far to find the shiny black rocks that set Claudia's hands tingling. My mother identified so many stone talismans and tools within a short radius of our front porch that I couldn't help but conclude that we were living on the very site of an extinct Indian village.

While my mother's skills were undeniable, I suffered from grave self-doubt. I didn't think I could live up to being the warlock she wanted me to be. "Are you sure I'm psychic, Claudia?"

"You are *very* psychic, Joshey. Don't you remember when you were sick?"

I did remember. A couple of months back I had been laid out for nearly two weeks with a wicked fever that ravaged my mind and transformed the tiniest noises into explosions and the slightest glimmers into violent lightning storms. I lay motionless for hours on end, barely able to accept the drizzle of miso soup my mother slid down my throat. Somewhere in the darkness I'd heard her booming whisper on the phone:

"He's *really* sick. He's burning up with fever. No, I'm not going to give him drugs. I'm giving him garlic and sponging him down with cold water. No. Where? I don't even know if there is a doctor in town. And how would we get there? No, I don't think so, Tony. What would a doctor do? Give him penicillin? Penicillin might make him get better a little faster, but in the long run he'll grow to be stronger without it."

One morning I lifted my sweaty head out of feverish oblivion and called for tangerines. As I caught up on two weeks' worth of food, Claudia told me: "You were *super* psychic while you were in your trance." She told me that at one point I'd sat straight up in the midst of a vision and announced: "I just saw a man in the water, wearing a blue shirt." A couple of days later, she turned on the radio and heard a news report about a local man who had drowned in a waterway. I had foretold his death.

I had to admit that my feverish pronouncement sounded paranormally prescient. But I didn't remember uttering it.

"Well you did, Joshey. Don't worry. I'm telling you, you have a special gift."

But I wasn't so sure. I didn't feel it within me.

One afternoon, I wrapped myself up into the deepest meditative trance I could muster and reached into the depths of my soul to project one solitary message into Claudia's mind like a thunderbolt: I wanted pizza toast. Minutes later, my mother slid a bowl of blanched beans and boiled bok choy in front of me. She was smiling down at me: "You looked hungry."

I could *not* communicate telepathically, I concluded. And I didn't have a third eye that could see through ESP cards either. I was faking it. But I forgave myself. My mind just worked differently from hers. I preferred to look around with my two regular eyes and catch the little details that Claudia didn't. I noticed the tremors in the puddle that heralded rain, for example, and the distinctive facelike contours of the burnt tree that marked the turn-off toward home. It wasn't clairvoyance, but at least it was something.

One day in November we ventured down into town for food and library books and found ourselves in a race against darkness to get home. My myopic mother had a hard time navigating the steep, winding roads at night. And then, halfway up the mountain, winter arrived. Snow poured from the blackened skies like milk. Fields and forests were quickly folded into a smooth new landscape of sparkling white. Our well-used egg-shaped Buick coupe (that I'd dubbed Victoria the Great White Whale) began to fishtail in the ice and snow. We slowed to a crawl. Claudia leaned forward over the white plastic steering wheel, peering into the whiteness that punctuated the blackness.

"Hang on, Josh. I can't see the road anymore."

I leaned forward too, looking for landmarks. "Look, Claudia, you can see the fence posts at the edge of the fields still. Try to stay in the middle between them."

We crawled forward for another half mile or so, churning up the snow in front of us. The Whale started to cough and buck. Then we very slowly slid into a shallow ditch, and the Whale breathed its last breath.

"OK, Joshey, let's take a couple of deep breaths and send our energy to start the car again." I closed my eyes out of respect for my mother but didn't even try to telepathically jump-start the car. I already knew the Whale was gone. We sat in complete silence for a few moments, the heat ebbing out of the expired Whale, the snow piling up around us. "We could stay in here, I guess, and wait for help," Claudia said uncertainly. She didn't know what to do.

"No, let's walk," I told her.

Claudia turned to me, her glasses fogging up: "Is that what your heart tells you?" I detected a hint of fear in her voice.

"Yes," I told her with certainty. But it wasn't my heart telling me anything. It was just facts. I remembered that the previous winter, when we were with Bob, they hadn't cleared the roads for weeks. And we'd be hard to spot in a white car covered in white snow. Plus, I was pretty sure from the length of the parallel fence lines that this was the last straightaway before the second to last fork on the road home.

We emerged Jonah-like from the Whale and scrambled onto the snowy beachhead of the roadway. The white powder was almost up to my knees.

"This way, Claudia," I called to my mother. My voice sounded tiny, the snowy air muffling my words.

We waded down the road together, holding hands. Claudia had to stop several times to clean her glasses, until finally she said: "Joshey, I can't see. Every time I clean my glasses they fog up again. I'm *blind*." She sounded panicked.

"It's OK, Claudia." I squeezed her hand. "I think I can find the way." I stepped forward, leading her by the hand.

"I believe you can do it, Joshey. Concentrate. Let your third eye lead the way."

I knew we went left at the fork in the road. "This way."

"Good, Joshey. Follow the blue energy."

We were in the forest now, and the flat roadway was easier to follow. At the second fork, I knew we needed to turn right. "This way, Claudia."

"You are *so* psychic tonight, Joshey. You always have been."

She was referring to my fetal telepathy again. The week before, my mother had finally told me the secret of what I had communicated to her in utero. She cried, and I held her hand, struggling to understand her words. She told me that back when she was first pregnant with me she had been living by herself in the Noe Valley of San Francisco. One night a man broke into the apartment and attacked her. A black man in dark clothes. He raped her and then went out through the fire escape. My mother lay there, sinking into the floor, into the depths of the earth, blood between her legs. It made no sense to her. None of it. How could she bring a child into this? What was the point of keeping me? Then, from the blackest depths, there was a sudden emphatic, brilliant twinkle. Like a new star at the edge of a dead cosmos.

"I know who you are," she had whispered to me. "You're my baby. Are you trying to tell me something?"

I had twinkled back exuberantly.

"Are you trying to tell me you want to live?"

"Yes!" I had signaled back.

Now I was almost six and I was leading us through the snowy landscape. Out of the frozen mist materialized the familiar burnt tree with its human face, bearded now with whiskers of snow. The flatness beneath it must have been our little dirt road. "Come on, Claudia, we turn up here."

"Oh, Joshey, are you sure? It all looks the same."

"I can tell by the tree."

"Are you using your third eye?"

"Yes," I lied.

The second break in the trees had to be our driveway, curving up and to the right.

She thought I was communicating with her telepathically when I was in utero. But now, as I led her through the frozen darkness to home, I realized she had gotten it wrong. What she sensed must have been my little fists pounding at the walls of her womb in rage, wanting to come out and protect her. Now I was almost six, and I was getting stronger every day. I didn't need psychic powers or a third eye or anything else. I just needed to be strong and brave, like a sharp-eyed shepherd guiding a lost sheep through the storm.

SIX

The Extraterrestrials

In the year 1165, the Jewish traveler Benjamin of Tudela left Spain to explore foreign and exotic lands. He met the wise men of Samarkand, the pearl divers of Bahrain, and the rabbis of *Mizraim* in Egypt. To his surprise, he found that people did things much the same as they did back home. I had the opposite experience. In the year 1981, when I was five, I journeyed no farther than it took to meet the neighbors, hitchhike into town, and attend school. The people I encountered were more foreign to me than the dervishes of Barbary or the fire eaters of Cathay.

Foremost among these strangers were our elderly neighbors on Mount Lassen, the Stiglers, whom my mother considered land barons of Hearstian proportions. "They're millionaires! They own half the real estate in Redding and Red Bluff," Claudia complained to me. "They don't have to lift a finger, and the money just rolls in." I'd never met rich people before and was duly impressed by the Stiglers' fancy doublewide trailer, what with the redwood porch they'd added on, and I stared in wide-eyed awe at the big color TV that dominated their living room.

But my mother's resentment of the Stiglers wasn't just class animosity. They'd refused to acknowledge that their St. Bernard, Champ, had killed our goat, Nancy. "Champ's a rescue dog," insisted Mrs. Stigler. "He'd never do something like that. Must have been wolves." But we knew better. Later, after we'd run out of firewood, old Mr. Stigler came down the hill and yelled at Claudia and me for chopping down an old dead tree with our chain saw. "That tree was on my property and you were trespassing! Next time you trespass on me, I'm gonna call the sheriff on you."

Claudia fumed: "He doesn't own the fucking land! *Nobody* owns the

Earth. *We* were doing *him* a favor, clearing out a fire hazard for him. Cheap old bastard! He could buy us a whole *herd* of new goats if he wanted to."

But, as time went on, the Stiglers slowly began to redeem themselves. A couple of weeks after the yelling incident, a full cord of chucked wood mysteriously appeared in our woodshed. Later, after our car had broken down and we were running dangerously low on food, Mrs. Stigler dropped off a bag of groceries on our doorstep. Most of the food was full of white flour and sugar, rendering it inedible for organic pioneers like us, but it was the thought that counted.

The Stiglers' upslope property deigned to meet our funky little lot along the fence line of the gardens. There, the worlds of the bourgeoisie and proletariat came together to celebrate the spring. On the upslope Mrs. Stigler daintily tended to her orderly flower beds in the shade of her yellow sun hat. On the down slope Claudia dug up to her elbows in chicken shit and dirt, raising beds of chard, kale, bok choy, and broccoli, her hair tied back with an old shoelace. But as they toiled under the same sun, the women began to make small talk across the low picket fence, and it seemed that some sort of friendship was possible. Until I accidentally ruined it.

Gardening—like meditating, dream journaling, and painting—brought my mother great pleasure. I considered it a form of torture. "I'm bored. I'm *booored*, Claudia. You said an hour. It's been like ten hours already and I'm *sooo* bored. And it smells bad."

"Joshey, you have to look at working in the garden as a form of meditation. Try it. Come down here and get your hands dirty. Let all your negative energy flow out into the Earth."

If redeeming your soul in the soil meant kneeling in chicken shit for three hours at a stretch, I didn't want any part of it. In desperation, I wandered off to pick through the last of the junk Bob DiNardo had stockpiled from the dump. Underneath the fire-blackened box spring, I unearthed a sad little tricycle, stripped of paint and afflicted with rust. The rubber grips on the handlebars were long gone, and metal stumps were all that remained of the pedals. I righted the thing and found that it was only moderately mangled. All three wheels still spun, and I could move the pedals almost one full rotation before they jammed into the front fork. Then I had to jump off and crank the pedals back again. It was just like our car. You lurched forward, stopped to fix it, and then lurched forward again.

It took me a full minute to cover ten feet. "At this rate, it'll take me all day to get back to the garden," I thought. But I couldn't think of anything more fun to do, so I seesawed my way forward. Half an hour later, I rounded the pine tree at the corner of the garden. "Look, Claudia, I'm driving my car!" I threw my head back as though enjoying the breeze flowing through my hair, and then jerked to a stop. I put an expression of shock on my face. "Ah, fuck! It's all fucked up! Look, Claudia, I'm meditating to fix it! Now I'm fixing it for real." Claudia looked up and nodded and then tried to continue her conversation with Mrs. Stigler. I lurched forward and then jerked to a stop. "Ah, fuck! It's all fucked up! It's fixed! Ah, fuck! It's all fucked up! It's fixed!"

I went on this way for another twenty feet or so until Mrs. Stigler stood up suddenly. Her face was flushed as if she were embarrassed. Her white gloved hands were trembling. "Oh . . . my goodness!" she stammered. "I can't believe what I am hearing." She looked off into the distance, scared and shaken, and then turned and hurried back up the path toward her palatial doublewide.

I stopped pretending to drive and dismounted from the tricycle. Something mysterious and horrible must have happened to Mrs. Stigler.

"Claudia, why did she run away?"

"You said a . . . well." My mother stopped pulling weeds and gave me her undivided attention for the first time that day. "You didn't do anything wrong, but she was probably upset by some of the words you were using."

Me? This was about me? The woman hadn't so much as noticed me all day. And *words*? I thought back on my day and was sure I hadn't said anything racist or sexist. "What words did I say?"

"Well, probably *fuck*. Just *fuck*."

Fuck? What was wrong with *fuck*? It was just a word you said, like *shit*, or *whoops*, or *ouch*. Claudia saw the confusion on my face.

"Joshey, I don't understand it myself. It makes no sense. There's nothing wrong with *fuck*, but some people just don't like that word."

"Doesn't it really just mean sex?"

"Yes, and there's nothing wrong with that. You can say the word whenever you want, but you should know there are some people like Mrs. Stigler—straight people—who will be offended by the word and won't like you if you say it."

Who were these people who went crazy when they heard a random word? "Straight people?"

"Yes. Straight people. You know . . ." Here, Claudia adopted a cold android face, stiffened her arms, and spoke like a robot. "Well. Hello. Josh-u-a. I am Missus Stigler. How are you. I am fine. Boop. Beep." I knew she didn't literally mean that Mrs. Stigler was a robot. She meant that she was rigid, unimaginative, and uncreative. And probably that, as a rich person, she could afford to buy a robot.

That night, lying on my sleeping bag, I felt like a GI who, having tromped around Tokyo for a year in boots, discovers it is considered offensive not to remove your shoes. I'd been saying *fuck* my whole life. I'd probably met maybe a dozen of these straight people over the years and unknowingly offended them. And now they hated me. I swore to myself that I'd never say *fuck* again.

As *fuck* slipped out of my vocabulary, spring slid into summer, and a new generation of Stiglers slipped across the property line. Amy was my age and had long, raven black hair. Jenny was seven, two years older, and possessed a fiery mass of red curls. They were the Stiglers' granddaughters, and they came fueled by curiosity and a hatred of boredom. When they discovered me, I was sitting on a stump in front of the cabin, packing unwilling kittens into a shoebox.

"Do you live here?" asked Jenny.

"Yes," I said.

"I always thought this was a shed."

"It's like a shed," I said, "except for humans."

The girls giggled. "You're funny," said Jenny.

I had never been so proud.

"Are you a boy or a girl?" Amy asked, crinkling her nose.

"*Amy*, that's rude," scolded Jenny.

I didn't mind. I knew it was because of my long hair. I went for the laugh again: "I'm a long-haired human boy."

That got the desired effect and, when they were done giggling, I showed the girls my kittens, my chickens, and my collection of sticks. Then I brought the girls into our half-built cabin, where they studied everything hesitantly and carefully like anthropologists in the highlands of Papua New Guinea. They marveled at the bookcase-lined walls, inspected our Indian tapestries, and commented on the inexplicable absence of a television set. In the next room, the paintings stunned them into silence: the massive collage of naked and copulating figures; the half-naked/half-skeletal woman; the peasants slaughtering the anaconda behind Victor Jara; the man clutching his bird-woman; the blue landscape of Sandinistas roasting a pig alongside Iranian revolutionaries, Menachem Begin, Virginia Slims, and Shirley Temple.

"Claudia's an artist," I offered, to coax them out of shock.

"Who's Claudia?" Amy asked.

"Here she is," I said, introducing my mother, who'd just returned from gathering pine needles for a new art project. Claudia smiled and gave each girl a slight bow of respect.

"You're his mom, right?" asked Amy.

"Yes, I have that great honor," Claudia said.

"Well, how come he doesn't call you Mom?"

"Because *Claudia* is my name." The girls were puzzled by this, but clearly entertained by the strangeness of their new neighbors. Soon they were peppering my mother with questions, and she seemed delighted to be interviewed by them. The girls looked anxious when they learned that television was a corporate trick that rots your brain and makes you buy things you don't need. The girls' eyes grew wide when my mother told them that a bum had been stabbed to death on the slide in our neighborhood playground in San Francisco. And they were impressed by Claudia's home economics when she explained how two hundred dollars a month in Welfare benefits could get you a lot farther renting in the country than in the city.

When their interrogation of my mother started to slacken, I invited them to consult the oracle of the I Ching with me by throwing coins. I wasn't surprised to find they didn't know the first thing about divining fate from the casting of lots. "Straight people," I thought, "you have to teach them everything." After the girls had posed their questions for the oracle, I taught them about yin and yang and the straight and broken lines, and coached them on how to throw the sacred pennies we used. Claudia looked on approvingly and gave us some background on the Shang dynasty.

In response to Amy's query as to whether or not she should get her hair braided, the I Ching advised that fear was natural in her situation but that sometimes war is the only path. We interpreted this as a *Yes*. Before we began Jenny's consultation, I excused myself to answer the call of nature: "I have to take a shit," I announced.

The girls snorted uproariously. Jenny turned to my mother: "Do you allow him to say that!?" she asked. Claudia shrugged and smiled and returned to gluing pine needles onto a picture of Fidel Castro. Jenny's question distracted me from my mission to the bathroom. The idea that my mother would "allow" me to do or say something was almost too strange to conceive of, but her question meant that Jenny and Amy's mother controlled what they could and couldn't say. Who were these straight people, fascists?

About then Mrs. Stigler rang a dinner bell and the girls jumped up with Pavlovian obedience. "We gotta go," said Jenny. "Or we'll get in trouble. Bye."

I only saw Amy and Jenny a few times after that. They weren't allowed to visit me anymore, they said, so our contact was limited to clandestine visits when old man Stigler was passed out in front of the ball game or when no one noticed their absence at a Sunday brunch. When they came, they smuggled contraband desserts to me in exchange for some time playing in the chicken coop or another peek at the illustrated Kama Sutra. I felt sorry for the girls. They had everything that money could buy, but their minds remained in total poverty.

Walking down the mountain toward town one day, Claudia and I passed a blonde girl feeding a donkey tethered to a tree at the side of the road. We stopped to talk with her, and to help with the feeding. The girl, Christine, was about my age and lived in the redwood house up the hill. We agreed to come back and visit her someday soon and then took to the road again, my hitchhiker ears desperate for the sound of some rumbling car that might spare me the forced march down the mountain.

A week or so later, I was overcome by boredom and begged Claudia to take me to visit Christine the Donkey Girl. My mother looked up from the mud pit she was digging in and decided she'd done enough work on her Chinese kiln for the day. We walked down the mountain, hand in hand. As we rounded the bend, we saw Christine leading her donkey and her mother toward us up the hill. We waved and quickened our pace to meet them.

"We were just coming to visit you," I called out as we got closer.

"We were just coming to visit *you*," said Christine, wide-eyed with wonder. "What a *coincidence* this is." She pronounced *coincidence* with great care as though the word was as magical as our serendipitous meeting.

I knew what *coincidence* meant too, and appreciated the girl's linguistic prowess. I repeated the word back to her: "Yes, it is quite a *coincidence*."

"It's because of *Jesus*," she declared.

A bolt of electricity seemed to course through my mother's body, and I winced as she suddenly clenched my hand tightly. I looked up to see that she was struggling to bring a forced smile to her face.

I'd heard of this Jesus guy a couple of times before, but it seemed to be all Christine wanted to talk about as we walked back to her house. Her mother with the long black braid was also very taken with Jesus and spent most of the walk talking about how he had saved her. Christine and I fed carrots to the donkey and ran around her rickety house bearing wooden crosses she made from kindling. After that, Christine told me very solemnly that Jesus had died, and that he'd died for *me*. I was still processing this information when Claudia politely but firmly declined a dinner invitation. I was going to throw a minor fit in protest but could see there was no changing my mother's mind. Plus I suspected that Christine's mother was preparing spinach, so I went without a fight.

As we trudged home, I asked: "Claudia, how come we couldn't stay for dinner?"

"Those people were fundamentalist Christians, Josh."

"They're what?"

"They believe in Jesus."

"Yeah, who is that Jesus?"

"He was a man from a long time ago but they think he's God." Claudia shook her head. "Christ, that woman wouldn't stop talking about Jesus for one minute. Did you hear her? 'My pastor this, my pastor that.' People have done a lot of really horrible things in Jesus' name, Josh. The inquisition, the pogroms, the Native American genocide."

"That's why we couldn't stay for dinner?"

"Yes. If we'd stayed, they would have tried to *convert* us."

That did sound unpleasant, even painful. "Would they have minded if I said *fuck* or *shit*?"

"Oh, definitely."

"So, they were straight people?"

"Well, yes . . . a kind of straight people."

Wait. There were different kinds of straight people? This was starting to get a little complicated. Straight people like the Stiglers were rich. But Christine wasn't rich. She only had a little tiny black-and-white television, and the car in her driveway was old and junky. So straight people could be either rich people or poor people who believed in Jesus. There must have been some connection between Jesus and the rich that I wasn't getting. I lost my train of thought, though, as Claudia began to point out the emerging constellations. There was the Big Dipper. And there was Orion's Belt, always leading to Sirius the Dog Star. If only people were as easy to read as the stars.

If Jesus was the mother tongue spoken by our neighbors down the hill, something called "sports" was the lingua franca in town.

"Hey, Buford. You catch your Rams last night?"

"Yup. Tyler's on fire pretty much, but Haden's a flop."

"Yessir, he ain't the fastest thing rushin' on two legs."

We were sitting at the counter in Annie Bow's restaurant, eating fried pie. Annie Bow's was the diner/bar that served as the town commons in the tiny community of Manton on the side of Mount Lassen. Fried pie was what it sounded like—deep-fried pockets of berry pie that my mother miraculously and mercifully didn't consider junk food. As I carefully scraped the last of the berry filling off of my plate, Darlene mussed my hair and offered me more ice water. Darlene was the waitress/manager/chef/informal town mayor, and she kept up a steady line of chatter with everyone who walked in the door of Annie Bow's.

"Carl, you thinkin' the Giants will shut out the Cubs again?"

"Dunno. All depends on Blue comin' off the bench and steppin' up. You hear? Shifty lost a whole pile a money on them Angels."

My brain hurt trying to figure out what these people were talking about. The guy chewing tobacco in the corner was catching sheep? Someone was on fire? Someone lost money on angels? I was utterly confused. "Claudia, what are they talking about?" I finally whispered, imagining it was some sort of theological debate about an epic clash of spirits like in the *Ramayana*.

My mother snorted dismissively: "Sports."

"What?"

"Sports."

"You mean like running?" That didn't make any sense.

"No, Joshey. You know." My mother hunched up her shoulders, furrowed her brow, and stuck her lips out like a gorilla. She let out a series of grunts, windmilled her arms around like she was throwing rocks, and then jerked her shoulders around like a drunk pushing through a crowd on the subway. She finished by compressing herself into a muscular squat, scrunching up her face, and growling with exertion. I was left to believe that "sports" was a Neanderthal soiling itself. But I knew that couldn't be quite right.

Whatever "sports" was, it could apparently be used as a pickup line. The logger with the red flannel shirt and lazy eye slid over to sit next to Claudia. It was only about three in the afternoon, but happy hour had come early for this gentleman, and he reeked of booze and slurred his words.

"Hey, baby," he addressed my mother. "You know why they call it 'Manton,' don'tcha? Manton is 'Man-Town' 'cause there ain't enough women to go around. You catch my drift, babe?"

Claudia didn't look at him. She stared straight ahead at the shelf of Tabasco sauce.

The logger tried again. "Who ya rootin' for tonight? The Giants?"

Claudia responded in a monotone. "I always root for the team with the largest fan base of urban poor."

The logger seemed confused. "Well, that's . . . That is . . . what now?"

"The largest group of urban poor. It's a known fact that when the home team loses, wife-beating spikes dramatically. So I want the winning team to be the one that will spare the largest number of women from domestic violence."

The logger now stared at the Tabasco sauce bottles too. Then he shook his head, wiped his nose on his shirt, and slid back down the counter to ask Darlene for some coffee.

Sports was such a passionate topic for these people that their team loyalties sometimes devolved into violence. One day at Annie Bow's a middle-aged man next to us explained his black eye and multiple gory face bandages to Darlene: "I ain't goin' to no more high school football games. That's for sure. I never shoulda worn that jersey."

Another time we entered the restaurant to find a trembling man standing inches away from Darlene's outstretched carving knife. Darlene spoke calmly: "Clem, if you ever talk about them Raiders in my place again, I'll cut your balls off. Got it?" Clem got it and sat down to enjoy the rest of his pancakes. A number of people clapped and then returned to their meals. It was a joke of some kind, but only sort of.

On one of the many evenings when we bivouacked in the corner of Annie Bow's, waiting to hitch a ride up the mountain, a group of men entered the restaurant taut with anger. Their jaws mercilessly worked their chewing tobacco, and their eyes bore the glassy invincibility of inebriation. Another group of men smoking cigarettes in the back of the restaurant stood up to confront them. Darlene ran out from behind the counter and put her hands out like a traffic cop. "Dusty," she barked at the ringleader of the newcomers, "I know you ain't comin' in here to yak about the game 'cause the game is over and ain't nobody goin' be talkin' about it tonight. Ain't that right, Slim!?" She shot this last question at the tweaky ringleader of the smokers at the back. There was a long silence as the two parties sized each other up from across the restaurant. My mother and I hunched down in our booth. I was scared but decided that if a riot broke out, I would leap over into the next booth and grab the fat lady's glazed doughnut in the confusion. Darlene didn't like the silence. "In all my years here I ain't never called the sheriff before to help me sort out my troubles. So, I'm real sure I ain't gonna have to start callin' the sheriff tonight and ruin my streak. Right, boys?" Dusty made some sort of executive decision, and he and his crew turned and walked out as silently as they'd come.

The fat lady got up and looked down at me curiously. "Are you a boy or a girl?"

This was one of only two non-sports-related questions that anyone ever asked of me. I knew the first was because of my long hair, and it was the easiest question in the world. I would answer in exasperation before it was even asked. "Are you . . ." "I'm a boy!" The second question—"What grade are you in?"—was harder to answer. I'd spent most of what would have been my kindergarten year traveling around in a funky blue van and a green bus. Now, it was summer and there was no school. And the plan for the coming fall was that my mother would home-school me. Sometimes I'd give this whole narrative as a response, which would leave the questioner silent and bewildered. Other times, I'd simply respond: "I'm home-schooled." This prompted the questioner to give a sad shake of the head and say to my mother: "Oh, so he's retarded, then?"

As we hitchhiked home through the tiny cluster of buildings that was Manton, I gazed at the one place in town I'd never been: the elementary school. It was dark, closed for the summer. But in my mind, it was full of potential for the fall.

My mother's eyes grew wide with alarm. "You want to go to *school*!?" She wouldn't have been more surprised if I'd told her I was leaving to join the Reagan administration. But she'd heard right. I wanted to go to school. "Are you sure, Josh?" I was sure. Deep within me I sensed that school was something kids *had* to do, even if their mothers told them they didn't. "You remember what I told you about school, right?" She wanted to make sure I knew what I was getting into. "Public school, it's run by the government, remember?" I assured her she'd trained me so well that I would have no problem withstanding the Capitalist lies and conformist brainwashing that made school so dangerous.

Once I'd made the decision to go, I began counting down the days to the first day of first grade. To avoid any further confusion about my gender, I asked Claudia to cut my hair. "Oh, your beautiful curls," Claudia lamented, as she fetched the scissors. Sitting on a volcanic rock in the sun, my long blond locks shorn into the wind, I felt like Pinocchio being carved into reality.

The appointed day came, and the babyish blond streaks were gone from my head. My big-boy hair was light brown now, and Claudia vigorously brushed it up into a frizzy bouffant. Then she adorned me with an elaborately embroidered vest she'd picked up from a Redding thrift store for just this day. "You look like Louis XIV," she said, admiring me. I knew he was the Sun King, and I beamed. We walked hand in hand the mile down the mountain to the bus stop. When the bus came, Claudia sent me off with tears in her eyes. I controlled my emotions and climbed onto the battered yellow bus bravely, reminding myself to censor my language lest I run into any straight people. The chatter of the children dipped toward silence as I walked down the aisle. "What is that thing?" someone called out. "Nice vest!" called out another voice. I smiled. The vest was a hit!

When I got to class, I was so excited I talked ceaselessly, introducing myself to and asking questions of my new classmates. But my day took a precipitous and traumatic dive a moment later when the teacher dragged me across the room by my hair.

"I said no talking!" the strange giant man castigated me. "You're all gonna learn to follow the rules in *my* class," he announced, and I was banished to a plastic chair in the hallway. I covered my face with my hands and shook with shame and humiliation until I was joined a minute later by a tall, thin boy named Travis.

Travis was mad. "That teacher is *so* mean!" he spat out.

I felt instantly comforted by having a cellmate confident enough to be outraged. "I guess he really doesn't like talking," I said.

"Yeah, I guess not," Travis said, and we both laughed. "Why are you wearing that vest thing?" asked Travis.

"My *mom* got it for me." I knew he wouldn't know who "Claudia" was.

"Well, you should get rid of it. It looks stupid."

I flung the vest down the hall. We both laughed again. We were soon joined by two more kids, also banished for talking, and a sense of desperation returned to the hallway.

When I got off the bus at the end of the day, and saw Claudia waiting for me with banana and carob chips, I started crying.

"What happened, Joshey?"

I told her what had happened.

"Oh, my God, Josh! You do *not* have to go back there."

But I wanted to go back. In part, because I didn't want to let the mean teacher win and, in part, because my trip to school brought me the same mix of fascination and fear that must have filled Pocahontas as she sailed up the River Thames for the first time. An alien and tremendous world awaited me.

"He dragged you by the hair!?" My mother's jaw hardened. When we got home she began working the phone like the harbinger of the apocalypse. An official investigation was demanded. The ACLU and class action lawsuits were mentioned. A protest march was threatened. Claudia told me the school "admitted" that Greg, the first-grade teacher, was ex-military. She wasn't surprised. "He still thinks he's in the Army. We'll see how he likes his court-martial." Greg remained my teacher, but he hardly even made eye contact after that, which made me feel powerful, but also invisible.

That night Claudia and I slept outside under the stars. My day replayed itself over and over in my head. It wasn't really the hair-pulling that stuck out in my mind. It was a thousand little clues that, taken as a whole, added up to a startling and unsettling conclusion. They were *all* straight. Every single one of them. I was the only kid who wasn't. It was *me* who wasn't normal. I'd started the day like a great American bison confident in his stature among the teeming kings of the prairie. I ended the day realizing I was on the endangered species list.

They couldn't tell I was from a different species just by looking at me, although my friend Travis told me I had the biggest nose he'd ever seen. Or, phrased another way, in front of some girls, he told me: "Josh, if you walked into a wall you'd hit your nose before your pecker." That was a good one. Ha! Pecker. Whatever that meant. It was the language that gave me away. I couldn't understand most of what they were saying.

At recess the dead leaves smelled of decay and manure. I was the last kid still buried in a generous pile of them on the playground. We were supposed to pop out when we heard the right pig call but I couldn't tell the difference between them. "OK, one more time, dummy," scolded Billy. "Heeey-yooo. Shaaaw-weee. Sooo-weee. Weee-yaaay." I popped out. "Nope, Josh, you missed it again. Git back under there."

Day after day, my ears hurt straining to understand what the kids were saying. My problem wasn't so much the words—which, when they weren't pig calls, were often English—but the context in which they were said. These were some of the incomprehensible questions they asked me:

He-Man or She-Ra?

Baptist or Methodist?
Bird or Magic?
Indiana Jones or James Bond?
John Deere or Caterpillar?
Christie Brinkley or Suzanne Somers?
Donkey Kong or Pac-Man?

I nodded knowingly and smiled deferentially but remained as bewildered as a Spaniard in Lisbon.

Over time I began deciphering some of the language and reported my findings back to my mother. "Remember how I told you that a whole bunch of kids are in love with Jessie's girl? That's because there's a song about that that kids listen to on the radio. Did you know that *getting physical* means sex? And *stocking stuffers* are on Christmas when you put red socks into a fire and put presents in them." Claudia nodded distractedly, adding another layer of bricks into the kiln pit in the ground, trying to get the temperature high enough to fire raku pottery.

She took full notice, though, when I told her that I'd been kneed in the head five times playing Smear the Queer. "Josh! That's homophobic!"

And she went absolutely bananas when she overheard me chanting: "Crack the whip . . . on the Japs!"

"Josh!" she screamed at me. "How can you say that!? Hiroshima!"

The next day I diligently tutored my schoolmates: "You can't say 'crack the whip on the Japs' because it's racist."

Bucktoothed Bo replied defiantly: "I'll crack the whip on anybody I want." I didn't have a response to this, so I let it go.

Later in the day, I got an even more surprising response when I told the football dudes: "My mom says you can't say 'Smear the Queer' because a 'queer' is a gay person, like Harvey Milk. Gay people are men who put their penises in other men's butts, and my mom says there's nothing wrong with that." The faces around me erupted wildly into a crimson flush. The dudes laughed themselves apoplectic, their open mouths wheezing for air and drooling with uncontrollable giddiness. As the laughter slowly died down, someone threatened to tell on me, and several of the dudes called me a "faggot." I decided to let this one go as well.

Most of the things I said sparked less of a reaction. Or no reaction at all. A blonde girl in my class named Misty would sometimes talk to me at lunchtime. We didn't so much talk as exchange mutually unintelligible soliloquies.

"Misty, did you know all the corporations are making the sky poisonous?"

"I got a lemon-lime sucker at the bank yesterday and two gumballs."

"Banks put all their money into nuclear holocaust development."

"I watched *Bambi* on TV after church."

"I never saw it but my mom told me that *Bambi* is really sexist. Girls should be able to save themselves. The worst thing a boy can be is macho. The *worst* thing."

"My big sister, Krista, came home from the rodeo after curfew last night. It was past my bedtime, but I was still awake, and she got into a huge argument with my mom, but then they said they loved each other and they loved Jesus. And I know Jesus loves them."

I didn't understand what a curfew was, although I was vaguely aware that Somoza's death squads imposed them on the barrios in Nicaragua. I didn't really understand what a bedtime was, either, but I inferred that it had to do with going to bed. "Misty, last night, before *I* went to bed, my mom was sitting on the floor painting with gouache and listening to Flora Purim records. And she was drinking wine, and I really wanted some wine too, but she wouldn't let me have any. But I kept asking her for some, and finally she gave me some, and I drank it, and the wine was really, like, sour, but I drank it anyway. And then I started jumping over her painting of a lesbian woman who slew a dragon saying: 'Tell Saint George to forget it.' And I kept jumping, and she grabbed me like: *Whoom!* Right out of the air, and I fell down, and I wanted her to be sorry for doing that so I started coughing over and over until I made myself throw up a little bit. But then she said: 'That's what happens when you drink wine.' Then I had to sleep in the cold room. Isn't that ironic?"

Misty stared at me in silence for a time, and then the bell rang.

Of all the nicknames I received in first grade—including Big Nose, Elvis (because of my hairdo), and Josh Doesn't Wash (which had some truth to it)—the most accurate was probably E.T. My failure to speak a common language undeniably set me apart, but my fundamentally differing conception of reality was positively extraterrestrial. I thought that school was an academy for learning knowledge, and I behaved accordingly. I diligently spent each minute of class time applying myself to the lesson at hand. My sense of self-worth rose and fell with the plus, check, or minus grading system. But performance in class seemed to be irrelevant to my classmates.

"Hey Dwayne, did you get all the way through to letter G by recess? I did," I called after the big kid with feathered hair.

"Shut up, nerd." Dwayne didn't even bother to turn around.

Nerd. This was another nickname and was proof positive that some other criterion for popularity was at work here. In fact, it seemed the *worse* you did at your studies, the more popular you were. Dwayne couldn't even recognize any lowercase letters, and he had a whole gang of boys that followed him around.

"Guys," I called out to Dwayne's gang. "Did you hear that Anwar Sadat was assassinated?"

Dwayne shook his head in pity, and his gang continued trading Matchbox cars.

The children weren't the only ones who thought I hailed from another planet. I spoke at morning circle about visions from my past lives too often for that. The teachers knew me as the boy who successfully lobbied to have his minus changed to a plus for putting the sugar cookie in the inedible column with the chair, rather than in the edible column with the carrot. And I was the boy who came to school regularly with notes from my mother requesting that I be given less conventional art projects and more creative math problems. The teachers rolled their eyes and set me up at my own special table so I could do addition with my finger in a tray of sand rather than with the unimaginative pencil on the boring paper.

From my perspective, the teachers didn't have a lot to offer. At first they came across as knowledgeable, but once I got the real story from my mother I realized they were almost as small-minded as the children.

"This is a toothbrush." The health teacher began her presentation on oral hygiene. I sat in rapt attention like Powhatan watching his first display of musketry. I returned home with brushes and floss and little tubes of toothpaste. "Claudia, I'm supposed to use these every day. Twice a day!" But I came back to school the next day, reeducated and armed with facts. "These," I began my indictment, holding out the unopened toothpaste tubes to the health teacher, "are poison! They have fluoride, artificial sweetener, and chemicals in them that will *kill* you."

The same cycle of enlightenment and counter-enlightenment repeated itself when I learned of the festive holiday of Thanksgiving that apparently everybody celebrated. I returned the next day preaching about Native American genocide. "Did you know," I asked the art teacher, "that Indians to this day are still being driven off of their land? The government took away their forests and meadows and now they want their rocks. For the uranium. So we can make atomic bombs to kill every last woman, man, and child." I shook my head in disgust. The art teacher shook her head too. We lapsed into silence. I sat with my hands folded while the other kids made paper turkeys out of their handprints.

Winter came soon after Native American Genocide Day, and the mile walk to the bus stop became an arduous trek through unplowed snow. I'd grown so disillusioned with school that after a few days of slogging my way to the battered yellow bus I decided to call it quits. We'd reached the end of the driveway when I announced: "Claudia, I'm done with school." She nodded knowingly, and we retraced our slushy steps back to the half-built cabin. She was right. School was no place for kids. At least not a kid like me, whatever kind of kid that was. We warmed ourselves by the fire and picked up where we'd left off in *A People's History of the United States*. Claudia began reading: "Even the school serves only the purpose of furnishing the offspring of the wealthy with those qualities necessary to uphold their class domination." This was more like it. I interrupted Claudia's reading in a contented alien voice: "E.T. phone home!"

School passed on into a memory of the fall. Now it was winter's turn, and icy winds howled up the mountain. Legions of snow buried the roads and barricaded our door. Our rickety little cabin was ill prepared. Half of the building was still a jumble of cinder blocks and rebar, and the half-inch of gypsum board that should have formed an interior wall now faced the full fury of winter. The single-paned windows provided no protection from the arctic wind that circled our cabin, so we bricked in the windows with stacks of books, pillows, and piles of old clothes. As temperatures dropped, two of our three rooms were rendered unlivable iceboxes. We retreated into my mother's bedroom, where the wood-burning stove kept us alive. We huddled around it for weeks on end, feeding branches and logs into the blaze.

After a month or so, the firewood ran out, and we stumbled through the snow drifts, looking for standing deadwood to bring down with the chain saw. Claudia pointed through the hazy, milky air: "Look, Josh. There's a dead tree!"

"Don't say 'dead,' Claudia." Something about our condition seemed too fragile to throw words like that around. We felled the old pine and dragged it laboriously through the mounting blizzard. We split it into rounds at the doorstep and shuttled the wood into our bunker of warmth so that it might sustain us for another week.

A deep freeze burst our water pipes, and the tap went dry. We took to hacking icicles off of the eaves and melting them down for drinking water.

Bathing was a trickier business, and I went several months without a proper bath. Cleanliness just wasn't important enough to bear scrubbing myself down in melted snow. With the cold persistently gnawing at my lungs, it was only a matter of time before I got sick. A deep bronchial cough plagued me for a couple of weeks and then I finally succumbed to a nasty fever that kept me sweating and hallucinating for a couple more. By the time I was feeling myself again, we'd begun to run out of food. We rationed what we had and miraculously managed to live the last couple of months off of kidney beans and ketchup, canned soup, and chewable vitamins.

As much as we subsisted off of dry goods, though, our real sustenance was books. The power of the written word transformed those unbearable cold and endless winter nights into fantastical voyages into worlds of imagination. By the light of the flickering electric bulb, we read about the Cherokee Trail of Tears, King Arthur, and CIA assassinations in Latin America. When the bulb burnt out, we read in the golden glow of candles the works of Marge Piercy, Ethel Cook Eliot, Ray Bradbury, Walter M. Miller, Jr., Ursula K. Le Guin, and Robert A. Heinlein. When these books ran out we began reading our 1967 *Encyclopedia Britannica*, beginning with Aabenraa-Sønderborg, a district of Denmark. Thus began a process that I completed eleven years later when I finished reading the final *Britannica* entry for Zworykin, Vladimir Kosma, an American electronic engineer and inventor known as the father of television, a device I still had not yet had the pleasure of owning.

It was April before winter's wrath finally abated. We were down to one can of minestrone soup and beginning to eye the dry cat food when spring suddenly blessed the mountain. The forest crackled and gurgled with the thaw, and soon the mountainside was awash in color. New life chirped and sang out on all sides as we unblocked the windows and let the light pour in. Ms.Ms. and her sons Farfel and Fluffer sunned themselves with blinking, ecstatic eyes. My dog, Babe, rolled exuberantly in the mud and caught up on the thousands of objects that needed sniffing. I ran around after him, soaking up the warmth of the sun. Then I remembered school. Somewhere down the mountain all of my classmates were still in school listening to teacher Greg, still trading Matchbox cars on the playground, still playing Smear the Queer at recess. I winced, waiting to feel pangs of guilt, anxiety, and uncertainty. But I stood my ground, feeling nothing amiss. Sure, everyone else my age was in school, but I'd seen school. It had nothing to offer me. I wasn't missing a thing.

Claudia, Babe, and I thaw out at the half-built cabin on Mount Lassen.

During the long winter, Claudia had explained the Doors' song "Five to One" to me. "Listen to these words, Joshey: 'They got the *guns*, but we got the *numbers*.' That means the government and the corporations might have the police and the means of production, but we outnumber them. So long as the People are being exploited, it's just a matter of time until we rise up and take this country back." But she was wrong. I knew that now. They had the guns *and* the numbers. They had everybody—except us. We happy few. We didn't care about sports or Jesus or television. We didn't need to go to school. We were free. Free to wander the world and choose our own destinies. I raised my arms skyward with a clear conscience. Nature was *my* classroom.

By day I wandered our rambling eleven acres of scrub forest with Babe at my side. I picked manzanita and blackberries and ate apples right off the tree. In the evenings, my mother read the Narnia books to me by candlelight, and we slept under the stars on our little wooden porch. Fueled by magical visions of Narnia, I saw the landscape with new eyes. This was a new world just waiting to be explored and, like Adam before me, it waited for me to name its every part. I dubbed the climbing tree "Smilax"; the new kitten was "Reepicheep"; the horse-shaped manzanita tree was "Bree." Our cabin was "Cair Paravel," and the little ribbon of water that ran by it was "Narnia Creek."

Over time the twin forces of confidence and curiosity pulled me across Narnia Creek. Babe and I began wandering up and down the mountain pine forests on our own, discovering hidden glens, babbling brooks, and sacred groves. We ranged for miles and miles without ever feeling alone. A guardian spirit seemed to course through the natural world around me, its breath on the breeze and its heart beating in the ground below me. During those golden months, the presence of that sacred spirit wove itself into my being and never left me. They were the happiest of my childhood. I woke when I wanted and slept when I felt like it. I played and wandered where I pleased. I experienced what few have: freedom to the fullest. There can be, perhaps, no purer freedom than that of a boy loosely supervised by a free-spirited mother in the midst of the wilderness.

SEVEN

Little Man Won't Get High

I was six years old and couldn't think of anything better than an endless summer on Mount Lassen. We had forests to explore, books to read, and carob chips to mollify dreams of chocolate. What more could we ever need? But, according to Claudia, our quest for Utopia had stalled out on Mount Lassen. To hear her tell it, we were stuck in sort of the *opposite* of Utopia. "Think about it, Joshey. The people in town are drunks, the teachers are violent, and the only acceptable topics of conversation are sports and Jesus." My mother told me she was lonely, still longing for that magical mix of consciousness and land-based living. She was *depressed,* she told me, which meant *always sad*. And just when I began to worry about her, she came running back from the mailbox, breathless with excitement. The Rainbow Family was holding a festival up in Idaho! A real gathering of the tribes! Brothers and sisters from every intentional community in North America would be there. *This* would be our gateway to Utopia.

When summer came, we left a mountain of kitty chow for our cats and dog and bused and hitched our way north on I-5. In Portland, Oregon, we stood in the pouring rain for three hours, our thumbs out at the end of an iron bridge. I glared at the passing cars. How dare you not stop for us? Can't you see I'm shivering?

Eventually some merciful stranger picked us up and carried us east on I-84 along the Columbia River Gorge. After several more rides, towering green forests wilted away into yellowing dusty flatlands and then high desert. Claudia and I found ourselves east of Baker City, Oregon, walking alongside a dry creek bed. My water bottle was almost empty. The steady rumble of cars had withered away until all that was left was the crunching of gravel under our feet. The creek bed narrowed until it finally collapsed into a mound of sand. My step soon began to falter. I had never experienced so much heat and light and dust. It was like walking into a ceramic kiln.

Suddenly, Claudia stopped. She pointed up into the sky.

"Look Joshey! A red-tailed hawk! It's your totem animal!"

Back home I had a *Ranger Rick* magazine with glossy pictures of birds. I had once told her I thought the picture of the red-tailed hawk in flight was "beautiful." This, she decided, meant that I had chosen my totem animal. Whenever we saw any bird bigger than a crow, she'd get excited and say: "Look! A red-tailed hawk!"

This bird was *not* a hawk but I recognized it from the same *Ranger Rick*. It was a vulture. A turkey vulture, if I remembered correctly.

"Look, Joshey! It's circling! It's a good omen!"

I knew what that meant and watched in horror as the circling vulture was joined by another.

"Look! Another one!"

A wave of dust blew across my face, stinging my eyes. My lips were cracked and there was nothing to drink. Out here I was just another lame animal condemned by the immutable laws of nature. I was walking vulture food.

My eyes narrowed, and I could see the horizon shimmering in all directions as the sun boiled the living vapors out of the land. The heat played tricks with my eyesight, distorting the dirt roadway so that it looked like it was moving. And then it *was* moving. From the west came a new column of dust, winding its way through the scrub brush. Out of the haze, a blue bus soon became visible. Its engine growled as it slowed. It was an old school bus, repainted so thickly blue that it looked as though it was hewn from cerulean rock. An array of feathers and crystals flashed from behind the windshield. The side windows were covered in Indian tapestries. The bus came to a stop in front of us. Although the door was opened with a manual handle, in my mind I could hear the dramatic *tshhhh* of a hydraulic chamber being opened.

The driver gazed down at us in amused contemplation. He wore round purple sunglasses and a Dr. Seuss hat. His long beard was pulled together in a braid that flounced across his linen tunic.

He addressed us with an air of deep solemnity: "I'm Driver Dave. You hombres goin' to the Rainbow Gathering?"

We grinned and rushed forward. The vultures would have to go hungry that day.

Driver Dave took a deep bow from the driver's seat, waving his white-gloved hand with a flourish: "Welcome to the Roach Coach from Roachberry Farms!"

We clambered onto the bus. Tapestry-covered foam mattresses lay where iron benches had once been riveted. Up front a couple of guys were sitting cross-legged smoking a hookah. A dreadlocked couple crouched in the back, playing bamboo flutes. These were our people!

After a couple of days of bucking and bouncing along dirt and gravel roads, the Roach Coach from Roachberry Farms suddenly stopped moving at the edge of an interstate. Nag Champa smoke and the goofy vibrations of the Bonzo Dog Doo-Dah Band filled the motionless air. Driver Dave broke the stillness with an announcement: "Dudes and Dudettes! We are about to hit God's own open road, which means we're gonna follow the Fifth Golden Rule. I'm gonna lay it down on you right now. Are you ready? Here it is: No smoking any of them *fuuunny* cigarettes or hittin' the *boooze* till we hit fifth gear! Got it!?" Everybody cheered.

The Roach Coach jolted forward, and I felt the blessed smoothness of pavement beneath us for the first time in two days. Driver Dave called out: "First gear . . . second gear . . . third gear." Everyone chanted along with him. The engine grunted and whined under Driver Dave's relentless command. "Fourth gear." The Roach Coach shuddered and creaked as we picked up speed. "Fifth gear!" The Rolling Stones' "Sympathy for the Devil" suddenly blasted from the Roach Coach's quadraphonic speakers. Driver Dave pumped his fist in the air and then victoriously produced a huge bottle of whiskey from beneath the dashboard and began swigging greedily from its open neck. He passed the bottle back, and smoldering joints were passed forward in return. "We're on our way, Joshey!" my mother whooped, one arm around her new best friend Michael, the other waving a wrinkled white spliff in the air.

I shrugged. I'd learned that adult exuberance rarely correlated with anything actually exciting, and this fifth-gear whiskey-ganja party was no exception. I turned back to my 145th hand of Go Fish with my new best friend and asked him if he had any sevens. Back home in New York City they just called him Rick. But I promoted him to Ranger Rick because he liked camping and bore a passing resemblance to the shaggy, saucer-eyed raccoon that graced the covers of *Ranger Rick* magazine. He told me he'd hitchhiked from the airport in Seattle down to Oregon and had been taking a piss in a ditch at the side of the road when the Roach Coach stopped to pick him up. Ranger

Rick was on his way to Rainbow to find a new direction for his crummy life, a life that had been sidetracked by an all-consuming job. "You know how crummy my job is, Josh? All I do is sit behind a crummy desk all day pushing crummy papers around while some crummy boss yells at me. Do you have any kings?" I didn't have any kings, but I recognized that Ranger Rick was a boy thrown into a thirty-year-old body, uncomfortable around adults, and happier playing cards with me than doing whiskey bong hits with the grown-ups.

My mother's new best friend, Michael Rodriguez, was also from New York City and about the same age as Rick, but he was a different kind of man-boy. He threw his lanky frame around like the star lacrosse player he was still proud to have been, earnestly trying to impress the other adults with how adult he was. He'd been the first one to throw off his clothes back at the reservoir, making a big show of his naked plunge into the frigid green water. And he'd jumped through the campfire barefoot just because Driver Dave said he used to do that back in Santa Cruz. When Gita told us she had smuggled opium out of India, Michael bragged about his backpacking trip through Nepal. And when Mike from Boston told us he'd overdosed on angel dust at Woodstock, Michael boasted that he'd once blown his mind on angel dust so bad he'd been arrested and then hospitalized for throwing himself through the display window of a department store.

Michael wore his wavy orange hair short on top and long in back because he played Riff Raff in the shadow cast of the midnight showing of the *Rocky Horror Picture Show* in Manhattan. From his reenactments, I gathered that Riff Raff was some sort of creepy hunchback who fondled my mother's breasts. Michael kept us guessing as to what his day job was. Claudia psychically intuited that he was a community organizer. Ranger Rick said that he probably worked at an ad agency. Gita and Mike from Boston both kept asking him whether he was a narc. But they were all wrong. I came the closest, he said, when I guessed that he was a rodeo clown, but he kept his profession a mystery.

Gita was from Austria. She was a terrorist in the Red Army Faction and had been on her way to receive explosives training in the Middle East when she met Mike, who was playing a gig in London. Because her period had dried up and she'd been vomiting, she suspected she might be pregnant with Mike's baby. She was on her way to Rainbow to have a hallucinogenic spirit quest to figure out whether the Goddess had cast her fate toward terrorism or motherhood. Claudia told her she didn't have to choose between the two, but Gita felt that changing the world and changing diapers were mutually

View from the Roach Coach as it hits the open road.

incompatible. Mike from Boston was from Philadelphia originally, and played bass, and no one could believe that he was forty. He had a twenty-year-old son out there somewhere. Gita and Mike had matching dreadlocks, nose rings, and tattered leather jackets. They rolled their own cigarettes and didn't know how to talk to kids like me.

The other two Roach Coachers didn't know how to talk to kids either. And they both had shaved heads. One was a young woman who was menstruating and had apparently taken a traditional Seneca women's vow of silence while she was bleeding. The other was a perpetually pickled British chap who was either narcoleptic or sedated or both. He stank of booze and drooled out phrases like "bollocks wiffout me giro got no quid wiffout me quid got no smack wiffout me smack got no bollocks."

We all relied upon Claudia's psychic powers to find the turnoff for the Rainbow Festival. But after several fruitless forays up rutted logging roads, even she conceded that we were lost. We skirted the edges of the vast Boise National Forest for about an hour until our sauced Briton yelled out: "Bloody 'ell! Look at dem geezers." His arm extended toward a muddy field in which two bearded men in tie-dye were hugging each other. A third bearded man waved at us with a huge pair of deer antlers.

Claudia rushed to the window of the Roach Coach. "Hey, brothers, which way to the Gathering?" Deer antler man waved his horns at a broad swath of mud that cut across the field and into the woods. Driver Dave gunned the Roach Coach forward and Claudia called out: "Thank you, brothers!"

All three men flashed us peace signs, and antler man called back: "Welcome home!"

As the Roach Coach struggled up into the forest, the curving muddy road widened, and a steady stream of smaller vehicles began passing us from behind: a pink VW van flying the Jolly Roger and a peace flag; a skeletal dune buggy loaded with yellow crates; and a convoy of battered pickup trucks bearing rainbow flags. The men and women clinging to the trucks were weatherworn and solemn, but flashed us the peace sign like the rest.

My mother had her head out the window, flashing peace signs back at them. "Oh, Joshey: rainbow, rainbow, rainbow! Go like this, Josh!" She was showing me the V of her first two fingers. "This is the symbol for peace. This is no hip thing to do. We don't grin and laugh at one another like straight people with their 'have-a-nice-days.' Here, we're eager to show each other how strong we are. This is not the sixties anymore, Josh. This is the eighties. We are for *real*. This peace sign is for *real*. It means courage, a pact, a dedication, a hope."

After an hour of muddy switchbacks, the Roach Coach finally came to rest in the clearing that served as the parking lot for the Festival. We staggered off of the blue bus and slogged through the mud toward the trailhead, where a crowd of people was singing "We are one with the infinite sun" and blowing bubbles. At the mouth of the forest we passed through a gauntlet of half-dressed white people wearing Indian buckskins and feathers. "Welcome home! *A-ho*!" they greeted us.

A young woman squatted down to greet me and stared into my soul with bright eyes. "*A-ho*, little man," she said and pressed her pointy little breasts against me in a deep patchouli-soaked embrace. "Do you know what *A-ho* means?" I shook my head no. "It means *peace* in Indian." I knew that couldn't be quite right since there were hundreds of Native tribes that must have had a multitude of mutually unintelligible ways to say "peace." But I didn't say anything. She had been dispensing some sort of treats from a paper bag, and I didn't want to risk offending her. Instead I stared with exaggerated curiosity at her bag. "Here, little man, have a halva from the Goddess," she said, handing me a brown flaky candy. I placed it on my tongue and gagged. It had the consistency of sand and the unmitigated taste of raw sesame. I spit it out onto the forest path and joined the pack of pilgrims stumbling their way through the dark fir forest toward redemption.

We finally emerged into the light at the edge of a broad treeless slope covered in thick, wet knotweed. The bottom of the hillside sunk into a murky stream, and the top disappeared into a fog-draped crest of Douglas firs. "Welcome home!" someone called. All the adults whooped, and most of the women around me took off their shirts. "Now we're free," one of them said. Ranger Rick later told me the disrobing ladies were his favorite part of Rainbow. Not mine. I shivered looking at all those naked breasts on such a chilly day. "Welcome home!" yelled a hairy naked man with a parasol. Up and down the wet hillside, people were unfurling tents and erecting teepees. We trudged up a broad, treeless slope for a while, slipping on the slimy green knotweed, before Ranger Rick declared he'd found a spot flat enough to pitch his tan pup tent.

My mother stopped with a stunned look on her face. "I didn't bring a tent," she said to no one in particular.

"Yikes," said Ranger Rick under his breath, his cheeks flaring in a sympathetic wince.

The earth tilted ever so slightly on its axis in that moment, and I saw Claudia for the first time from a new angle. She was no longer omniscient. She was still my mother, but she was also a pale-faced city slicker woefully unprepared for the reality at hand. Ranger Rick's subtle "Yikes" meant that I was not alone in this conclusion. I gained in that moment the ability to see my mother through the eyes of others. She was an imperfect person, just like any other. "Does this mean I'm growing up?" I asked myself. This thought was closely followed by "Where the hell are we going to sleep?"

"Hey, Josh," called Ranger Rick. "Come help me hammer in these tent stakes. They keep slipping around in the mud." I busied myself with the tan pup tent and eyed Claudia and Michael Rodriguez skeptically as they ran around the hillside like children, gathering up discarded plastic bags, bumming plastic sheeting off of better prepared Rainbow warriors, and raiding a pile of construction debris dumped at the edge of the woods. They soon had a tiny garbage wigwam formed over a skeleton of fir branches.

On cue a Native American guy in a leather jacket emerged from the woods and inspected their handiwork. He straightened the eagle feather in his hair and nodded approvingly. "This is the way the ancestors would have done it, even more than these store-boughts." He waved his hand at the conical white canvas teepees studding the hillside. "You used what's provided, what the land had to offer." He bid them *"A-ho"* and went off to escort a new crop of topless women up the mountain. Claudia and Michael did a little celebratory dance, basking in the affirmation of their authenticity. The garbage wigwam then collapsed under its own weight. As Claudia and Michael set about rebuilding it, Ranger Rick and I trudged up the hill in search of food. We followed the sound of conga drums and panpipes to the Rainbow Family kitchen, where a pungent cluster of bedraggled rainbow warriors held out their battered bowls for lentil slop. I lost sight of Ranger Rick in the jockeying for food, but he found me gnawing on a crusty round of bread by the fire.

"Buddy, didn't you bring a bowl?"

"No. I don't have a spoon either."

"You want to use mine?" Ranger Rick offered me his yellow plastic camping bowl and spork.

"No thank you."

A sweaty naked white man with dreadlocks stopped to gyrate between us, firelight and shadow dancing across his streaky body.

"You don't like the lentils, huh?"

"Not really. I took an extra loaf of bread for later," I said, patting the hard round protrusion under my shirt. A group of fire dancers began spinning burning sticks in the air.

"Hey!" said Ranger Rick. "Should I try to put out the fire on her butt!?" A topless brown woman in a grass skirt was shrieking as smoke curled up her backside. I nodded yes, but a muscular young man in blue body paint had already thrown her to the ground and was now on top of her, grinding the fire out with his hips.

After dinner we slid and stumbled back down the hill, and I crashed with Ranger Rick for the night. The floor of the little tent was wet, and I shivered as I tried to fall asleep. A few yards away, underneath Michael Rodriguez and a pile of plastic and sticks, my mother was moaning loudly like a cat in estrus.

"I'm real sorry, buddy," sympathized Ranger Rick. "That must be real embarrassing."

"It is," I said and wrapped the end of the towel that served as my surrogate pillow over my head.

"I can't believe what a wuss I am," Ranger Rick regretted. "I coulda been over there like a tiger. That girl's butt must have been on fire for a full thirty seconds before anyone else noticed it. Man! I coulda been the hero up there."

"Maybe someone will catch on fire tomorrow," I offered hopefully.

"Ha, that's a good one."

The next morning, Ranger Rick spoke from the haze: "Hey, buddy, you can see a little sky peeking out from behind the rain clouds." I rolled over and covered my face with a damp towel. It was drizzling and gray by the time the reek of recycled breath and rotting knotweed finally drove me from the tent. A thick mist blanketed the hillside, and nothing moved. For a moment I thought that everyone must have died during the night, leaving us as the only survivors, but then I saw a hunched figure scuttling down the hillside in the direction of the shitters. And I noticed the arrhythmic pounding of drums from up the hill. The perpetual drum circles were such a fixture of the environment, I'd momentarily forgotten that untalented humans were responsible for the noise. I donned my last not-completely-filthy garment, an orange-and-white-striped wool turtleneck, and began the climb up the hill into the woods. I wandered through the trees until I came upon a cluster of people packed into a big canvas tent called Madam Frog's Tea House. I squeezed myself between muddy legs, sniffing for food. I smelled coffee, marijuana, and bitter medicinal odors, but nothing resembling breakfast. I turned to force my way out and bumped into my mother and Michael Rodriguez sitting together on a tree stump. They looked blissed out of their minds.

Claudia saw me and gave me a warm embrace. "Oh, Josh," she purred. "Isn't it wonderful! The whole Gathering is like a metaphor. You come in at the parking lot at the lowest point, and a lot of people never get past that point. The bikers with their Harleys are all still down there drinking beer. Then you get everyone strung out along the hillside trying to get higher. And the higher you climb, the higher you get. And if you can make it to the top, you get to the kitchens of the tribes, and *you* made it all the way to Madam Frog's!" She lowered her voice to let me in on a secret. "But, Josh, you can get even higher. There's a trail up here that goes to a higher ridge, a higher level. That's where the healers are—at the very top—giving massages, acupressure, chanting, meditations. There's even a healing commune."

Someone brought Claudia her order of ayahuasca tea at this point, and her face disappeared behind a mug sculpted to look like a green goddess with snakes emerging from her nipples.

"Josh, come with us!"

I declined and excused myself to go look for Ranger Rick and, more importantly, breakfast. As I lifted the muddy canvas flap of the tent to leave, the drunk Briton from the Roach Coach shrieked and stumbled backward, shouting: "Look, it's a bloody dwarf, it is."

A woman with a conical black witch hat comforted him: "Relax, it's a child."

"Like 'ell it is! Why would a child be in a place like this?"

I passed the Krishna Kamp, where freaky men and women with bizarrely shaved heads danced around in saffron robes, and found Ranger Rick around the fire at the Rolling Turtle Tribe.

"Hey buddy!" called Ranger Rick. "I'm glad you're here. Let me take a picture of you. Sit on that log in front of the ladies." Ranger Rick took several photos of me sitting in front of a group of three women shaking themselves vigorously to the conga drums. Their naked breasts slapped around rhythmically, and the bands of white seashells wrapped around their ankles and wrists rattled like a hundred rattlesnakes. Rick seemed satisfied with his documentation and put his camera away. "Man, the guys at the office are never gonna believe this. Did you eat yet?"

I shook my head no, trying to look as starved as possible.

"OK, let me get you something."

I stared into the bonfire and closed my eyes, trying to project my spirit into the fire where it would be warm. I heard Ranger Rick somewhere behind me. "Uh, hey, brother, what's your name again? Dog-worm? Dog-wort? Dagwar? OK. Hey, I've got a little buddy over here who didn't get any breakfast . . . Really? . . . Well, what about that big pot? . . . But it's still steaming. I can see it . . . Come on, please, man? . . . Look, he's a kid . . . Well, can't you just *pretend* he's part of the Rolling Turtles? . . . OK, what about for five bucks?"

Was I really hearing this? They were refusing to serve me? Ranger Rick returned triumphantly with his yellow plastic bowl overflowing with hot corn gruel. The day before I'd been too squeamish to share germs by using Rick's unwashed bowl and spoon, but now I shoveled the tasteless grainy mash down with gusto. "Boy, were you hungry. You going to be OK here? I got myself invited on a hike up to the summit with a couple of the dancing ladies."

"I'm good," I said. There was no way I was going to go tramping off into the woods. Besides, I had a little score to settle with the Rolling Turtles.

"OK, just bring my bowl and spoon back to the tent with you when you go."

I nodded. The bowl and spoon weren't all that I was going to bring back. When I was done eating, I wandered around the Rolling Turtle Tribe's camp, trying to appear innocent and curious. I ducked under the blue cloth flap that hung from their tarp-covered yurt and walked into a wall of hashish smoke, thicker and more pungent than your run-of-the-mill marijuana. A tangle of naked people were engrossed in massaging each other, so no one

Taking refuge in Ranger Rick's tent at the Rainbow Gathering, Boise National Forest, Idaho, 1982.

noticed when I liberated a green wool army blanket, a bag of apples, and a Tetra Brik of soymilk. I felt this was a fair trade for violating the creed of the rainbow warrior to feed all who were hungry.

The rest of the gray, drizzly day was spent hunched in front of dying bonfires under my new vaguely water-resistant blanket. When the Rainbow Family Tribe fire fizzled out, I moved back to the Sun Tribe, and from there to the Shambhala Circle. Toward evening I was drawn to a little drum circle mostly populated by black men. There was something special about these guys, and it wasn't just that they were the only black people on the mountain. For one thing, their drums didn't have the high, tight percussive whine of the congas. These were deep, low, hourglass-shaped African *djembes*, whose trancelike rhythms sounded truly tribal and ancient. These guys also weren't high energy, trying to whip up crowds with their music. They were slow and steady, chanting with low, harmonic confidence. And they were dressed alike, with matching knit red, gold, and green tams and dark patterned robes. They all boasted serpentine, ropy dreadlocks and scraggly beards. They were the first people I'd seen at Rainbow, besides the Krishnas, who actually looked like they were members of a "tribe," and not just a loose affiliation of hippies who'd come together to bake hempseed bread.

The leader of the group spotted me across the fire and called out: "Ay, boy, what you called?"

"I am called Joshua," I announced, trying to sound regal.

"Joe-Shwa! None other! You know what old Joe-Shwa do? Back in Zion?"

I nodded. "He brought the walls tumbling down," I said. "I was named after him."

"Name for him!? Joe-Shwa!" The leader turned to the man on his right: "Brother Gregory, you know what him remind I of?"

Brother Gregory took a deep drag from his water chalice and nodded absentmindedly.

"Him remind I of when we was all in Jericho, knocking down Jericho walls."

Everyone around the fire murmured in agreement. "Joe-Shwa, you ever hear a vice speaking fah you, telling you everyting's gwan be alright?"

I nodded.

"I and I hear it, lawd and clare," declared the leader, and he began a chant that was immediately picked up by his tribesmen and accompanied by the low, heavy rumbling of the *djembes*:

> *I hear da vice of the I-a-mon saaay:*
> *Babylon, you trone gawn down,*
> *Ga-awn down,*
> *Babylon, you trone gawn down,*
> *Ga-awn down,*
> *Jah come wit' tunder and lightning and trow dem awaaay.*

I soaked up the chant, intuitively understanding the cosmic dynamic wherein Babylon was the powerful evil that oppressed us downtrodden sufferers, but that we should hold our impoverished heads high, confident that Babylon's omnipotent days were numbered.

That night I lay wrapped in my new blanket on the clammy marsh that now lined the bottom of Ranger Rick's pup tent. The Rasta chants continued on in my head while lightning split the sky and thunder shook the ground.

Many days' worth of meals gathered together in one place at the bottom of my belly, and I awoke in the middle of the night at the beckoning of my bowels. Ranger Rick lay snoring next to me, stinking of wine. I swept my arms around in the wet muck until I found his flashlight and stumbled down the hill to the engorged stream that marked the edge of camp. The path to the shitters led across a slimy log bridge. After I took a few tentative steps, I concluded that the log was too slippery to be safe. But then my bowels convulsed, and I figured that the risk of drowning was better than crapping my last pair of pants. I slid my feet forward like a cautious ice skater and nearly made it across to the other bank before I tripped on a branch stub and fell into the water face-first. The ice-cold stream leapt over my head, and I flailed in the water, shrieking into the night air, more from the shock of the cold than fear. The stream wasn't deep, and the current wasn't strong, and I was able to pull myself onto the muddy bank in a few sea lion–like lunges. I stamped around shaking the water off of me, and my body convulsed with a shiver from deep in my core. My bowels clenched within me again, and I hobbled exigently down the path toward the shitters.

The shitters were the communal restroom for the entire Festival and consisted of nothing more than slit trenches carved into the mud with a few logs thrown down to hang your butt off of. My two previous pilgrimages to the restroom had ended in self-inflicted constipation. It was hard enough setting my naked nether regions on a slimy log crawling with ants and flies over a muddy sluice flowing with excrement. But having to do this in front of two dreadlocked women crapping while they played Filipino nose flutes, or in the midst of a group of diarrheal bikers, was too great an offense to my dignity.

What sort of vile animals would condemn themselves to this? Before coming to Rainbow, I'd already concluded that Claudia and I were rare outliers, alienated from Straight Society. At Rainbow, Claudia had promised, we would meet others of our own kind. When we arrived, Claudia was confident we had. I wasn't so sure. Straight Society clearly didn't have a place for me, and now I was convinced that the counter-culture didn't either. I was trapped on an island between the two worlds, able to navigate in both, but without a home in either.

In the privacy of the muddy darkness, I finally found relief and struggled to wipe myself with a pilfered Tibetan prayer flag and scraps of tapestry I had pocketed over the course of the day for just this occasion. Then the flood began. Lightning ripped open the sky and a torrent of rain plunged upon the land with a biblical fury. The slit trenches below me jumped their banks, and the ground morphed into a marshy morass of human waste that surged over my ankles. I churned my feet through the foul muck in grim resignation as I made my way back to the stream.

The stream was already swollen with rainwater, and the slimy log bridge I'd crossed over before was now mostly submerged. I stood shivering in the rain, paralyzed with indecision. "Help," I said to no one in particular, in the off chance I wouldn't have to be brave. When no one responded, I drew strength from the Rasta teaching about Joe-Shwa knocking down Jericho's walls and waded into the water. Straddling the log, I shimmied myself across slowly, the numbingly cold water flowing over my lap. This kept my head above water until I got to a point where the log was too far submerged. The vigorous current pushed me off firmly but gently and sent me sputtering downstream. I clawed at the dark water in a panic and managed to keep my head up long enough to grab at a sturdy clump of weeds. The wet, stringy plants supported my weight, and I pulled myself up onto my belly, spitting out muddy water. Exhausted but safe, I rolled onto my back and let the cold rain wash the mud and filth off of me.

As I slithered back into Ranger Rick's pup tent, I realized I'd lost his flashlight somewhere, but was too tired to care. I wrapped myself in the wet army blanket and fell into a deep sleep.

From somewhere a thousand miles away, Ranger Rick was talking to me: "Hey, buddy, we're sliding down the mountain. Crapola, we're really sliding." When I came to, Ranger Rick was panting and cursing somewhere outside. The bottom of the tent was filled with muddy water. "Don't worry, Josh, I'm tying us to a tree."

When I finally climbed out of the partially submerged tent the next morning, I saw that the muddy hillside had been swept clear of people. In the forest on both sides of the field, hillside refugees were lashing themselves to trees and fighting one another over the scarce pockets of dry land. Ranger Rick and I spent the rest of the day wandering around like turtles with a length of salvaged brown tarp over our backs, squatting around smoky smoldering campfires, trying to ignore the rain and the dissonant non-rhythms of wet drums. We crashed that night under our tarp on the floor of Madam Frog's tent, listening to old burnouts tell their tripped-out stories about peyote vision quests and LSD-induced hallucinations in the desert.

Sometime before dawn's light broke over the mountain, Madam Frog's Tea House broke over us. Perhaps the waterlogged walls of the canvas tent just couldn't take any more weight or perhaps the spells of protection woven by Madam Frog just weren't strong enough to hold off Mahpiyato, the Lakota sky god, any longer. Whatever the case, it took us a few minutes of crawling through mud in the darkness before we found high ground and settled ourselves back down to sleep, wrapped in our brown tarp in the lee of a big tree.

We were eventually awakened by some dedicated rainbow warrior who obviously believed it was never too early or too rainy for a drum solo.

"Maybe the sun will come out today, Josh," volunteered Ranger Rick, whose hair, like mine, was filled with pine needles.

"It won't," I said.

"I know," laughed Ranger Rick. "Boy, I really need some coffee."

"Why?"

"Because today's the big day, and I want to be awake for it."

"What big day?"

"The Fourth of July."

"What's that?"

"You know, July Fourth, Independence Day."

I shrugged.

"You know, the fireworks and parades and everything? The Fourth of July, it's like America's birthday."

"Never heard of it."

"Man, you really gotta get out more. Anyway, here at Rainbow it's supposed to be like the main event, except instead of fireworks and America's birthday, they have a big parade celebrating the whole world."

"But it's raining too hard."

"Yeah," said Ranger Rick, lying back down against the tree root that served as our pillow. "Hey, buddy, you know what else? Today's my last day. I gotta get back for work on Tuesday."

This was not good news. I suddenly felt alone and desperate, like I was losing a parent. "Ranger Rick," I began.

"Yeah, buddy."

"I'm really sorry, but I lost your flashlight in the river."

"It's OK, buddy. I have enough light in my life." And he smiled like he meant it.

As we talked, we splashed through the dank forest in the direction of a growing chorus of voices and a clanging gong. The wet woods around us were soon filled with hunched human forms splashing in the same direction. We picked up speed instinctively like a herd of anxious zebras fleeing a grass fire. We emerged into a muddy clearing and joined a thousand other dirty pilgrims in a loose, chaotic circle.

No flood of biblical proportions was going to keep the rainbow warriors from celebrating the Fourth of July. I perched myself on a log at the edge of the clearing and peeked out from the protective shelter of my tarp to watch a muddy circus of unrestrained revelry unfold before me. The rain pounded down, and drum circles within drum circles pounded back. The drums were accompanied by clattering cymbals, babbling marimbas, a braying tuba, and the croaking of a thousand untrained voices. Amid the would-be musicians, a churning maelstrom of freaky dancers flung their bodies about in frenzied celebration. Topless women wearing skirts over corduroys paddled at the air like dogs in water, and shirtless bearded men shook to the music with epileptic convulsions. Pairs of jugglers slid muddy rainbow pins back and forth while a circle of men in rags kicked at a waterlogged hacky sack. A soot-faced anorexic woman massaged the air with tai chi movements. The balding man with the massive beard was wearing only a loincloth and he teetered back and forth, balancing an upright closed umbrella on his chin. Here and there a naked couple slow-danced, pawing at each other's mud-streaked hindquarters, oblivious to the wild rumpus all around them. Occasional lone trippers weaved through the throng, their arms extended as if in flight, their minds consumed by pharmacological visions more powerful than reality.

What little ground cover there had been was quickly chewed up, and muddy water began splattering into the air with each footfall. Thousands of feet kept digging at the ground, churning the soil into a muddy soup. On all sides, dancers were soon slipping and falling onto their asses. The Earth was striking back at the rainbow warriors, bringing more and more of them down until the ratio of vertical to horizontal gyrating bodies became nearly even. This absurd development was met with euphoric howls from the downed warriors. The raw mud was a new medium for their sacred art, and the congregation converted to muddy contact improvisation, massage, wrestling, and just plain rolling around. Many now stripped off what wet clothing remained and painted themselves with mud, spinning, grunting, and howling like primordial simians rising from the muck of prehistory.

From the safety of my tarp, I was happy to enjoy the spectacle with the same detachment as an anthropologist witnessing a primitive mating ritual. But when a group of mud people took notice of me and began pulling at the tarp, beckoning me to come out and dance, I concluded it was time to move on. It wasn't just the sheer madness of their invitation that motivated my departure, it was also the sudden realization that if all the rainbow warriors were here wallowing in the mud pit, no one was left to guard the kitchens.

I padded down the trails, pilfering dried apricots from Everybody's Kitchen and heavily tithing the banana and carob chips at the New Dawn Tribe camp. After the initial exhilaration of stuffing my face, a deep exhaustion took hold of me. I found myself standing back in front of the great tarp-covered yurt of the Rolling Turtle Tribe. The place still reeked of hashish but was impossibly and tantalizingly cozy. In the corner of the yurt, a big round propane heater was dishing out warmth. I glided across the mud floor in an incandescent trance and curled up in the embrace of a vacant blue sleeping bag and slept.

Many hours later, I awoke to voices floating over me.

"I don't know," a woman was saying. "I just found him here."

"Moonflower, we can't keep him," a man decided. "What would we do with a kid?"

"We've gotta find his parents," said another woman.

I kept my eyes closed, trying not to freak out. Nothing was going to pull me away from this heater. Nothing. But what could I say that would make them leave me alone? I sat up to confront those who would decide my fate. Their eyes were unnaturally dilated, and their deeply tanned faces were framed with golden dreadlocks.

"My pyarents," I began in a deep Slavic accent, "are still in Soviet Union." I jutted my chin out, as though pondering the next words of English I would need to convey my solemn announcement. "CIA and government police, they are look for me. I must rest chere before continue on for Syan Franchesco." The Rolling Turtles were stunned by the revelation that they had a brave little fugitive in their midst. They whispered among themselves and concluded, as I knew they would, that they couldn't betray a little comrade to the cops. I lay back down and grinned into my sleeve. This sudden turn of events was a lot for them to handle, and they quickly medicated themselves with billowing clouds of Moroccan hash.

I stopped smiling to myself when I realized that Ranger Rick must be gone by now. We'd never had a chance to say good-bye. I consoled myself with the hope that he was in a warm, dry car out there somewhere, satisfied with his haul of photographic evidence to prove to the guys at his crummy job that he had had a great time.

Beneath me the cardboard was dry, and thick enough to soften the rigid ribs of the wooden pallet that I'd adopted as my bed. As I drifted off, floating on a sea of welling mud, I dreamt up a Russian fugitive backstory, and hummed myself to sleep with the stirring bars of "The Internationale."

Throughout the next day a steady stream of sodden refugees cycled through the yurt to warm their hands, smoke grass, or impart nonsense packaged as wisdom. Eventually none other than my mother popped into the Rolling Turtle tent. "There you are," she said dreamily. She came and wrapped me in a deep embrace. Her eyes looked crazy. I put a confused expression on my face, fearful that she would blow my cover. Claudia swirled her hand slowly over her head, trying to capture something in words. "Joshey, thousands of lives, life's incantation, thousands of eyes!" She sat by me for a time, rocking back and forth, smiling. Then she stood up suddenly, and stuck her hand down the front of her muddy bellbottom pants. When she pulled it out, her hand was bloody.

"Hey, sister," someone called out, "you cut yourself."

"No, I'm menstruating. Does anyone have a sponge? Anyone?" She turned back to me, saying: "I've got to go clean the blood off my hands."

I was afraid she'd out me as her American son. Luckily she didn't come back. But had her visit already compromised my identity? I was worried. Luckily, the Rolling Turtles seemed to have dismissed her as just another tripper, like the rest of the visitors, living with one foot in the astral plane.

Toward evening, I was asked a few probing questions by my hosts, who seemed newly curious about me. I told them my name was Ilyich Ulyanov and gave them details of my life, inspired by what I could remember of Lenin's early years. Then I told them that I had been sent to the United States to be raised as an American, to take over the System from the inside. They seemed duly impressed and began giving me lessons in Americanism.

"Look, Little Man, all you gotta know about America is this: Everyone's greedy and racist and sexist, and they'll try to pump you full of corn syrup and sugar, and the next thing you know the bank will end up owning your life."

"Yah," chimed in one of the women. "And money. Everyone loves money more than people."

"Yeah," joined in the alpha male, cupping the breasts of the woman who'd been speaking and running his lower lip up her neck. "You have to remember to love *people*, more than *money*."

I raised my reused glass bottle of rainwater into the air and saluted them: "We must to loves the peoples more than the monies!"

Everyone cheered, and the alpha male declared it time to break open the last brick of hashish. The yurt soon filled with thick, clingy smoke and the gamy smell of skunk filled my nose and burrowed into my skin, hair, and clothes.

"Little Man! Take a hit from the chillum," ordered the shirtless alpha male, offering me a long straight pipe. No way. I'd smoked pot before, and a helpless veil of cannabine confusion was the last thing I wanted draped over my mind.

"No to thank you, *tovarish*," I said, holding my hand out like a stop sign.

"Come on, Little Man!"

"He doesn't want to," suggested one of the two women now snaking their bodies around my would-be pot pusher.

"My friend," I tried again, but the alpha male thrust the pipe into my face. I stared at him, summoning my toughest, most defiant man-face.

His hazy eyes sharpened, and he stared back at me, determined to crack my will. We faced off for what seemed like a minute, before he threw his head back, laughing: "Little Man won't get high!" This was apparently quite funny. When the snorting died down, the talking stopped, and the dirty naked bodies of the Rolling Turtle Tribe began slithering toward one another in a carnal convergence.

I covered my head with a musty poncho, muffling out the noises around me, and thought of all the wonderful things money could buy: food, shelter, clothing. If only the Russians knew—I was a double agent.

Water, at volume, plus gravity is greater than Rolling Turtles divided by poor planning. The mud level rose steadily overnight, and near dawn I awoke embedded in a clammy quagmire. At about the same time, the steady leaks in the roof matured into a catastrophic failure of the waterlogged felt ceiling. A pent-up cascade of water plunged into the center of the yurt, and groggy grunts of protest went up from all sides. I shook my head in disappointment. I'd had a hunch the dry warmth wouldn't last. I collected my tarp and plastic bag of food and sloshed through the bedraggled band of still-stoned flood victims. "Thanks, guys, and good luck," I called over my shoulder. I couldn't tell what stunned them more: the flood or my suddenly accentless voice.

I slogged down the trail looking for new shelter. Up ahead, the sound of Vedic drums and hand cymbals beckoned me forward. As I crested a little ridge, a beautiful scene filled my eyes. The Krishna Kamp spread out before me—dry, orderly, full of dancing people and, most importantly, steaming pots of food. I felt like some lucky sinner who'd had the good fortune to bump into Noah's ark just before it launched.

The finger cymbals chanted, and so did the people:

Haray Krishna, Haray Krishna;
Krishna, Krishna, Haray, Haray;
Haray Rama, Haray Rama;
Rama, Rama, Haray Haray.

Over and over.

The cymbals and the people never stopped. Ever.

But it didn't matter. Their camp was perfect. I walked the perimeter and stooped appreciatively to pat the French drains they'd installed all around. The gravel-filled ditches conveyed the runoff away from the kitchen. Genius. Above, they'd anchored to trees a series of interlocking plastic tarps that directed the rainwater into a catchment tank that could be used for washing. Beneath this structure was a huge canvas tent that housed the kitchen itself—a seamless production line manned by saffron-robed Krishnas—and a series of wooden benches. The focal point of the camp was a massive bonfire around which paraded the swaying musicians, the dancers, and the singers who continuously praised Krishna in the simple repetitive formula that indelibly seared itself into my brain after the first few thousand times I heard it.

"Well, I've finally found the adults," I thought to myself. "And they're a bunch of weird chanting people in yellow robes with funky shaved heads." The chanting didn't matter. Nor did the robes or the oddly shaved heads. The hot food and dry ground were all that mattered. I took my serving of hot, pasty, sweet basmati rice and sat cross-legged under one of the serving tables, staring out at the leaping orange flames of the central fire. I had arrived. I was safely aboard the ark now and, whatever happened, I was going to be one of the survivors.

Two days later, the rain finally let up. But it didn't matter. Rainbow was over, and the Krishnas began dismantling their spectacular camp, chanting all the while. I ran into my mother on one of the trails back to the parking lot.

"Wasn't Rainbow amazing, Joshey?"

"It was *something.*"

"I know!"

We hitched a ride into the town of Council, Idaho, where I found my way into the public library and finally used one of the real porcelain toilets I'd been dreaming about all week. Afterward, my mother and I stood outside, looking to hitch another ride. Across the street, Michael Rodriguez was leaping around, playing frisbee with some other guys.

"Josh, you'll never believe what Michael's day job is. He's a *stockbroker.*"

"It doesn't matter," I said. "He's not really a man."

"You're right about that," my mother said.

I nodded. No, Michael wasn't really a man. But I could think of somebody who was.

EIGHT

Wanderings in the Wilderness

The Rainbow Gathering had set my mother on fire with visions of idyllic intentional communities that might be out there waiting for us. She sensed that the elusive combination of rural agriculture and urban intellectualism might be down the next off-ramp, somewhere in the hills beyond the Burger King and the laundromat.

Hitchhiking with Claudia through the backwoods of the American West, I began to develop something of a hitchhiker's guide to the road in my head. No matter how hard I smiled, most folks driving by wouldn't stop to pick us up. I hated them, those smug rich people who could afford to own cars but pretended not to notice us. The ones who did stop for us came in two flavors: slow and fast. The slow stoppers were open to the idea of picking up a hitchhiker, but not just anyone. They passed by slowly, swiveling their heads to run their eyes over us. When they pulled onto the shoulder ahead, we had to smile, grab our gear, and run to catch their idling good graces before they changed their minds. We ran up the road, knowing they'd only stopped to pick us up after they'd calculated that they were bigger and stronger than we were. I couldn't blame them, but I couldn't entirely trust them either. The fast stoppers, on the other hand, would hit the brakes immediately when they saw hitchhikers ahead, pulling over before they could tell who we were. We could have been angels or we could have been ax murderers for all they knew. We walked back to them, grinning in their headlights. It was easy to love them for trusting us, but I'd always shake my head a little. You had to be a crazy person to blindly stop for total strangers—a real angel, or an ax murderer.

The big rig that gave us a ride outside of Klamath Falls was a fast stopper.

The truck driver with the leather vest didn't care who we were. He just wanted someone to talk to. "Where d'ya call home?" he asked me.

I had to think about that one. We'd lived in that half-built cabin on Mount Lassen for a year and a half. An eternity in my memory. But that was a freak occurrence, the longest we'd ever stayed in one place. We had to keep on moving.

"I guess this out here is home," I said, waving my hand at the darkening road ahead.

"I hear that, muchacho," the truck driver said. "I hear that."

Claudia had decided that one place in particular promised to be the perfect community for us: a survivalist settlement along Pokey Creek in the mountains of Northern Idaho. She had met two of its founders, Greg and Mary, at Rainbow and had been impressed by the way Mary used spiritual terms to describe gutting a dead deer. With their homemade buckskin clothing and adamant refusal to participate in American society, they proved to my mother that they were "for real." These people considered themselves white Indians, living off the land as the Great Spirit intended. They used every part of the kill, and smoked, dried, canned, and pickled all summer to survive through the brutal winter. It was almost too good to be true. But by the time we'd purchased long underwear and packed our bags, it was October, and the snows had already barricaded the place shut for the winter.

We sat out the intervening months in a rundown little shack in the woods of Shasta County, California. The nearest store was in Shingletown, a tiny cluster of dilapidated buildings. Shingletown was the kind of place you went to restock your propane, chewing tobacco, and ammunition. Unemployed loggers and drunken hunters gathered at the restaurants. Klansmen frequented the general store. On more than one occasion, we were cornered by a talkative young man with a hunting dog named K, as in KKK. He told us little K had been trained to "smell out Jews and Niggers." My mother went cold and rigid every time we bumped into him, until one day she overheard him talk about drowning unwanted kittens in the river. Then she lunged at him, gesticulating wildly and calling him a murderer. "What?" he sputtered meekly. "I don't want no kitties, *you* want 'em?" My mother *did* want them and quickly became known as the crazy lady who loved cats. Over the winter, we harbored sixteen feline fugitives, and the air of our home hung heavy with cat hair, dander, and piss. As the temperature dropped in the evenings, the cats sought the warmth of my body heat and burrowed into the bed all around me. I slumbered warmly but uncomfortably in my lumpy, purring feline blanket. When Uncle Tony visited for my seventh birthday, he stayed awake all night, pulling cats off of my face, afraid that they were going to smother me to death.

We didn't have a car so we hitchhiked into town regularly to buy supplies until some of the rides began to feel like attempted kidnappings. One guy wouldn't let us out of his truck until a sheriff's deputy fortuitously drove by. Another told me he was going to pump my mother full of quaaludes so he could sling her over his shoulder for some "R&R."

When Claudia and I finally received word that the snows were melting in Idaho, we took to the road again, leaving fourteen of the cats behind to fend for themselves in the woods.

The settlement at Pokey Creek was a dusty, eerie collection of subsistence homesteads carved into a thick evergreen forest in the Clearwater Mountains of Idaho. During the brief summer months everyone lived outside in teepees, laboring in a panic to prepare for the long winter when they would retreat back into their subterranean silos. The residents were lanky and pale, adults and children alike, collectively struggling with seasonal affective disorder and feverishly bracing for winter or the apocalypse, whichever came first. My mother had proudly agreed to be the schoolteacher for the community and, in exchange, we would receive meat and root crops to help us survive the winter. After a few weeks of inspecting potential building/excavation sites and getting to know the community elders, Claudia was ready to get to work on building a subterranean silo of our own. But not me. All those nights sleeping on the loose dirt under the drying racks of deer innards and the never-ending battles against mosquitoes, black flies, ticks, and fleas were too much for me. And although I could barely communicate with some of the jittery barefoot kids my age who spoke in a pidgin English of their own creation, their fear of the impending winter needed little translation. "Snow-snow back quick."

I was planning to stage a coup d'état.

After our final "interview" with the elders around the communal fire, they prepared to formally accept us into the community. But I sabotaged our whole venture by instigating a fistfight with one of Greg and Mary's feral boys in the middle of the ceremony. Mary's leathery face howled down at me: "At Pokey Creek we do *not* strike other human beings!" It was my first act of premeditated violence, but I forgave myself by invoking a broad definition of self-defense. In my mind, the alternatives were: a little fisticuffs or a lifetime spent underground gagging on half-cooked moose meat.

Hitchhiking away in disgrace, my mother told me how ashamed of me she was for wrecking everything. But she was quickly distracted by the artful contours of a mountain, and I sensed she was nearly as relieved as I was. We spent the next few months exploring less severe communities throughout Oregon and Washington State. We hitchhiked when we could and rode the Green Tortoise bus the rest of the time. Our fellow passengers on the Tortoise were typically radical international students, American rainbow warriors, and a few very distressed Midwestern tourists who had mistakenly assumed that the Tortoise was going to be a cut-rate version of Greyhound when they bought their tickets. The main differences between the Green Tortoise and Greyhound were tapestried beds in place of seats and luggage racks, and, instead of a men's bathroom, an oversized garden hose, called a "piss-tube," disappeared into the dashboard and reappeared somewhere beneath the bus. For women, the bus simply pulled over, and they squatted by the side of the road while everyone watched.

I loved the Tortoise. I made the rounds of the pretty European college girls, impressing them with my knowledge of Reagan's demonic foreign policy, and they rewarded me with hugs, massages, and sometimes candy. Federico, the dissident Argentine poet, carried me on his back into the deep waters at the nameless lake where we stopped for lunch. At the hot springs, I had the honor of rubbing down the naked zaftig form of Sølvig, the blonde Danish backpacker. Astrid, the Swedish dancer, invited me to be her teddy bear when she went to bed. I spent the night in an upper bunk nuzzling against her chest, drunk on her redolence of lavender and fresh rain.

In this manner we crisscrossed the Pacific Northwest until Claudia heard about Skagit County, Washington. There, the brave people were opposing the construction of two nuclear power plants and were even floating a ballot initiative to enact a nuclear weapons–free zone. These were *our* kind of people. In the county seat of Mount Vernon, we discovered the food co-op where the tie-dyed and patchouli-scented came for their organic produce. The Spirits guided Claudia's eyes to the billboard, where she saw a listing for a little cabin on Guemes Island out in the San Juans.

Our one-room cabin on Guemes was smothered by a tight canopy of evergreens that relegated the sun to more of a concept than a reality. Stinging nettles blanketed the web of little trails that ran through the forest, and every trip to the outhouse required a machete. My face, arms, and legs soon became a patchwork of white itchy bumps, and I took to peeing in a jar next to my bed.

Trying to stop Uncle Tony from boarding his train back to San Francisco at the end of a 1983 visit to Washington.

The cabin didn't come with running water or electricity, so we lugged bottled water over by ferry from Anacortes and read at night by the light of candles and kerosene. My mother still read to me, but I was increasingly decoding the magic of the written word for myself, carrying myself off into fantastical times and places where boys could be kings for a day and come home to use warm running water at night.

Claudia found employment on the island as a house cleaner, scrubbing toilets at a rustic waterside resort run by an old guy we called "Fat Butt Charlie." I helped out by making beds and stealing toilet paper. After work, we took saunas with Tara and Tolly, the lesbian couple down the trail, or wandered the roads collecting dead branches for the woodstove.

In the evenings, Claudia made masks from clay and plaster bandages with the hopes of selling enough of them to buy her own kiln. We invested in a table at an Anacortes street fair, wedged between the kids selling caramel corn and the lemonade stand. A lot of people wandered by, but no one wanted to spend fifty bucks on a twenty-six-pound clay mask of Eleanor Roosevelt or a bust of Archbishop Oscar Romero, the saintly Salvadoran clergyman gunned down by US-backed death squads. Nor did they want shaman-grade sun and moon masks, appropriate for the Longdance at the Autumnal Equinox or for the fertility dance on Beltane.

After a few months, Claudia decided Guemes Island just wasn't the community for us. Too many rich people from Seattle were buying everything up. We needed less pretentious, more down-to-earth folks. This led us back to the mainland. More specifically, this led us to the muddy corner of a hayfield east of Sedro-Woolley, Washington, the home of the Loggerodeo, where chain-saw carvers and log lassoers regularly competed.

The hayfield was owned by a long-haired, pot-smoking contractor named Frank. He and his wife wanted my mother to home-school their two little blond children, Sequoia and Samish. In return they agreed to let us live rent-free at the corner of the field in a dilapidated trailer and decommissioned ice cream truck.

Maybe every child is born with an innate desire to live in an ice cream truck. I was. I'd never even seen an ice cream truck before, but I already knew all about it. It was a big white refrigerated van that roamed exotic and faraway suburban neighborhoods playing metallic clown music. When the clean, well-groomed children came tumbling out of their fancy, running-water-equipped houses and streamed across their manicured lawns, a side window opened up, offering ice cream by the scoop, soft serve from a lever, ice cream sandwiches. And popsicles. Not the crappy kind we made in San Francisco by freezing apple juice on a plastic spoon. No, the genuine artificial article, glowing in unnatural colors and brimming with ingredients like FD&C Yellow No. 5 and enough preservatives to embalm a mammoth. Here, at long last, was going to be the kind of Utopia I could get behind.

"You know the ice cream truck doesn't drive anymore, right, Joshey?" I did, but I figured they'd probably left behind a few dozen popsicles. Maybe we could get the thing running again.

My nice dreams melted when I saw the big box of rust sinking into the mud. The cab area was thick with spiders and their webs, and the blackberry vines were snaking their way through the holes in the windshield. The back of the truck was free of debris but fettered with the sharp odors of rust and mildew and a little, taunting hint of curdled cream. The green trailer with the vaguely whitish racing stripe next to the truck wasn't much better. But these immobile vehicles became home. We stored our things in the ice cream

In front of the trailer where Claudia and I lived, east of Sedro-Woolley, Washington. The ice cream truck is on the other side.

truck—my books in the top freezer, art supplies below—and slept in the trailer.

For a couple of hours a day, my mother schooled Sequoia, Samish, and me in English, political science, and sculpture. We also learned some history and feminist theory. Math and science, not so much. During our lessons I'd daydream about hot water and flushing toilets. After we'd finished our William Carlos Williams, we'd race along the edge of the hayfield to watch *The A-Team* on the little black-and-white television that Frank and his wife left out for the kids while they were at work.

What was now three kids diagramming sentences in a moldy trailer, my mother saw as a powerful seed with the potential to germinate and grow into a national system of alternative education. But the seed's promise would not be realized. Frank's wife had started working the night shift, so now she could stay home and teach Sequoia and Samish herself. This meant no more "free rent" for us. Our Welfare check would have to stretch a little further if we were going to pay Frank for the right to continue living in our decrepit vehicles in the mud.

Claudia felt like the Spirits were giving her a sign: Now was the time to really make it with her artwork. She sliced up her twenty-five-pound blocks of moist red clay from the art supply store in Seattle with new urgency. She woofed as she flattened it with her fists on the old water-warped door that served as a table. A half dozen clay plates with shallow-relief carved images of women in the woods soon took form. They were joined by several large pinch-pot bowls. With a little sweet-talking, we were able to fire her work after-hours in the studio kiln at the local community college. Now we were ready for market.

We purchased tables and displayed our wares for sale at all the local venues: Loggerodeo, the county fair, and various flea markets and arts-and-crafts shows. We sat for hours, shivering in the fog, staring hungrily at passing faces, trying to catch their gaze and trick them into buying something with frozen smiles and plaintive eyes. But the results were disappointing. The old biker selling bookends welded from horseshoes did pretty well. The husky couple in the matching Hawaiian shirts did even better with their novelty fisherman coffee mugs. The skinny Asian guy sold out his entire supply of tube socks. And the two blonde ladies selling hot dogs walked away filthy rich. We failed to sell a single piece. Instead, we were out the price of admission and lost a moon mask when I tripped carrying it back to our car.

Claudia hated to admit it, but she recognized that Capitalist market forces were at work here. It couldn't be that there was *no* demand for her artwork. It had to be that there was no demand at the *high prices* she was charging. But she couldn't lower her prices because it took so long to make each piece, and her overhead was high and fixed. What she needed was a product that she could manufacture assembly-line style. And her own kiln. This was her Henry Ford moment, and I reluctantly set aside my Land of Oz books and rolled up my sleeves to help out. Together we dug a trench across the hayfield from Frank's house to lay down a phone line and a series of extension cords. We dug a pit for the fifty-five-gallon water drum and affixed it with a hand pump. We worked the phones to Grandma Harriette, appealing to the frustrated artist within her that never got to express herself, and successfully obtained a loan for a kiln and high-fire glazes. Finally, we laid a concrete foundation for the kiln and built it a rain shelter.

With our innovation laboratory completed, I watched as my mother conceived of the perfect, replicable product for the market. After a day and a night of furious pacing and frenzied pounding at the blocks of red and white clay, she got it. It was a duck. A clay duck sculpture with outstretched wings that would double as a hanging planter.

To be successful with a product like this, my mother finally concluded, we needed a more moneyed, sophisticated audience than the Logerrodeo set. We tried our luck instead in one of the bustling stalls of Pike Place Market in faraway Seattle. As we passed through the sad, soggy suburban netherworld north of Seattle, we did the math. We needed six hundred dollars a month to survive. That meant selling six ducks a week at twenty-five dollars a bird. No problem.

It turned out to be kind of a problem. The artisanal marmalade woman was doing OK, and the Starbucks coffee shop was moving product like it was unstoppable. But the ducks weren't flying. I wandered around the marketplace by myself, staring longingly at the squares of rich fudge and the shining samurai swords, hoping that when I got back to our table it would be empty. But when closing time came, we hadn't sold a single duck planter. We left in a deficit. We were out the money for the table and for gas and morale was low. When we got back to our hayfield, I tripped in the dark and went down with a duck in my arms. Its wing was smashed, and I cried. Claudia didn't care about the duck, but she was crying anyway.

We tried our luck at Pike Place Market a few more times and finally did sell some of the birds. But it wasn't enough. Besides, whatever money she made had to be reported to the awful people at Welfare, and they just deducted it from her check. "What's my incentive to work if you just take my earnings away?" Claudia reasoned with the pudgy lady who was chewing gum behind the counter. "I've got to put the money back into my business if I'm going to be successful." But the Welfare people wouldn't listen to reason. They wouldn't let us invest in plaster of Paris molds to streamline production and bring down costs. Claudia even pitched the idea of the Welfare system investing in the molds and sharing some of the return. But the woman just grunted: "Next." We seethed out the door, Claudia hissing, "Shortsighted bastards!"

It was time to concede defeat. Claudia turned her back on her visual art and submitted to a series of menial part-time jobs. She trimmed evergreen trees on a Christmas tree farm, cleaned disabled people in a care facility, and provided home care to the elderly. This work left her depressed and demoralized. In her diary, Claudia struggled with her fate: *I keep telling myself, "when I'm settled, I'll lead the disciplined life that will turn me into a saint—or at least a psychic healer/teacher." How many years since I promised this to myself? When is "settled"? Where is community?*

After several months of emptying bedpans and wresting cat food away from elderly mouths, Claudia decided it was time to take up our search for community again. We took to the road via Green Tortoise and rode through Oregon, chanting alongside a band of Australian Bhagwan Shree Rajneesh devotees dressed in lavender and orange. We met with a group of self-identified Native Americans who believed that Mount Shasta was the center of UFO activity on Earth and were preparing to walk barefoot up the mountain to be teleported home. We made a lot of inquiries, but my mother was too independent-minded for any of the cults that we visited. She didn't want leaders to follow, she wanted partners to build with.

For a time, Claudia found a partner in Thaddeus, a Mennonite Rastafarian carpenter and pot dealer who owned a huge vinyl collection and a warm wooden house outside of Mount Vernon. After their relationship failed, Claudia began dating a perpetually stoned Norwegian carpenter named Gunnar who lived in a ganja-farming settlement at the end of Janicki Road up on Cultus Mountain, above Clear Lake, Washington. The place was owned by a stout, dark, and hirsute herbsman named River Kerry who was perpetually clad in raw wool and splattered in mud and patchouli. He was a frenzy of dreadlocked energy, cultivating marijuana and overseeing the swarm of quasi-indentured servants like Gunnar who worked the land in lieu of rent.

From the road above, River's settlement could have been the cover of a sci-fi novel. Down on his Forest Moon of Endor, Ewok huts and rammed-earth sculpture houses dotted the hillside. Out of the valley sprouted boat-like structures on stilts and, in the foreground under a cloud of construction, was rising a colossal wooden pagoda with cantilevered roofs. About thirty feet up, the belly of the pagoda was pierced horizontally by a giant tree, its massive root structure bursting into the air on one side and its expansive tangle of branches blooming from the other. How it got there was a mystery of physics.

Gunnar lived in one of the stilt houses, and we had to pull ourselves up a long ladder to get to him. We were rewarded with soup. And then my mother received sex in the back room. I curled up on a little couch next to the door with *A Prairie Home Companion* blasting from the radio to drown out the rhythmic squeaking and my mother's yowls. The carnal visits to the house on stilts became more frequent, and my mother bought herself a tubal ligation for her fortieth birthday. We stayed at Gunnar's stilt house for days while she recovered. Mercifully, the Walkman Uncle Tony sent me for my ninth birthday arrived just in time to drown out the sounds of renewed lovemaking.

Claudia wasn't ready to move in with Gunnar on River Kerry's ganja farm, but she found a cabin nearby. "Just wait till you see it, Joshey!"

"Does it have running water or electricity?" I asked hopefully.

"No, but it's hidden in the middle of the beautiful woods on Cultus Mountain. It almost looks like it's part of a big mossy tree stump. You'll love it!"

Just as she promised, the evergreen canopy swallowed the one-room cabin whole and enclosed it in a thick, perpetual mist. It never received a photon of direct sunlight. The one room housed a bed, shelves, and a propane stove. Up a worn homemade ladder, an enclosed little platform jutted out from one wall. This was my "loft." It was just big enough for me to unroll my sleeping bag, put my books on a shelf, and deposit my toys into a trunk.

Down the trail was the tiny elfin cabin of Michael McNeary, a pale little man with an oversized Adam's apple and a deep thirst for whiskey. He dressed like a leprechaun and communicated primarily through his violin. He was rehearsing Bach's Mass in B Minor, accompanied by a glass of grog, on the day we met him. When his blood alcohol level passed a certain point, his violin became a Scottish fiddle, and he was known to sing to himself as he stumbled half-blind up and down the trail. In exchange for free classical violin music, Claudia sometimes gave Michael chakra readings and administered psychic healing to his pickled soul. He showed us how to skin a rabbit and how to dump sawdust down the outhouse hole to keep the smell under control. Michael sometimes drove us into Mount Vernon in his little blue pickup truck to the food bank. There we waited in line with bedraggled elderly people and seasonal laborers. Former drug addicts served us fresh eggs, milk, and bread. We gave Michael our block of yellow cheese since Claudia thought it had too many preservatives in it. We didn't have refrigerators, so we had to wolf the food bank fare down quickly before the salmonella could set in.

The day after we moved to Cultus Mountain, Gunnar broke it off with my mother. Claudia processed her feelings of hurt and abandonment with me, and we made ourselves feel better by building a wood shed. On our way back up the trail from the hardware store, a massive white ape-man stumbled out of the bushes and came thumping down the trail at us. He was completely naked and bushy clumps of red hair bulged out of his head, eyebrows, jaw, and genitals. His body was littered with pine needles, cedar sprays, and dirt. "They're all lying!" he hollered our way. "They don't care about *people*! All they care about is *money*!"

I nearly pissed myself with fright and jumped behind my mother, fingering the smooth wooden handle of the hammer in my right hand. Every other woman on Earth would have turned and fled. But not Claudia. She actually took a step toward the ape-man and yelled back in encouragement: "You're damn *right* they're lying to you! The corporations have one objective, and that's to maximize shareholder profit! That don't give a *fuck* about the People!" Claudia kept advancing up the trail, gesticulating wildly: "The tin conglomerates *napalmed* half of Vietnam to keep their stock prices up! The copper companies overthrew Allende in Chile and a hundred thousand men, women, and children were *tortured* and *murdered*. Even now, as we speak, the fruit companies are bankrolling the Contras in Nicaragua and the *death squads* in El Salvador!"

The naked ape-man stood still, a stunned look sweeping his face. His eyes focused on us, and he stopped grabbing at the air. "I'm John," he said, suddenly apologetic. "They call me Crazy John, but I don't feel like I'm crazy."

"You sound like the sanest person I've met in a long time," Claudia reassured him. "I just broke up with a guy who listened to Paul Harvey and thought the rich people deserved to own all the land just because they're rich." We invited Crazy John in for peppermint-rosehips tea, and he sat down agreeably on the towel my mother draped over the milk crate for him. Claudia redubbed him Red John for his brilliant thatches of hair. But he still seemed pretty crazy to me. Crazy John emerged from the woods regularly after that to discuss politics, ethics, and the concept of so-called reality. He became my mother's closest friend on the mountain.

My closest friend was a boy named Eli who lived down the road. Eli was smaller, darker, and more bucktoothed than I, but we complemented each other well. He had a room full of new toys—Transformers, action figures, and Legos—but no one to play with. He prized his shelf of Douglas Adams and Lloyd Alexander books, but couldn't read them by himself. Though he was my age, the self-actualization-and-positive-thinking-based private schooling he'd been receiving had left him nearly illiterate. I stepped into the void to read to him and to enjoy the warmth of his home.

Eli's mother, Karma, looked like Sacagawea and spent most of her time stoned in a back room behind a tapestry. Her husband Richard, Eli's stepfather, was a much older, fast-talking marijuana grower/dealer with a ponytail of frizzy white hair. He slept in a separate cabin out back but would come to the main house for dinner and tell us stories about barfing up his innards on peyote or wedging bags of cocaine into his ass crack to smuggle them up from Mexico. I liked Richard, but he could be mercurial. Sometimes he'd spend three hours with me and Eli, letting us fire his hunting rifle at water jugs. But other times, he'd kick me out of the house, brusquely: "Josh, you gotta go home now. Hit the road, man."

Back home, my mother told me she was sick of cleaning up after Alzheimer's patients. "I can't wipe another wrinkled bottom, Josh, I just can't." But what to do? Until the Revolution came and people didn't need straight jobs anymore, she had to find a way of pairing her artistic talents with a paycheck. Ideally, she should be able to use her art to help heal all those zombies out there who had covered over their third eyes with Society's lies. Maybe, she thought, going to college for an art therapy degree could be the path forward.

With this in mind, Claudia applied to Seattle's Antioch University, a progressive adult school with a social justice focus. A few student loans later she was a college student, poring excitedly over the course catalog. When she announced that her class schedule would require her to spend three nights a week in Seattle without me, I felt the mountain tremble. She was leaving me behind? This was a foul betrayal of her maternal oath.

"Joshey, you should be happy for me."

"But you're basically going to abandon me!"

"Are you kidding me? You'll be having so much fun with Eli you won't even notice I'm gone."

She told me she'd arranged for me to stay with Eli while she was down in Seattle, but the arrangement proved to be less than formal. After the second week embedded with his family, Karma told me she felt like Claudia was dumping me on the doorstep like an orphan. Richard continued sending me home whenever the mood struck him, and even Eli began telling me he needed some time to himself. I received the message like a door slamming in my face. Fine. If they didn't want me, I didn't need them. Imposing myself where I wasn't wanted was worse, I decided, than the specter of loneliness. The result was a lot of time home alone, improvising to take care of myself. I learned that paint thinner applied to kindling was a real time-saver in firing up the woodstove. A handful of brewer's yeast could turn a can of minestrone soup into a rich and hearty meal. And the darkness wasn't as scary when I pretended to be a samurai warrior, slashing at the shadows with my white plastic sword.

My mother was off on a new journey, but this time I'd been left behind. She had her destiny, but where was mine? Was this my fate, to be imprisoned in a temperate rainforest reading the same books over and over again? No, my mother had told me a warlock could shape his own future. If she was going to abandon me now, maybe it was time to give my father another chance.

I shared the idea with Claudia when she came back from Seattle, and she chewed on it slowly. Why not, she concluded. My father had never come through for me before, but maybe he'd be willing to spend some time with his boy now. After a few phone calls from the food co-op pay phone, we found Claude living on the Lower East Side of New York, trying to make it as a musician. I breathed very quietly, trying to shut out the noise of the freeway to overhear his response. His baritone crackled back. "How about for the summer? That would work."

When summer came, I packed my bag and grinned at Ms.Ms. "See you later, cat. I'm gonna go stay with my *dad* in the Big Apple."

Claudia put me on the plane to New York with a list of ten must-see destinations, including the Empire State Bulding, Central Park, and the Metropolitan Museum of Art. Claude dutifully promised to take me to all of them, but we didn't make it to any of them. Instead, we spent most of the summer in the apartment, where life followed a regimented structure. We woke up every day sometime after noon, fried hamburgers for an hour or so, and then ate them on bagels for lunch and dinner. The rest of the day I split between sitting on the toilet, looking at the *Playboys* and *Penthouses* that were stored in the bathroom, and watching *Batman* reruns on TV. In the evenings we went to band practice in a windowless basement walled with black foam. My father played bass, a heroin addict named Johnny played drums, and an assortment of guitarists and singers cycled through, joining and quitting the band after each failed gig. I usually sat in a corner, stuffing cotton balls into my ears and playing with guitar pedals. Once the novelty of indoor plumbing and meat-eating had worn off, the days blended into each other with tedious sameness.

At the end of the summer, Claude looked at the list of places he'd promised to take me and realized he was 0 for 10. He hustled me uptown and sent me alone into the Guinness World Records museum in the basement of the Empire State Building. "Well that's one we can check off," he said. I flew back to Washington the next day thinking that New York was the most boring place on Earth, even worse than Cultus Mountain, where at least I could wander around outside by myself. I'd spent years thinking about my father, hoping that someday I'd get a chance to spend time with him. Then he'd get to know me. He'd see what a smart, funny, amazing kid I was. How could he not? Having proven my worth to him, he'd start his life over again. He'd choose to be my father in Washington instead of wasting his time in a dark basement in New York. But, after our summer together, he didn't choose me. He preferred, instead, the most boring place on Earth.

NINE

Decepticon

When I was nine years old, a little ray of normalcy came shining my way. My buddy Eli got a television set. I still struggled with chores, like hauling water and chopping wood, and boredom for most of the day, but here and there, windows of opportunity opened up. If I raced down the mountain at the right time, and if his parents weren't watching the news or meditating in the living room, I could watch cartoons with him. Sometimes for hours.

Our favorite show was *The Transformers*. We'd stretch out on his soft green carpet and get transported away into a galactic struggle between evil Decepticons and heroic Autobots. A place where there was always more than met the eye. Where a car or a stereo or an airplane could suddenly transform into a robot warrior. A place where boys were never left alone to fend for themselves, and goodness always triumphed.

The spell of the Transformers would last for days. I'd replay entire episodes in my head, identifying narrative inconsistencies, and reconciling them with elaborate back stories that I'd compose in a little journal. Sometimes I'd stare intently at my broken Walkman, half believing that if I stared hard enough it would transform into a little talking, walking friend for me.

But it never did. Instead, I was left to ponder the essence of Transformer nature. Were they fundamentally people that could disguise themselves as cars, or were they cars that could suddenly become human? I posed this conundrum to Crazy John, who became very skittish and paranoid, wondering aloud whether *he* was actually a transforming robot. Then he took off his pants and disappeared into the woods yelling: "I'm not part of your System!" When I posed the question on a long-distance collect call to Uncle Tony, he explained to me that the Transformer conundrum I was describing was just the latest in Cartesian Dualism—a struggle between the mechanical body and the immaterial mind. And when I asked my mother what she thought, she responded decisively. They were people. Every person, no matter what shape they took, bore a fundamentally pure soul. You had to see through the rough exterior and recognize the shining light of human goodness. She applied this conviction to the Transformers—and to a man named Leopoldo.

At the time, Claudia was consumed by her History and Culture of Central America class at Antioch University. Her homework was to interview someone who had been directly impacted by US foreign policy in Central America, and she knew why the teacher had assigned it. Her class had been reading about US atrocities on foreign soil and looking at grainy black-and-white photos of disturbing consequences. But none of it was real. It took a living face sitting across from you, crying three-dimensional tears, to bring it to life. At the food co-op she'd heard that one of River Kerry's new migrant workers at the ganja farm was a refugee from El Salvador and had many stories to tell.

When she reached the doorway of River's pagoda construction site she paused, and the Spirits whispered something in her ear that gave her the courage to cross the threshold. Inside, she found Leopoldo, wrapped in a woven blanket, shivering under the burden of so much pain, still tortured by memories of the death squads.

"Are you Leopoldo?" she offered him. "I want to interview you . . . to hear your story."

"You have come to see *me*?" He was full of humility, surprised and honored to receive this unexpected guest. He sprung out of his chair, gently took her hand with a chivalrous bow, and then moved the greasy hot plate that served as his kitchen from the other chair. Once she was seated, Leopoldo squatted and gathered up scraps of wood to build up the fire in the little black stove. "I make it warm for you."

He answered all of her questions and brought her to tears. He had been tortured by the death squads. Tied up for days at a time. Beaten. There was a tough interrogator who'd been trained by the Americans. He'd kicked Leopoldo in the head over and over until he thought his skull would break. They beat and tortured everyone: *campesinos*, students, old men, women, children. Leopoldo escaped from El Salvador, but the death squads were still tearing him apart inside. When he'd unburdened all of his pain onto her, Claudia could hardly move. He told her it felt good to finally talk about these things. Could he talk to her again? Of course, of course, she promised him. *Of course.*

She walked down the mountain in a daze. When she got back to the cabin she told me that her world had just changed. That our war in Central America had just become real. That there was a living martyr up the road, a beautiful man full of so much suffering. But she didn't tell me then what the Spirits had whispered to her at the threshold of his door. She only told me later. The Spirits had whispered: *husband.*

I hadn't seen him yet, but I already knew what Leopoldo's whimpers sounded like. He was sitting on the bed down the ladder from me, pouring out his heart to my mother. He was telling her about his son back in El Salvador. The boy's grandmother had written him a letter. It was almost too hard to put into words. The boy . . . there was shooting . . . cross-firing . . . he was cut down. The boy . . . was dead. I shut out the grieving man below me and focused myself on the epic dragon war unfolding in my book.

Eventually the whimpering petered out and new sounds caught my ear. Slapping and grunting, animal noises. It had been several months since the last time sex had trapped me up in my little loft. When Claudia brought a man home during daylight hours, I'd usually pop down to say hello and then excuse myself to wander around in the woods until he left. But this visit had caught me unprepared. The refugee was now going at it below me, and there was nothing left to do but wait it out with my head buried in a pillow.

A few days later, Claudia led me up the rickety steps of River Kerry's pagoda and introduced me to Leopoldo. He stopped smiling when he saw that I was in tow, and nodded at me—man to man. I extended my hand and stepped in for a handshake. He crushed my fingers in a vise of callused, scarred, and nicotine-stained digits. Then he brought out his jar of fermenting fruit pulp to share with us. It was called *chicha*, and it was fuzzy and mildly alcoholic. Claudia purred over her mug. I sipped the rotten brew, spit out a hunk of moldy orange peel, and tried to be polite. "Wow!" I said without a hint of sarcasm. "This tastes like the nectar of the gods." Leopoldo shot me a look that I would come to know well. It meant "Why are you talking?" and it also meant "You think you're better than me?" I quickly learned that I was his competition for my mother's affection, so the more noise I made, the more I pissed him off. I also learned that his command of English was quite limited. And it wasn't just English. He'd never gone to school past fourth grade and didn't even know the Spanish alphabet in order. So when I pulled out a phrase like "nectar of the gods," it translated into "These are fancy words that you'll never hope to understand, you fucking peasant."

The *chicha* flowed and fizzed, fueling the air between my mother and Leopoldo until it grew heavy with romance. I excused myself to take a leak off of an unenclosed wooden ledge. The root structure of a tree was inexplicably protruding from the side of the pagoda above me, and I grabbed on to a gnarled root for balance while I stared out at the mist-laden trees. I felt sorry for myself, trapped out on a ledge, trying to estimate how long it would be before I could safely reenter the amorous construction site behind me. And then how long would I have to wait for this relationship to end? Three more weeks? Three months? Hopefully not. Thaddeus the Mennonite Rastafarian, Gunnar the Norwegian carpenter—none of them had been longer. I gave it six months, tops. Six unbearable months. Then my mother would process all of her feelings of hurt and indignation with me, and then we'd be back to our manless status quo.

Ignorant of the short life expectancy I'd given their relationship, Leopoldo became a persistent visitor. He came down the mountain every day or two for counseling sessions with my mother. The ratio of therapy to sex dropped so quickly I barely had time to put on my jacket before Leopoldo was dropping his pants. Outside the dripping forest was growing brittle and frosty. The mud underfoot was turning crunchy. I stamped my feet to keep my toes warm and imagined transforming into a Porsche and driving off to someplace warm.

Throughout his many consultations with Claudia, Leopoldo remained oblivious of me. I was a wraith in the shadows, a stranger he passed at the door of his therapist's cabin. Then one day he took notice of me. He and Claudia were sitting cross-legged on her bed, enjoying a postcoital joint. Leopoldo was saying: "River Kerry, him exploit me. I am like a slave to him. In the pagoda, no heat, *no hay nada*. I almost slip on the ice and fall. He exploit me, Claudia." There was an insistence in his words and a plea in the way he said her name, *Clow-thia*. He looked up to watch me climb the ladder to my loft and then called out to me: "*Chosh*," which was his way of pronouncing Josh. "What you have?" He was pointing at the white plastic samurai sword hanging from my belt loop. "Come, *venga aquí*," he said, waving me down.

Suddenly I was the full focus of his face. Between deep drags off the joint he began to tell me a story. His voice grew lyrical, and he waved his fingers as he serenaded me with a remembrance from the *Revolución*. My mother translated earnestly where his English failed, and where the Spanish was too obscure for her, I flipped excitedly through the pages of our yellow paperback Spanish-English dictionary.

The samurai sword had brought him back to the darkest days of the Revolution. They were low on ammunition and hungry up in the jungled mountains of the North. The cells of the National Liberation Front of Farabundo Martí were being hunted down one by one by the death squads. A traitor in San Salvador was giving the army the coordinates of their camps. Leopoldo's squad had been on the move for days and was laagered in a streambed when a lone figure darted out of the woods. They nearly shot him, but spared his life when they saw that he was a small Chinese guy, armed with nothing but a couple of samurai swords. He was all smiles, scraping and bowing.

"What are you doing here?" they demanded of him.

"Ah-soh, yo quiero Revorrución," he said, squinting at them.

He'd come all the way from China or Japan—one of those—to join in their Struggle. They didn't believe him at first, but he brought a sack of rice with him and was hardly a threat, so they let him stay. They called him El Chino—the Chinaman. A few days later, they were ambushed by a troop of soldiers in the heat of the afternoon. Leopoldo's squad had been caught napping, and now they were pinned down. A little guy known as El Gigante was hit in the arm. Leopoldo was about to risk a hail of bullets to come to El Gigante's aid when El Chino leapt up, yowling and howling, his two swords flashing in the afternoon sun.

Leopoldo leapt out of bed at this point in the story, wearing only his gray briefs, to pantomime the ensuing fight. Jumping around with my plastic sword, he yowled like Bruce Lee, his chiseled muscles rippling as El Chino whirled and deftly stabbed at the soldiers. In five minutes flat, all the soldiers lay dead. Leopoldo and his comrades sat up with wide-eyed astonishment. They began shaking their heads and then laughed. And that was the story of how El Chino came to join the Revolution.

It was a good story. He was a great storyteller when he was high. Compared to all of the other men who'd come to my mother for counseling, this guy wasn't that bad. My mother beamed with delight, seeing her two men connect over something so deep as the Revolution. Leopoldo slept over that night, and in the morning I heard him tell Claudia: "That boy, he need a father." A couple of days later, Claudia wrote in her dream journal: *"How very open and tumultuous it was the night before last with Josh, Leopoldo, and I all intensely interacting. That scene seems a faraway dream now. Can hardly believe that he will be back tonight."* And then, to Leopoldo, she wrote: *"I have taken another bite of you and spent this time of separation digesting your being into mine."*

Leopoldo would have slept over every night if he could have, but Claudia was still spending three nights a week down in Seattle to attend Antioch. Most nights she crashed on the couch of a Seattle commune, but sometimes she had to sleep in her car when the commune was overrun with other couch surfers. Some weeks she would stay in Seattle for a fourth day, doing research for a professor in exchange for a free course on the literature of black women writers.

Even when she was home, Claudia didn't have a lot of time for me; she was absorbed in books, writing papers. Leopoldo found her preference for schoolwork over him unbearable. When my mother began studying for fall quarter finals, Leopoldo paced around below me like a panther in a cage. He stopped his pacing and spoke: "Claudia. Claudia! *Hay algo* to tell you. I love you."

A long silence followed and then Claudia chose not to hear it. "Sweetie, I *have* to study. I have a big test tomorrow. I told you today wasn't a good day for a visit."

Leopoldo stomped his way out and slammed the door behind him.

My mother sighed and breathed heavily. She cried for a time and then resumed flipping pages. After the final exam, she wrote: *He tells me he loves me. I feel guilty because at that moment I am unable to answer . . . less song-in-the-heart because of this . . . guilty and fearful of losing him.*

A couple of evenings later, Leopoldo was back to spend the night as though nothing had happened. In the morning, my mother was almost inaudibly talking to herself: "That's weird. I had a five and two ones. Where's the five? Not in here. It couldn't have fallen out. Leopoldo, did you borrow five dollars?"

"What!?"

"It's OK if you did, you should just tell me."

He was screaming at her. "You call me a *ladrón*!? I'm a robbing to you!? Now I am a liar!? You don't trust me!? What I need!? Money!? It is a nothing to me. You think I am stealing from you!?" On and on it went. He ended with a cold, disappointed "I am so hurt, maybe I don't come back," and he walked out the door without closing it behind him. Downstairs, she was crying again.

The next day, she wrote in her dream journal: *"After the indescribable closeness—the incident of lost money—today's terrible fear waiting for L—as though his vision of me will condemn or absolve me in my own eyes, and as though the possible dissolution of this relationship were like the doctor's announcement of a cancerous growth."*

The controversy of my mother asking Leopoldo whether he'd borrowed five dollars continued to rage. A couple of days later, she wrote:

L is sleeping home tonight but will come for coffee tomorrow. The intensity of the storm has died down having lost momentum in distrust . . . now that seeming distrust on his face produces guilt in me—even when I'm innocent. Fear that he will refuse to believe in and therefore make room for my love for him.

Lost in all of this, of course, was the mystery of what actually happened to the five dollars. *I* hadn't taken the money, so in my humble opinion that left only one suspect. But when I asked my mother about it, she told me the whole thing must have been some sort of a test, challenging the sincerity of her love for him.

The next morning was filled with laughter. Claudia had apologized for asking if he'd borrowed money. He'd told stories about the death squads. And then they'd made loud and incendiary love. I was holding my bladder upstairs, weighing whether I should sprint past naked sweaty bodies to take a leak out in the snow or whether I should top off the putrid apple juice jar I kept by the bed for just such occasions.

Then they called me down. Claudia had figured it out. It was so simple. Why hadn't she thought of it before? Leopoldo was moving in! That way River Kerry couldn't exploit him anymore, and I'd finally have someone to look after me while my mother was at school. "Joshey, doesn't that sound crazy?" This rebel leader was going to trade in his AK-47 for a babysitting job. I agreed that it *did* sound crazy and then excused myself to take a wizz outside. Dancing around to keep my bare toes from freezing off, I took measure of my new reality. On the one hand, Leopoldo was scary and casting some sort of a spell over my mother. On the other hand, the single greatest trauma of my latchkey existence was boredom, and Leopoldo promised to be interesting.

As my mother's Chevy Citation sputtered down the mountain, Comandante Leopoldo moved in and embarked on his first day of babysitting. Everything he owned fit inside an army footlocker: a few changes of clothes, a couple of books in Spanish, and a whole bunch of bandanas. These he folded up carefully and wore as headbands—blue, black, or red—depending on his mood. With his headbands, shaggy black hair, and well-worn white shirts, he looked like an Apache brave from a distance. But up close, his face was all wrong. His cocky sneer was too cowboy and not enough Indian. And it just wasn't a warrior's face. His features were too thin and delicate, bunched up together over high cheekbones. He wore a wispy goatee to make his face look tougher, but it was still too slight and birdlike to inspire fear at first sight. He relied on a pronounced swagger for that.

My mother thought he looked like an Indian. She was convinced that Leopoldo was as indigenous as the ancient Mayan shamans who had perfected astronomy when the West was still in the throes of the Dark Ages. But Leopoldo set her straight. One night on a romantic walk, she later told me, they stopped to kiss, and she caressed his face, cooing: *Mi Indio*, "My Indian."

"What!?" he sputtered. "I'm Spanish," he spit out. "*¡No Indio!*"

Indians, Leopoldo later explained to me, were sneaky little fuckers who spoke like birds. He hunched his shoulders, covered his mouth, and gave me a taste of the peeping gibberish the *Indios* spoke. He shook his head, dismissing their primitive stupidity.

Gringos, on the other hand, he told me, were OK. But you had to watch them. They'd exploit you every chance they got, people like River Kerry. But some of them, like my mother, were good people. Augusto Sandino said that the white people from the cities would support the Revolution, and those were the people you had to get close to. They had the money.

"The Blacks" were another story. They were mean and tough, but not too smart. If you stood up to the Blacks, and popped them in the nose before they had a chance to try anything, they would respect you. He illustrated his point with a story about a time in Seattle when three of the Blacks had tried to jump him. They thought they spotted a little Latino guy they could push around, but they hadn't been expecting Leopoldo. They were big, but Leopoldo was stronger and faster. They punched and kicked each other until they were all panting and wheezing. Neither side could get the upper hand. Then the cops showed up. Leopoldo and the three Blacks looked at each other and nodded. Then they joined forces and beat up the cops.

The worst, he said, the absolute worst, though, were the Mexicans. They were liars and cheaters and would smile and then knife you in the back without hesitating. You could never trust a Mexican. This was a lesson Leopoldo had learned the hard way, and he showed me a couple of long knife scars that he'd received from Mexicans trying to murder him.

Leopoldo's body was an essay on people trying to kill him. Knife scars, jagged broken bottle marks, rough patches from being dragged through gravel, and rounded bullet scars. One bullet left a blackened little bowl in his bulging bicep after the Salvadoran nurse pulled it out. The rebel veterinarian who worked on the other bullet couldn't pull the whole thing out. Underneath the mound of scar tissue on his lower back, lead fragments still reminded him of the war.

With his shirt off and arms cycling through his martial arts routine, Leopoldo looked every bit the black belt in kung fu he claimed to be. Each muscle was rounded and fully defined, firing and retracting with each move. He scooped at the air, lunged gracefully, and ended each movement with a punch or a kick. "Josh," he instructed me. "This . . . the big cannon, this . . . the box punch, this . . . the back fist. No, Josh, like this . . ."

I stood next to him, fumbling through poor imitations of his liquid movements, but he was going too fast for me to keep up. He quickly lost interest in the lesson and dropped onto the ground for a flurry of push-ups. I tried to keep pace with him, but he finished his set of fifty before I was at ten. I struggled to twenty with his foot on my butt while he yelled at me: "Straighten to your back! Flat, *cabrón*!" Then I gave up and sat on his feet while he did his sit-ups.

I never saw him exercise more than that. Five minutes of punches and kicks, fifty push-ups, and fifty sit-ups. No running, no stretching, no breaking a sweat. Somehow this base level of exertion was all he needed to maintain a superhero body, even with all the booze, pot, and cigarettes.

After the sit-ups, we crunched through the snow to my mother's pottery shed, where Leopoldo had transplanted his marijuana crop. He sang a Spanish children's song to the little feathery plants and told me that they should have died in the winter cold but his energy kept them alive. On the way back to the cabin, he showed me how to walk noiselessly. "This is how they teach in the army, Josh . . . look." He walked in slow motion, stepping gently with the sides of his feet, swiveling his head from side to side on full alert. He was so fully invested in the slow, tense movements that I could see a flash of him picking his way through the jungle, with a pack and rifle, stalking someone. I pulled us out of the moment by saying I could hear the twigs snapping under his feet. Leopoldo shook his head at me. "You not very smart, huh? In the army, they teach how to walk in the jungle, the *jungle*. No one can walk quiet in the snow."

We finished out our first day together with Leopoldo showing me how to roll him a joint. His eyes narrowed as the THC hit his brain. I brushed my teeth while he told me how to really make the *womens loco*. "You just put the *maria juana* oil on you fingers. And then you shake to they hands or rub to they shoulders. And then they open up the legs for you and give you they pussies." It had been a strange, perplexing day, and I needed to go to bed.

It was a day full of contradictions. Little contradictions, like the way he kept criticizing me for being lazy when smoking weed and napping seemed to be the highlights of his day. Or the way he could tell me that his spiritual life force nourished plants and then boast about his one-day kill record (sixteen soldiers). Or the way that one story cast him as an army soldier and the next as a rebel fighter.

And then there were the big contradictions. The racism, sexism, homophobia; the glorification of violence. These went against everything my mother had taught me, against everything she stood for. Yet she was hearing the same things I was, and he was still a romantic hero in her eyes. The way Leopoldo talked about black people as stupid animals was so taboo to my ears that I cringed with every reference to "the Blacks," fully expecting lightning to strike him down.

This was rivaled by his thoughts on the ladies, or "bitches," as he often called women. To hear him tell it, women primarily walked the Earth "to give you they pussies." He didn't have a single female character in any one of his stories who didn't follow the narrative arc of frigid bitch to horny sex slave. One of his favorite stories was about the time he was kidnapped as a teenager by three uptight businesswomen in San Salvador. They kept him tied to a bed and took turns pleasuring themselves on his ever-rigid cock. He finally escaped after making all three of them climax so hard they passed out.

This blasphemy could only be outdone by his hatred of "the Faggots." He spent a full ten minutes explaining to me all of the insulting Salvadoran nicknames for *Los Maricones*. His favorite was *Culero,* which literally meant "diaper," so called because "after they ass-rape each other all day, their buttholes don't close and they have to wear the diapers."

Why was this man living with us? My mother had explanations.

First of all, it wasn't racism when black or brown people criticized each other. A black person could call another black person a "nigger," and, however disturbing that was to us, it wasn't racism. It was an oppressed person taking back hurtful words from the Man.

Second, Leopoldo didn't mean it. The words coming out of his mouth were learned behavior from an oppressive patriarchal culture. They didn't reflect what was *inside* of him. He had told her stories with eyes full of wonder about the brave *campesinas* who took up arms beside their menfolk. He had told her, with eyes full of tears, about his father's cruel and abusive treatment of his sweet mother. His trash-talk was just a thin veneer of machismo holding together a sweet but traumatized refugee who had suffered so much. Oh, the things Leopoldo had experienced. "If only you knew, Joshey."

Third, he was a hero, a freedom fighter. Violence wasn't a bad thing when it was brandished against the System. Capitalism was itself a systemized form of violence, therefore resistance to it was, by definition, an expression of anti-violence. As a freedom fighter, you had to cut the man some slack. Serving as a rebel fighter in the guerrilla front of Farabundo Martí's *Liberación Nacional* essentially earned you a lifetime credit for crude behavior.

But my mother had glossed over the biggest contradiction in my mind: Leopoldo's dueling roles as refugee and rebel. The way he switched back and forth so deftly between the two made me think he was intentionally transforming his identity to suit the audience. He was a Transformer. With me, he was a shiny racing car with blazing guns. With my mother, he was a human with feelings. Unless she was in the mood for a ride. Then he was a shiny racing car for her too. Sometimes he would transform in midsentence as he calibrated my mother's mood.

"Three of us went to rob the bank—Martillo, El Flaco, and me. We had on the masks. It was one of Duarte's banks, with big bags of *dolares* from the CIA . . ."

"Leopoldo, when are you going to get a job?"

" . . . that they give to the death squads. I saw them once pull up in a white truck, they jump out and grab my friend, an *estudiante* from the university, a girl. They pull her in, and I never see her again. A week later, we find her arm floating in the river, with the bracelet I give her still around the wrist."

It wasn't just the narrative that had changed. It was his face, his voice, his body language—from open and boastful to downcast and pained. He had transformed before my eyes.

I tried to get to the bottom of Leopoldo's shape-shifting one day by telling him about the Transformers—how the heroic Autobots and evil Decepticons could transform from car to person and back, depending on who was around. "Do you ever feel like a Transformer?" I asked him. He didn't. Instead he told me that these kinds of robots already existed. The CIA was developing them. In El Salvador they already had a plane that could saturate a square kilometer with bullets in five minutes. He knew because he'd once taken one down with a rocket launcher.

In the end, my mother, Leopoldo—they all got it wrong. The only person that got it right was my friend Eli. He said: "Who cares if it's a car or a person? What you really want to know is whether it's an Autobot or a Decepticon."

TEN

On Bended Knee

It was my turn. I rolled the ten-sided blue crystal die and moved my way through the graph-paper dungeon Eli had spent all day constructing for me. My elf character fumbled his way a few more steps into darkness.

"Who's that guy that was doing push-ups at your house?" Eli wanted to know.

"That's Leopoldo, Claudia's boyfriend."

"Isn't your mom in Seattle?"

"Yeah. But he's staying with us now."

"Like, living with you?"

"For now."

"Or for forever."

"No, he won't stick around too long."

"Why not?"

"He's like ten years younger than Claudia, and he's from El Salvador and, I don't know, he just won't stay."

"That's what I said about my stepdad. He's ten years older than my mom and he just came over for oolong tea one day and then he never left. Now I have to ask his permission to watch TV."

"At least you have a TV."

"What are you complaining about? You don't have a curfew or bath time or even, like, a bedtime."

"Is that a good thing?"

"Heck, yeah."

Eli's jealousy of my lifestyle made me feel better. "Eli, you think he'll stay? None of her other boyfriends lasted very long."

"You never can tell with these guys. It depends on what they're looking for."

Leopoldo finished his fiftieth sit-up and came up frowning.

"Why you go to Eli house all the time? You are a faggot with him?" He grabbed his crotch. "If you want to be a *maricón*, I show you what it feel like." He spit on the ground and reached for a cigarette.

It had been three days since Claudia left for school in Seattle, and Leopoldo was growing testy. It wasn't fair, he told me, for him to be trapped on the mountain with no car and nothing to do but watch over a "pussy" kid like me. I was useless. I was nine years old, and I didn't know how to cook him dinner. I couldn't even shine his boots. I was worse than useless. I was weak. So weak I couldn't split wood. I couldn't even do push-ups. In El Salvador, he told me, the strong boys would have beaten me to death long ago.

When Claudia got back, Leopoldo gave her a grim assessment. She'd been spoiling me, he said. I was soft. I would start menstruating soon if he didn't toughen me up. My mother took the news like a man. She admitted she'd been so busy with school and her artwork that she hadn't stopped to see that I was sliding off the rails. The good news was Leopoldo was there to help me get back on track.

It was already afternoon when Claudia dropped us off by the river in Mount Vernon on her way back to Seattle. Leopoldo had some work lined up, he said, and he was taking me with him. From the river, we followed the train tracks through a part of town I'd never seen before. Little wooden houses drooping with peeling paint and rusting chain-link fences. Little apartment blocks here and there. No trees.

"Where are we going?" I panted, trying to keep up with Leopoldo.

"We go to Rodolfo house. He owe to me money."

We turned onto a little street, and Leopoldo's swagger grew more pronounced. He threw his head back, jutted his jaw forward, and worked his shoulders up and down like a boxer at the side of the ring. We stopped at a ramshackle green house, and Leopoldo flicked his cigarette into the patch of weeds that served as a front lawn.

"This Rodolfo," he pointed, and waved for me to follow his swagger up onto the little porch. Leopoldo paused before the door, clenching and unclenching his fists. The air was sharp and cold. He blew his nose carefully into the clutch of his thumb and first two fingers and wiped the mucus on the door frame in front of him. An airplane droned far overhead. And then action. Leopoldo struck the door with his fist—*bam, bam, bam*! Not so much knocking as punching. The door rattled on its hinges. Flakes of green paint flurried into the air. Somewhere nearby, a dog barked. But the house remained silent.

Leopoldo backed down from the unanswered door and pulled me around after him. I followed his swagger down the narrow driveway that hugged the side of the house. My feet crunched in the gravel, and Leopoldo turned to scowl at me. He pointed at the band of grass that sprouted like a mohawk between the strips of gravel. This was where I was supposed to walk. Chastened, I tiptoed through the wet grass after him. We rounded the back of the house in silence and stopped and stared at the back door. It was boarded up with sheets of graffiti-smeared plywood.

Suddenly the silence shattered with crazed barking. Snarling, yellow teeth lunged at my face. I fell backward with a girlish shriek. The dog—the *monster*—was huge and black and muscles, awash in drool. It hurled itself at me, closing in for the kill. But it was stopped short with a clank in midair. It had reached the end of its chain and fell back. In an instant it righted itself, barking and snapping at my feet.

Leopoldo hadn't flinched. He stood and stared at the snarling dog for a moment and then strode over to a pile of construction debris, beyond the dog's reach, and selected a length of copper pipe. He tested the weight of the pipe in his hand and then rushed at the dog. It leapt up to meet the challenge, its neck straining against the taut chain. Leopoldo growled back at it, *"¡Hijo de puta!" Son of a Whore!* and arced the pipe down hard onto the dog's skull. Its bark cracked in mid-roar and the dog stumbled backward. They stood staring each other down, man and dog. Leopoldo wielded the copper pipe like a slugger at bat. The dog bared its teeth and gave a low growl. Then it convulsed with a bark, and Leopoldo brought the pipe down with a crack onto its back. The dog sat down for a moment and then wobbled back onto its feet. They were frozen, staring at each other again. Every time the dog opened its mouth to bark, Leopoldo waved the pipe and hissed: *"Chhhht!"* The dog finally conceded defeat and retreated back to its lair under the house.

Leopoldo dropped the pipe where he stood and turned to look at the old, beat-up black Camaro that was parked next to the debris pile. After some contemplation, he pointed at the Camaro and said, "This my car." My chest was still heaving from the dog attack. Adrenaline was pumping through my veins, still pushing flashing images of the snarling mouth into my brain. But Leopoldo seemed to have forgotten about the dog. Now, all he saw was the car.

The doors of the Camaro were locked, so Leopoldo took a brick and smashed out the little triangular window behind the passenger door. Once inside, Leopoldo fumbled around with the steering column. Then he bent down under the wheel, pulling panels and wires apart.

After an eternity of Leopoldo cursing in Spanish and yanking at wires, I asked him: "How come you don't have the keys?"

He looked up with the first smile of the day. "I have them right here." His hands conjured yellow sparks from the darkness, and the slumbering engine of the Camaro came to life with a thunderous howl. Leopoldo grinned and revved the engine several times. We launched down the driveway, leaving the emasculated dog barking behind us.

Now, I figured, we would finally go work at that job Leopoldo had mentioned to Claudia. But we didn't go to work. Instead we drove to old town Mount Vernon to pay a visit to Leopoldo's friend Fabricio. He invited us into the cozy little house he shared with his fat wife, Trina. They were in their fifties and held real jobs. Fabricio was a construction manager and Trina worked as a Spanish translator over at the courthouse. It was unclear how or why Leopoldo knew these mainstream people, but Fabricio was also from El Salvador and that seemed to be all the explanation that was needed. Trina was Mexican and, even though he thought Mexicans were the worst, Leopoldo told me she was all right because she worked to support her man. And she made authentic *pupusas*, a kind of stuffed corn pancake, which we stayed to enjoy for dinner. Leopoldo later told me that *pupusa*, like nearly every other word in El Salvador, was slang for "pussy."

After dinner we were joined by two other Salvadoran guys who worked on Fabricio's crew. The men sat around the table drinking beers and trading stories in incomprehensible Spanish. They were all from El Salvador, but Leopoldo looked as different from them as he did from me. They looked like the weary workers I'd pass in the discount grocery store. Thick, heavy faces. Wearing jeans with plaid shirts tucked in over their paunches. And then there was Leopoldo, perched at the edge of the table, doing most of the talking. His shaggy hair flaring out from under his red headband. His Andean sweater hanging loosely over his army pants.

Leopoldo drained bottle after bottle of Miller High Life, three beers for every one consumed by his countrymen. It was dark and lightly snowing when he stumbled out of Fabricio's with me under one arm. Leopoldo started the car and sunk into a paranoid stupor as we pulled onto College Avenue. He was ranting about the *policía*. He was convinced that every flicker in the rearview mirror was a cop car. "We going trick them, Josh. You see." We swerved between lanes and braked suddenly every few hundred feet until we hit open farmland at the edge of town. Then Leopoldo turned off the headlights and we surged forward in the dim moonlight, meandering across the roadway without regard for the arbitrary yellow lines the *policía* had thrown down to control us.

We picked up speed when we got to Highway 9, the rural route that ran north past Cultus Mountain. As we fishtailed through the gravelly shoulder of the road and lurched into the lane reserved for oncoming traffic, I gripped the door handle with both hands and checked and rechecked my seat-belt buckle. An uncontrollable panic welled up inside of me, and I began calculating my survival rate if I were to jump from the moving car. But we were going too fast. The inky roadway hurtling past my window would chew me up on impact. I would have to wait until he slowed to turn up Old Day Creek Road.

We blew through the little town of Clear Lake. The turnoff for Old Day Creek Road was up ahead, but Leopoldo, who was now screaming at no one in particular in Spanish, took the turn without slowing down. The tires shrieked as we slid off the roadway, and then the Camaro kicked and bucked wildly as we churned our way across the lip of a field. Rubber met road again, and we shot up the mountain. The engine clattered and coughed as Leopoldo tried to keep our speed against the winding incline.

"Lights! Lights!" I was screaming at him. "Turn on the lights!" It was only a matter of seconds until he was going to send us careening off the cliff into the reservoir below. *"¡Luces! ¡Luces!"* I screamed, pulling the Spanish word out of nowhere. Twin beams of blessed light streamed forth onto the chaotic shifting patchwork of road, trees, and sky swirling in front of us. Leopoldo slowed slightly and pulled the Camaro back into the right lane.

"You learning!" he said proudly, as he slouched behind the wheel. "You learning Spanish!"

"Sí, sí," I assured him. *"Español muy bien."*

He took the turn up Janicki Road more slowly. Slow enough, I thought, that I could make the jump. But I lost my nerve and continued gripping onto the door handle with both hands. The next bend in the road proved too much for Leopoldo. He failed to follow the road, and we slammed into the muddy hillside with a solid thud. Dirt and rocks sprayed across the hood and windshield, and somewhere glass shattered. Wheels spun against the hillside and the smell of burning oil filled the Camaro.

I wasn't too bad. I'd smacked one shin pretty hard into the dashboard, but I could tell nothing was broken. Leopoldo was slumped over the wheel for a moment, but then sat up suddenly and launched into a stream of expletives. *"Hijo de puta, chingada sucia pinche madre."* His hands slapped at various levers and dials. The windshield-wipers diligently went to work on the dirt obscuring the windshield, and the smooth voice of the DJ from KBRC floated out of the dashboard, promising us more rocking with the oldies. By the time Leopoldo had found the reverse gear, I was out the door and hobbling up the road.

"Josh! *¡Venga!* Come to here!"

I kept going, rounding the bend and limping my way up the straightaway. All I wanted was to lie down. To zip myself up in my sleeping bag, to bury my face in my pillow. I would have trudged through a minefield to get to bed. Behind me I could hear the wounded Camaro stalking me, huffing and pinging as it came. I stepped down into the ditch at the side of the road and kept sloshing forward. Leopoldo pulled alongside, the passenger side door still open.

"Josh! Come to get in!" He was waving me in.

"No. I'm gonna walk."

"Josh! Get in to the car!"

"No."

Leopoldo stopped the car, but he wasn't looking at me. He was staring straight ahead, his eyes wide open. A deer stood dramatically illuminated in his one remaining headlight. It was a buck, replete with majestic antlers, staring back at him. They stared at each other, deer and man, locked in an impasse. Then Leopoldo began revving the engine. The deer still didn't move. Leopoldo popped the Camaro into gear, and the car lurched forward. The deer turned and bounded into the forest, Leopoldo screeching after him.

The chase was on—for about two seconds—and then Leopoldo slammed into a tree. The hood of the Camaro came flying up in a cloud of steam, and the windshield shattered with a pop, sending a spray of broken glass into the air like confetti. Maybe he's dead, I thought. But he wasn't. A moment later the wheels were spinning uselessly in reverse as he tried to back himself out of the forest.

"Josh," he was yelling again. "Josh, come to help me. Move the car, push the car back. You need to push with me."

Up the road ahead of me, a mile or two, was my bed. I limped forward toward that modest dream and didn't stop until I was safely zipped up in my own sleeping bag.

Leopoldo slept through most of the next day. I walked down Janicki Road in the afternoon and watched as a sheriff's deputy tagged the demolished Camaro for towing. When Leopoldo finally recovered from his hangover he didn't mention the car or the ride home. It was as if it had never happened.

Well, *he* could forget about it if he wanted, but *I* wasn't going to. When Claudia got back from Seattle, I could barely contain myself, thirsting all day for the opportunity to pull her aside and tell her what had happened. Toward evening I finally got my chance when Leopoldo went down the trail to trim his pot plants.

"Claudia, did you see the black car crashed down on Janicki Road?"

"Yes, Leopoldo told me all about it." Her voice was flat, restrained. She was angry. "He told me everything that happened."

"He did?"

She looked at me, trying to control her emotions, her lips pursed, her watery eyes magnified by her glasses. "Yes, he did. And I am so disappointed in you."

"What?"

"When Leopoldo was your age, he was working a part-time job, taking care of his little brothers and sisters, *and* helping out around the house. And now, here he is in the First World, trying to take care of you, trying to teach you how to cook, how to cut firewood, how to clean, and you're running off to Eli's to play instead of helping. And then he takes you to work with him, to show you how to fix cars, but you were too scared of a dog to help out. A dog!?

"Then he introduces you to his friends and you didn't even help clean up. He said that you just sat there watching TV the whole time. Josh, really!? You know how television rots your mind. Then, Leopoldo tells me the roads were icy on the way home and the car slipped into a ditch. And you *refused* to help him push it back onto the road!? You just said 'no,' and walked home!? Josh, that was his car. His friend Rodolfo gave him that car but he didn't have the papers for it. So now it's just gone.

"After all he's been through, Josh, he doesn't need someone else exploiting him. Leopoldo's been talking to me, and he's right that you need a father. Someone to teach you how to be a man."

My chest was so tight I couldn't breathe. I was crying and gesturing wildly, unable to get out anything more compelling than "He's lying!"

"See, Josh, this is what he's been telling me about. You can't just cry and get mad every time someone tells you, 'You have to be more responsible.'"

I slammed the door behind me and ran over to the chopping block. She wanted a man? I would show her I was man enough. I shook with rage, but underneath my indignation was the gnawing possibility that maybe some of what he said about me was true. I stood up a thick piece of wood and brought the ax down with all my strength, but it bounced impotently out of my hands.

They were fighting again. Yelling and screaming. Leopoldo was convinced my mother was cheating on him. She was sleeping with one or more guys down in Seattle. He knew it. Why else would she spend three nights a week down there? Who were these commune people? What bed did she sleep in? A different bed each time! Why else was she so tired when she got back? He slammed the door. She was crying. I'd try to comfort her, but she was usually inconsolable. He'd be back an hour later and apologize for losing control. He just loved her so much he couldn't stand to be apart for so long. I used to excuse myself at this point, knowing that the make-up sex was on its way. But it was too cold to go outside now, so I stuffed toilet paper into my ears and focused on my book, trying to read slowly, lest I run out of words before our next trip to the library.

The only thing worse than these cycles of fighting and fornicating were the intervening days with Comandante Leopoldo as my babysitter. So I had to admit a sense of guilty relief when Claudia finally gave up on her dream of an art therapy degree. She said that she wasn't giving up, that she was only taking a "maintenance" quarter for now. But she was jeopardizing the scholarship she'd received and, absent a sudden change of fortunes, there was no way she could afford to go back.

She'd been going to Antioch for almost a year, and I was looking forward to having her back. But so was Leopoldo. Since meeting my mother, the months of intermittent separations he'd had to endure were like a crushing weight on his heart. Now that weight had been lifted, and he was free to love again. And he had so much love to give.

When he returned from Thrifty Foods, he had red roses for Claudia. He sang to her. He danced with her. He purred: "Oh, honey, after everythings I was been through, the war, the torture. I think I been through it all just so I could meet you. How lucky I am to have your love." He lit candles for her every evening. Admittedly, we lit candles every evening anyway because we didn't have electricity, but when he lit the candles for her he did it with a sweep of his hand. It made the dinners very romantic. And the dinners were special now because they cooked them together. He showed her how to fry plantains, how to pickle *curtido*, and how to fold an *empanada*. He couldn't show her the secret of frying *chicharrones* because we were vegetarians, but he taught her how to make *pupusas*. "If anything happens to me, Honey, and I am killed, you go to another man. He will be happy you can cook this."

He loved my mother so much he agreed to read her his poems. These were secret, spiritual incantations that had never before passed through human lips. Her love gave him the strength to read them aloud for the first time. Composed in flowery script, these writings were bordered by pyramids, adorned with ankhs and hieroglyphs, and crowned with the All-Seeing Eye. They spoke of love and war, fire and occultist magic. He gave them utterance and then returned them to the bottom of his footlocker, where they awaited their next summons. He wrote from the heart, she said, and she cried. After everything he'd been through, after everything he'd seen, he had chosen to open his heart to *her.*

Leopoldo wasn't just a rebel, a refugee, a cook, and a poet. He was also a student of the occult, obsessed with the All-Seeing Eye and the energetic properties of pyramids. He told me he was a disciple of Saint Germain, an "ascended master" who reincarnated often through the centuries. Through his teachings, Leopoldo hoped to learn physics and then the greatest of all arts—alchemy. All he had to do was learn the alphabet in order, and math, and then he'd be turning iron into gold.

Leopoldo was also a spiritual healer. He'd learned from a medicine man in El Salvador and a real Native American shaman in California, and now he could cure the afflicted with the most ancient of formulas. He told me his antidote to black widow bites was a medicinal brew that included human excrement. When I came down with the flu, he promised that he could cure me overnight if I would submit to inhaling the ashes of cedar bark that he had urinated upon. I managed to prop myself up on one elbow and, through the haze of fever, croaked out: "No, I'm OK. I'm actually feeling all better now."

When I recovered from the flu—without the help of urine-based medicine—we went out to eat at a Chinese restaurant in Mount Vernon. As the fortune cookies arrived, he told the waiter: "This my woman. You see how beautiful is she? And this . . . this my boy!" The waiter replied: "Cash only, no check." And we walked out of the restaurant with our arms around each other. Then we strolled through the halls of the Skagit Mall like a father and a mother and a son. Like a family.

The next day Claudia took me with her to the county auditor's office. We waded into an endless line and shuffled through a sea of poor and desperate people before we finally took our turn at the shabby window. The rotund, pale lady with the thinning hair and generous eye shadow patiently answered Claudia's questions. I was watching the old man next to us pop his plastic teeth in and out of his mouth, so I wasn't paying close attention as my mother's voice started to climb. She was asking something about divorce, which was strange since she wasn't married. "I don't know. I have no idea. I haven't seen the man since 1970."

On the way back home she explained that she'd technically never gotten divorced from Frankie Rhys, the Black Panther she'd married when she was twenty. I asked her why she wanted to divorce him now after all those years. She said she wanted closure, but I suspected it was because Leopoldo was jealous. He'd freaked out so dramatically when my mother was spending the night in Seattle, it must be driving him crazy to know that "his woman" was still legally hitched to another man. When we got home I helped her write the requisite legal notice for the divorce. Even though she hadn't seen Frankie in two decades she still had to place an ad in a newspaper back in Toronto, where she'd last seen him, even if he'd gone off to be a Coptic monk in Ethiopia as she suspected. This farcical process would take two months and almost a hundred dollars, but, in her words, that was the government for you.

By the light of the smoky kerosene lamp we talked about Frankie. He was half Jewish and half Carib, from Belize. Claudia had thought he was going to be a real revolutionary leader. And he was, in New Haven, where he burnt the draft offices to the ground. But when they slid into Canada to elude the FBI, he became more concerned with screwing grad students down at the jazz club than smashing Capitalism. After Frankie, she thought she'd found the real deal again when she met Uncle Tony, but he was more comfortable discussing Greek mythology than trying to build a new society. And now, at long last, she'd met the genuine article. Leopoldo was Che Guevara and Archbishop Romero all in one.

We ate out at the Chinese place again the next week. We all savored the warmth in the restaurant, marveling at the way the heat kept rolling out of the wall. When the bill came, Claudia concluded that the three of us

Looking up the snowy trail at our little wood-plank cabin on Cultus Mountain, Washington.

weren't going to survive off of Welfare. She and Leopoldo needed jobs. On the way home we talked about what we were going to do with all the money they'd be making with all the jobs that were waiting for them. With jobs, we could buy a reliable car. Maybe rent a house in town with a heater and running water and electric lights.

Claudia found a job as a care worker at the Monte Vista nursing home, where she rolled incontinent old people in and out of beds. She changed them and she powdered them. She hoisted them into a wheelchair and stuck them in front of the TV. Then she did it all over again. They gave her so little time with each patient that she sometimes had to leave the folks who'd merely pissed themselves to languish in wet sheets. She came home exhausted, smelling of ammonia and degradation. Leopoldo had a harder time finding work. He worked a couple of odd jobs but the bosses always disrespected him too much for anything to pan out. He eventually found part-time employment at an auto body shop. We tried to bring him lunch there one day but he waved us away, annoyed at our surprise visit. He didn't want us to see him that way. Just one of many little illegal immigrants sweating in oversized blue jumpsuits and face masks, coated in Bondo and white dust. It was one of the rare occasions I saw him looking powerless. The auto body job didn't last through its second week.

During this time, I had been attending a one-room New Age private school where we wrote poems and used a geode to interpret each other's dreams, but when our money ran out, I was back home with my least favorite babysitter. I wasn't the only one unhappy with the new arrangement. Leopoldo was in the corner, clenching a cigarette to his face, pulling disturbing images out of the smoke. "She cheat on me," he concluded to himself. "She fuck with the other mens." It seemed like a good time to pay a visit to my friend Eli, and I slipped down the mountain.

When I came back, Leopoldo was in Claudia's face, snarling with paranoia. "Where you was!? Why you was so late!? You go to someone house? Me and the boy waiting and waiting for you." My mother turned away from him, her face blank as she transferred her salad fixings to another corner of the driftwood that served as a counter. Leopoldo whipped around her, shoving his face back into hers. "You no talk with me now? You no tell me *la verdad*!"

"Honey," she explained to him like he was a child, "I told you. I went to work. Then I went to the co-op to buy veggies." She offered up her paper bag brimming with carrot tops as her alibi. "Are you jealous of the lettuce or the carrots?"

"You went to the co-op?"

"Yes. And now I'm tired and hungry for salad."

Leopoldo took a step back like a cat releasing a motionless mouse, and eyed her carefully, waiting for a deceitful movement. Claudia stood in silence, peeling carrots robotically, one after the other, until they were all smooth and innocent. Leopoldo went out for a cigarette. When he stepped back in from the forest, he partook of the salad, and all was forgotten.

Until the next day when the whole thing repeated itself again. Rifling through her abalone shell of trinkets, Leopoldo held up her used costume jewelry from the thrift store. "You know how much this cost in El Salvador? Only the rich peoples have this kind of thing! Who giving this to you? You boyfriend?"

I was up in the loft, skimming across the Marvel microverse. Uncle Tony's latest package of Micronauts comic books had arrived, and it would take more than a little shouting to distract me from Acroyear's duel with

Psycho-Man. In the background somewhere, Claudia was shouting back: "You think after washing old people's asses all day, I'm going to pop by some guy's house to have sex for ten minutes before coming home to make dinner!?" And then reality pulled me back from inner space with a new sound. *"Ow!"* Claudia's voice was high pitched and startled. *"Ow!* Stop it! You're hurting me!" A chair hit the floor. "Stop it!" A long volley of Spanish expletives rang out, ending with *pinche, dirty,* and the slamming of the door.

"You all right?" I called down.

"Yes, I'm fine." The chair was righted below me and silence prevailed.

In the morning, I was summoned to help push my mother's car out of the ditch. Leopoldo had almost made it home the night before, but the combination of twelve beers and that last curve in the road proved to be too much for him. The car still ran, even with the busted headlight and leaking radiator. But Leopoldo didn't want Claudia to drive with it in that condition. "It no safe." And there was no way he was going to let her take it to a mechanic. *Pay* a stranger to do what he could do for *free*!? It was crazy.

One missed day of work turned to two, with Leopoldo and Claudia passing the time by arguing. First they bickered over how long it would take him to fix the car, then they moved on to how annoying it was for her to keep nagging him. On the third day, Claudia made an executive decision and limped the car into town on her own. The last of our savings went to the mechanic.

"You disrespect me!? I tell you 'I fix it!' "

"I had to go to work!"

"Why? To see you boyfriend!?"

Up the ladder, I turned my ears off and opened a new comic book, savoring every stipple of shade, every contrast of color. I had to make them last though these dark nights. The screaming droned on. Movement, creaking on the floors. Screams of "Let me go!" and *"Ow!" Slam.*

Claudia went to work the next day with a black eye. In the middle of her shift she broke down. She finished changing the demented patient in 3B and then sat on the bed beside her and cried. The woman sat up with a look of wonder. "You know how I feel, dear?"

The next Saturday we went to Fabricio and Trina's for dinner. In the kitchen Trina told Claudia that Fabricio's drinking had gotten so bad he couldn't even get it up to make love anymore.

"Why do you stay with him?" my mother asked.

"He's my husband."

I shuttled back and forth between the uncomfortable conversation in the kitchen and the ominous drinking in the dining room. On the way home, Leopoldo wrenched the car back and forth across both lanes, skimming along the edge of the precipice and ranting about my mother's alleged infidelity. "Who you fuck!? You tell to me!" If she had really been shopping on Friday, where was the proof? "Where the receipts!?" he screamed over and over as we fishtailed through the snow.

The next day Claudia and Leopoldo came to a settlement. My mother would give him all her money when she cashed her paycheck. That way he could keep track of how much she spent and make sure she wasn't cheating on him. Watching her count out her money for Leopoldo, I didn't understand the logic behind the agreement, but was relieved that the matter was settled.

"Claudia, why you keep ten *dolares*?"

"For coffee."

"Why you need money for coffee? We have coffee here."

A new argument began, but it was mercifully short, ending with the surrender of my mother's last ten dollars.

A few days later, my mother came home from work sweaty. Leopoldo inspected the wet stains under her arms with suspicion.

"You trick me. You fuck the men at you work!"

"Who, Leopoldo, who? The old people? Lupita, the sixty-three-year-old nurse? José, the fat orderly?"

She kept presenting her defense, but it was no use. José had been named, so José was the man. The smoking gun, of course, was that José was Mexican. Everybody knew you couldn't trust Mexicans around your woman. The door slammed. I slipped in and out of sleep.

Near dawn, Leopoldo came crashing through the door. "*¡Mis manos!*" *My hands!*, he was screaming, holding his frozen paws up in front of him. He was shivering, covered in snow and dirt and twigs. I helped Claudia wrap him in blankets, and then she sent me outside for more firewood. As the house began to warm, Leopoldo volunteered bits and flashes of drunken events. He had seen the police on the way home. They were parked on the side of the road above Clear Lake. They were up to no good, waiting for him. Waiting to send him back to El Salvador, to the death squads. He had to hit them first. He did. He came at them with full force. Their car went flying and sank into the lake below.

"That didn't happen, Leopoldo," my mother assured him.

"It happen."

"It didn't. If you'd drowned a policeman, they'd be all over the place right now." I looked out the window to see if a SWAT team was descending on us. Nothing, just darkness and flashes of snow.

"I got away. They no find us. *¡Ay, mis manos!*"

His hands were thawing out, but nearly frostbitten. He'd left the car in a ditch down on Janicki Road and then climbed straight up the hill. No trails, just a vertical climb through icy brambles and frozen forest, screaming *¡Mis manos!* as he came.

It was morning. The car was totaled. They were laughing. When I came down for granola and soy milk, they called me over to the bed, giggling like children.

"Did you hear that, Joshey? It's been so hard on Leo for me to be apart from him, but we figured it out."

He completed her idea: "We goin' get a job together, work at the same place, be together every day."

They were laughing again. I was happy they'd figured it out, but we were out of soy milk.

Leopoldo sang to Claudia, and she wrote in her dream journal: *Working on a divorce from Frankie . . . dreaming of having the real thing with Leopoldo. Love him enough to be happy . . . to be lovers. To be Partners is a little like the dream of enlightenment. A focus. A reason to be strong and beautiful inside and out.*

I was still looking for breakfast when Claudia came running back from the mailbox. The government had declared that her divorce from Frankie was final. "Now I'm free, Joshey!"

ELEVEN

The Groom

"Joshey?"

"Yeah."

"Are you awake?"

"No."

"I'm worried."

"He'll be OK. He always is." Leopoldo had hitchhiked down the mountain that morning to find work and he still wasn't back. Maybe he just couldn't find a ride back home. But then he would have called. We had a telephone now. Claudia had finally committed the paperwork and the dollars to get a little piece of the twentieth century strung up the hill. The phone was working—she'd checked for a dial tone five times already—and yet, it refused to ring. Leopoldo was more likely drunk behind a wheel somewhere, crashing into deer or policemen. I could see him now in a drunken rage, storming his way through a phalanx of police. How many cops would it take to bring him down? Three? Four? He was strong and fast, a kung fu master. Five? And my mother loved him, and I had to support him for her. I had to want him to be OK, to root for him. Six, seven, eight. I could see him whirling in the air, fists and feet flying, knocking cops around like socks in a dryer. Ten, twenty, or more. It would take a hundred cops to subdue my mother's lover.

As it turned out, it only took two cops to arrest him. One threatened to shoot him, and the other put on the cuffs. The phone went limp in my mother's hand. She rolled her head back and exhaled like she was giving birth to a nightmare. "Joshey. Leopoldo is in jail. Aw, Joshey, what are we going to do?" I suggested we go to visit him, which I intuited to be the proper etiquette in this sort of situation. My mother nodded her head in assent. "What else *can* we do?" she choked out, mashing her lips together to keep from crying. We plodded down the road in the rain, holding hands like the family of the condemned. By the time we picked up a ride on Old Day Creek Road, we were soaked and shivering.

"Where you guys headed?" said the fat white woman with the yellowed glasses.

"Believe it or not, to visit the jail," my mother apologized.

"Huh! Me too. What's your man in for? Drunk and disorderly?"

"Something like that."

"They're all the same."

I felt sorry for the poor fat woman. Her man was some drunk hick. Ours was a Central American refugee, a revolutionary poet. A man who drank not because he was an alcoholic, but to kill the pain of what he had seen. At least that's what Claudia had told me. We were trying to heal him. But now he was locked up in Skagit County Jail.

They wouldn't let us in. "Suárez, Leopoldo? He ain't here," said the sheriff's deputy with the REEL MEN FISH coffee mug. "They just took 'em next door for arraignment." The deputy returned to his fly-fishing magazine, and we were left to wander our way into the neighboring courthouse. There, a redbrick facade concealed a cavernous chamber where the defeated came to be humbled. Out they herded Leopoldo, the middle man in a string of five prisoners, shackled together at the ankles, waist, and wrists. He shuffled forward with the others, his face pale and lined, framed with the limp blackness of his unkempt hair. They'd taken his headband from him. He was left small and vulnerable in his oversized blue jumpsuit and clanking shackles.

Various men in suits and ties spoke, and at one point Leopoldo had to say "yes" and "no" and "not guilty." He only looked over at us once. A sideways glance, a raised chin of recognition. He had to look tough. I got that. Even Claudia, who was usually so sensitive about being slighted, got it. One look at the four grizzled men he was hitched to told us he had to appear like the toughest son-of-a-bitch he could be. After they led him away, my mother worked the pay phone, calling Grandma Harriette collect and pleading with her for an hour. She invoked our Hebrew ancestors, she appealed to Grandma's Communist sympathies, she catered to her social justice appetite. Leopoldo was Joseph thrown into the pit, Julius Rosenberg, and Martin Luther King, Jr., all rolled up into one. I knew Grandma Harriette would cave in eventually. Yes, she thought her only child was totally *farblunget*—a lost, dysfunctional fuckup. But doling out money in times of crisis was her only contact with her estranged daughter, and some combination of guilt for past mistreatment and fear for Claudia's future compelled her to open her pocketbook. By the time my mother hung up, Grandma Harriette had committed to paying for bail and wiring another three hundred dollars to buy a used car.

Leopoldo's face was light and clear as he left the jail. He breathed deeply the sweet air of freedom and hugged us, going so far as to drop to one knee to hug me.

We met with his lawyer a few days later. He wore a tie and kept referring to Leopoldo as Mr. Suárez, which demonstrated to me that he viewed Leopoldo as an important person. He knew what was at stake. "There's some indication in the police report that the car was stolen. It is registered to a Mr. Sosa. Mr. Suárez, do you know Mr. Sosa?"

"Yes, Adolfo. He my friend, he no talk to nobody," Leopoldo reassured us all.

"Yes, well, apparently he's not cooperating with the prosecution, so I think that issue will go away. There's a DWI charge that will be hard to shake, but we can probably divert that with a twelve-step program. The thing they really care about, of course, is the resisting arrest. But I think we can probably plea-bargain that down to time served and some community service. Mr. Suárez, I think the main thing you have to worry about here is your immigration status. You're an undocumented alien and now you're a criminal defendant. That's a combination that usually leads to deportation proceedings. Do you know what that means, Mr. Suárez? That you could be sent back to El Salvador?"

He nodded. He knew.

The lawyer continued: "Immigration issues are outside of my scope of representation, but I do want to tell you that there really aren't any defenses to deportation. It's the federal government, and if they want you back in El Salvador, there's not much you can do. That said, there are pathways to citizenship available to you, Mr. Suárez. The main one of course is marriage to a US citizen. I know that's worked for some of my other clients in the past." The lawyer specifically avoided looking at my mother for this last part. It was beyond the scope of his representation.

Leopoldo was silent on the ride home in our new, very used Ford Pinto. This was unusual. He usually insisted on driving himself or on ceaselessly criticizing Claudia for her *loco* handling of the car. But this time he was distracted, running through possibilities in his head. When we got back to the cabin, he began to tremble and shake. I rushed to build a fire for him. When the warmth and some coffee had soothed his anxiety, and his hangover, he began to confide in us. If they deported him, he would be shot in the head. There was no other way to put it. The secret police would be waiting for him at Cuscatlán Airport. They'd execute him on the tarmac. "We've been waiting for you, Señor Suárez." They wouldn't say "Suárez," of course, because that wasn't his real name. He couldn't even tell *us* his real name. But they had his photo on a "Wanted" list. They had not stopped looking for him since he escaped from the detention center in San Salvador. And now the US government was going to package him up and deliver him with a bow right into the arms of the death squad. His feet would hit the tarmac, and they'd blow out his brains with a bullet to the back of his head.

And, if they deported him, he wouldn't be here for us. To protect us. He knew how far the government would go. He'd been a follower of Cayetano Carpio, a guerrilla leader. Cayetano was surrounded by guards twenty-four hours a day and hid out in a dormant volcano. But one day, the government announced he had killed his lover in a jealous rage and then committed suicide. But Leopoldo knew better. "They killed Cayetano Carpio! They even killed too Cayetano Carpio's woman!" Even now, the Atlacatl Battalion was being trained by the CIA right here in America in the arts of assassination and counter-insurgency. They could be slipping into the surrounding woods, coming for all of us as we spoke. Who would protect us if not Leopoldo?

This was his proposal for marriage. There was no down-on-bended-knee, offering-of-a-ring silliness. There was only the case for marriage spelled out in cold, hard facts. And it was a compelling proposal: Marry me to save my life, marry me to save yours. A fount of energy welled up inside of my mother, and she threw herself into the cause of Leopoldo Suárez with a dedication and fervency not seen since her anti-nuclear days with the Three Mile Island parade. She began making calls and running errands as though our lives depended upon it, which, of course, Leopoldo had convinced us they did. She found a pro bono immigration lawyer in Seattle who would take the case. She enrolled Leopoldo in Social Security, filed his applications for entry into the United States and a driver's license, and began drafting a history of genocide in El Salvador to use in a request for amnesty. And, of course, she began planning the wedding.

Leopoldo wanted to consecrate the union in the occult traditions of ancient Egypt. He planned on building an immense lattice pyramid for the ceremony, but an errant hammer blow to the thumb scuttled the project on the first day. He designed outfits for my mother to make. White tunics made from used bedsheets, held together with golden cords. White pharaonic head cloths fastened with blue headbands for the two of them and a plain white headband for me.

For the ceremony, Leopoldo was adapting some of his occult Spanish poetry into a song he would play on my secondhand guitar. But the guitar didn't sound quite right, even after Claudia bought him all new strings, and he had to abandon the idea. For her part, Claudia wrote poems that included lines like: *your music hums in the quietest places in my soul* and *together we can generate enough energy to light up a part of this dark world.* She planned on talking about how Leopoldo had caused a physiological change in her. She needed less food and sleep when he was around. He enabled her to gain strength and peace, to feel clean, beautiful, strong, and innocent.

As the appointed date on the second Friday in May of 1986 came closer, they invited Fabricio and Trina to serve as Leopoldo's family, and Crazy John and his girlfriend Erica to play the same role for my mother. Because no priestesses of Osiris were readily available, Reverend Carol Taylor, a Sanctuary minister who sheltered undocumented Central American refugees, agreed to preside.

The day before the wedding, I walked alongside my mother in the narrow pungent aisles of the food co-op. We had come to buy blue chips, black bean dip, and a big glass jug of red Gallo wine for the wedding celebration. It was hard for me to believe that it was all really happening. Leopoldo wasn't going away like all the other men. He was going to be my stepfather. I'd never had a father before, and I wondered how it was all going to work. Leopoldo still scared me half the time, but I knew this wasn't about me. This was about the smiling woman next to me, waving her hands in conversation and scrutinizing the ingredients in the soy sauce. My mother was so visibly addicted to him, so elated with being loved and wanted by such a heroic man. There was nothing for me to do but throw my support behind this pending union.

Leopoldo had given me a line in the ceremony. *Today, Leopoldo becomes more than a husband, he also becomes a father.* I was up-the-ladder in the little loft, practicing the line, repeating it over and over. Did I want to emphasize *also* or *father*? Below me, Leopoldo had taken a head start on the jug of wine and was now yelling: "What you say!? You think I no do nothing for to make the wedding? It was my idea! Maybe you want to marry other mens!?" I shut it out and focused on the line: *Today . . .* becomes a *father.*

You fuckin' bitch! The concussion of shattering glass announced something new. Crashing, clattering. A chair burst into kindling against the stove. Claps and cracks. My mother shrieking. Choking and cries for help.

What was going on? It couldn't be what it sounded like. I slid over to the square hole in the loft that served as the door to my room and hung my head down. The world was upside down. He was in his red tank top, standing over a crouching form, beating it with both fists, his elbows taking turns to pull back in my direction. Under his fists was a flurry of waving white palms, fingers fluttering to absorb the blows. That couldn't be my mother, under there, the anvil for all that fury. There must be some other explanation. What was he doing!? A need to scream and jump and kick overtook me. *Do something! Say something, anything! Command him to stop. Tell him I see what he's doing.* But I couldn't move, couldn't even speak. He was clawing at her now, trying to grab her by the wrist, latching on to her hair. Finally a tendril of resolve slid out of my throat. *Shhhhhhhh*! Was this the best I could do, to shush him? Yes, it was. He had her by the collar now, hoisting her up with two fists. I caught a flash of her face, red and recoiling with terror.

I rolled back up into the stillness of the loft. I goaded myself. *He's going to kill her! You fucker, he's going to beat her to death, and you're not doing anything.* I finally sprang into action, scrambling around my room for a weapon. The samurai sword? I'd relied on it to overcome my fear of the dark, swinging it up and down into the eerie night air to guard me on the forest trails. But now, it was plastic and hollow. A toy. What was there? Somewhere outside was the machete, but I didn't even think of it until later. My desperate eyes came to rest on my aluminum globe piggy bank. I weighed it in my trembling hands. Below me he was bellowing, smacking, and slapping. The globe was half full of change, but still puny. It was the heaviest thing I had.

I crawled over to the opening in the floor again, huffing air fast, preparing myself to do something heroic. I slung my head through the divide and yelled: "Hey!" She had crammed herself into a corner, her back to him. He stood over her, prodding her with his foot. "Get up, *pinche puta*!" *Dirty whore!*

"Hey!" I called again, fingering the piggy bank next to me. "Hey!" He couldn't hear me. I felt frustration, at first, that I wasn't pulling his attention off of my mother. But I felt something else too, more powerfully. Relief. He couldn't hear me. He didn't know I was there. I crawled back into my bed, crying and convulsing with fear. I was agonizing over my mother, but was also scared for *my* life. I knew that made me a terrible, cowardly, selfish little wimp. I knew that, and I was still too frightened to do anything.

Below me the destruction went on and on. How could he still be at it?

Wasn't she dead yet? How could I be nodding off in the middle of the storm? But I was, my head jerking up suddenly with the louder screams and crashes. And then blackness.

The sun rose on the day of the wedding. Could it have been? Could last night have been true? All was so still and calm. Light trickled in through the mist. Then, the moaning began. "Oh, my honey . . . honey. I so sorry. Drink this, baby, please." Leopoldo was in a squat, shifting back and forth on his toes next to my mother, who was laid back in the armchair. He looked up at me with pleading eyes, his face carved with deep lines of anxiety. My mother looked like a car crash victim. She gazed up at me and didn't even attempt a wincing smile. Was she judging me for not coming to her defense? One eye was nearly swollen shut, purple and monstrous. Her face was a succession of lumps and swellings. Her lips were cut and raw. Even her fingers were swollen, as she clumsily spun the dial on the rotary phone.

"*Hola*, Trina, *tenemos que reprogramar la boda*." And: "Hi, John, we have to postpone the wedding, I'm sick." Lisping through fat lips, her voice was flat and dead. Reverend Taylor's phone rang and rang. Oh no, had she left Anacortes already? She picked up on the seventh ring. "Hi, Reverend, we have to reschedule." There was no question of canceling. It was just a matter of postponement.

Leopoldo came home with flowers, and a card, and the chicken soup she wanted, and plenty of makeup to cover up all the carnage. They calculated that between the natural healing process and the generous application of pancake makeup, her face would be presentable again in a week, and the wedding was reset for eight days later.

Leopoldo groveled and explained himself for two days. "I was all *loco* from the stress of the wedding. The night before, was very much pressure. We should not have the wine around the house." He sang to her and coaxed her up onto her feet to dance with him. They swayed together, and finally she smiled, and eventually she laughed, and all was forgiven. Their love was strong, and they would work through this together.

When the rescheduled wedding day arrived, it unfolded around us in a daze. We went through matrimonial motions: I said my line, we took three photos, Reverend Taylor signed the papers, and everyone went home.

Another week went by, maybe two, and then he was at it again. Bellowing about something or other and beating her. I played my role, hiding upstairs, hating myself for it. When there was a break in the storm, I popped

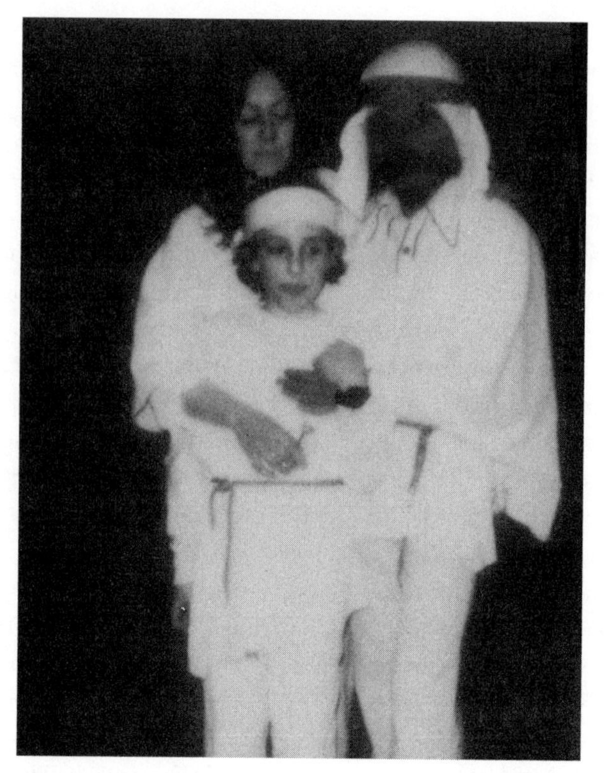

Claudia, Leopoldo, and me at their ancient Egyptian occult wedding in 1986.

my head down. He was standing with his face in my line of sight, bristling. My mother was rising to her feet on wobbly legs. "What, Claudia, you mad at me? You hate me? What you wanna do? To hit *me*!? Hit me? Go ahead, hit me." And then he was yelling: "Hit me, hit me, hit me!" My mother slapped him with an open palm clean across the face. The slap rang out into silence. He stood there stunned for a moment and then punched her square in the face. She flew backward out of sight, crashing onto the altar of incense and little gods and goddesses we had by the fire.

The destruction was so loud that Michael McNeary, the drunk violinist who lived down the trail, must have been able to hear it. And now he was banging at the front of the cabin. Leopoldo threw open the door and charged out at him. "What you want!?"

Michael stumbled back gracefully in his green frock coat and knickers. "You need to stop," he said in a lilting slur.

"She my woman!"

"Then all the more reason to stop. It's too much." He gave a little bow as he pronounced the words, challenging and deferring all at once.

"I love her!" Leopoldo shot back.

"I love her too," Michael volleyed back without a trace of irony.

"I love her. She *my* woman!"

"She's your woman, and we both love her," concluded Michael.

"Go home!" Leopoldo ordered him.

"If you stop, I'll go home."

I couldn't believe that he wasn't tearing apart the tiny man with the Renaissance haircut and tights. But he wasn't. Michael was just too slight and silly for Leopoldo to know what to do with. Instead, he slammed the door in Michael's face. Silence followed, and then he laughed. *"¡Maricón!" Faggot!*

I cried silently, more ashamed than ever. The little leprechaun was braver than I was. After a while the beating resumed.

The aftermath was more or less the same. This time he had punched her with her glasses on, so both eyes and the bridge of her nose were swollen and black and blue. This time the excuse was that Leopoldo had been stressed out about money problems. Once they had jobs, he said, the whole problem would go away. Claudia froze him out for a day or two, and then the song and dance thawed her love again.

Always the song and dance. The sweet, melancholy crooning of José Luis Perales spilled out of the tape player. The orchestra swelled behind his voice as he sang of the thief who had robbed him of his woman, and Leopoldo and Claudia swayed together as one. My mother wrote in her dream journal:

> *The heat of this relationship is almost unbearable . . . this is no dreamdance but more like a walk in a minefield . . . yet I would not avoid this connection any more than I would avoid the heat of enlightenment . . . this relationship is not haunted by a longing for anyone else except for my fullest self when I feel her slip away.*

And to me, in the privacy of a walk out into the tall dark forest, my mother told me: "Don't give up on Leo, Joshey. He's seen so much hurt. I have to heal him. You have to help me heal him. Joshey, you have to understand how important he is. What he saw happen in front of him, what he did in the Revolution. Even though he had no formal education, in El Salvador they were inviting him to speak to the university students, to share his story, to bear witness."

"But he gets so angry," I protested.

"You let me worry about that," she said, "he's getting better."

A few days later, he got worse. In the middle of his opening tirade, I could hear my mother interrupt him: "Let's go outside. I don't want Josh to have to hear this." They screamed and shrieked their way down the hill. At the bottom of the trail Leopoldo smashed his way through the locked door of a vacant cabin, and he beat her up in there for a change. In the middle of the night, they came crashing back into the cabin, screaming for help. My mother's arm was drenched in blood. Leopoldo was bare-chested, fumbling to wrap his T-shirt around the wound.

I stumbled around at my mother's side, one foot still in the dream world. "What happened? What happened?" But no one would notice me.

Leopoldo was now on the floor, sparking his lighter, setting fire to a newspaper. "Here, honey, here, wait!" The newspaper flared at my feet, and Leopoldo picked up the fire, juggling it in his hands, and then rubbing the flames out on the wooden floor. He swept the hot ashes up with his hands and turned back to my mother. With the gentleness of a pediatric surgeon he unwrapped my mother's arm, exposing the long grisly gash in her arm to the smoky air, and then began packing her open wound with newspaper ash.

"Ah!" my mother winced, but she kept her arm still.

"Hold to be still, be still," he counseled her. The ash-packing was one of his shamanic healing treatments. My mother would later tell people, with a tone of wonder, about the time he miraculously healed a deep cut of hers with ash from a newspaper. She just neglected to share the part about how he caused the wound in the first place. Down in the vacant cabin, Leopoldo had pulled the "Hit me, hit me!" routine again. And she had. And he'd hit her back again—in the face. Then he'd raised the stakes, pulling a long serrated bread knife out of a drawer. "You hate me? You want to cut to me!?" He'd exposed his neck to her and handed her the knife. "Cut me! Cut me!" She knew where this was going, and she didn't see any way out, save one. She slashed at her own arm, hoping that the sight of so much blood would calm him down. It worked. For a week or two, and then he was drunk and violent again.

This was my mother, and this was my stepfather. This was our new pattern of life.

TWELVE

The Descent of Man

Darkness was finally gone, but echoes of screaming and smashing still reverberated in my head. Normally, I would have just peed in the apple juice jar and gone back to sleep. But not today. It was Saturday, and on Saturdays I had to walk down the mountain.

My boots were all I needed to get dressed. I'd slept with all my clothes on. I always did. If he came up after me, I could just leap out the window of my little loft onto the roof of the outhouse, and from there run into the forest. I backed down the wooden ladder slowly, breathing through pursed lips like a diver descending into a shipwreck, breathing out of my mouth because I didn't want to smell the aftermath.

The cabin was a crime scene. Broken dishes littered the floor; books were strewn in an impact radius around the smashed shelf; muddy footprints led to a pool of vomit. My mother was asleep in the easy chair and, even in the dim light, I could see the bright red of her swollen brow. Leopoldo was passed out facedown on the bed. One muddy shoe was still on, and the naked sole of the other foot sparkled with hints of broken glass.

Normally, I would have stayed to help pick up the pieces. But not today. It was Saturday. I checked to see that my mother was still breathing. She was—deep, almost peaceful breaths. Her lips were cracked and puffy, and I looked away before I saw more. I didn't want to know the extent of the damage. I pulled on my boots and stepped down with a crunch. Underfoot was a smashed picture frame. Me, as a baby, smiling up at me. Most of the glass was in shards, obscuring my little face. The rest of it was undoubtedly embedded in Leopoldo's foot.

The cabin air was full of puke and malt liquor, and I gladly traded it for the mud and moss carried on the breath of the forest. The dark gray mist accepted me without question, and I plunged into the wet gauntlet that led down the hill. The salmonberry bushes and ferns struck at me with wet, harmless blows. I plowed through them, remembering that the trail hadn't always been this overgrown. I used to clear it regularly, enthusiastically, charging into the thicket, hacking at all sides with my machete, pretending to be Richard the Lionheart. But that was before the coming of Leopoldo. The day of the wedding I'd thrown the machete into the nauseating muck of the outhouse, where I knew he wouldn't go after it.

At the bottom of the trail, I followed the path to the muddy circle, where the top of the driveway collapsed into the trees. Two useless wrecks greeted me. Michael McNeary's rusting blue pickup was still pinned onto the stump where he'd crashed it. Next to it was our gray Chevy Citation, its face bashed in where Leopoldo had rear-ended the police car. The mangled vehicles were sinking into the forest, and they looked like a still life from the End of the World.

As the driveway spiraled its way down the hill, mud gave way to smatterings of gravel and finally the road. I followed Janicki Road as it dipped down the mountain to the right. The logging trucks rumbled down the road from the clear-cut. It was Saturday morning, and Eli was waiting for me to watch cartoons.

Karma opened the door, and I saw myself in her eyes. The greasy-haired, big-eyed, big-nosed kid in rumpled clothes. The kid from the forest whose mom had taken up with one of the illegal immigrants from River Kerry's crew. Whose mom had started showing up at the food co-op with black eyes and fat lips.

No one said anything, but Karma always invited me in, now without question. And Richard would let me stay all day, until every last cartoon was over, and I had no further excuse to ignore reality.

A few days later, my mother and stepfather were dancing again, enjoying the honeymoon period between Leopoldo's storms. My mother thought the lyrics from the tape player were revolutionary and romantic all at once, just like Leopoldo: *And you and I will be a pair of crazies again, turning the wrong into right, letting our love live in freedom.* They swayed together, letting the music erase all their memories of darkness.

When we were down to our last ten dollars, Claudia and Leopoldo finally got a job together at the RoozenGaarde bulb factory outside of Mount Vernon. There they stood side by side, hunched over a conveyor belt, separating tulip bulbs from clods of dirt. Sometimes on their lunch break at the bulb

Claudia posing in front of a sacred pole she and Leopoldo erected, adorned with her sun and moon masks, on Cultus Mountain. Claudia was the "moon" to Leopoldo's "sun."

factory, they would drive to a little hill and gaze down at the long fields of tulips, laid out in gigantic stripes of red, orange, and yellow. Leopoldo would roll himself a fat joint and capture the energy of the landscape on a little canvas with watercolors. "*Las flores* are in love, honey." This, she thought, was Leopoldo's real soul, loving, and moved by the beauty of the natural world.

Although I was home alone all day, I suffered the hours of loneliness and boredom happily, knowing that they were working side by side. Now that he could monitor her all day long, he wouldn't have any excuse to be jealous. But Leopoldo still found ways she could be cheating on him. If she took too long at the store, he was convinced she was screwing the box boy out back on a bed of lettuce. Every trip to the post office was a chance for her to have sex with a mail carrier on a pile of packages. Even visits to Fabricio's became uncomfortable. When he introduced Claudia to other Salvadoran guys, he'd say: "You see how beautiful is my woman?" They knew him well enough to nod yes or risk offending him, but they couldn't agree with any enthusiasm or he would start yelling, "You looking at my woman!?" when he hit the malt liquor tipping point.

One afternoon in June, Eli and I climbed up to the new clear-cut above River Kerry's place. We sat on one of the raw, wet stumps and mourned the death of the trees together. Then I spent an hour complaining to him about my unraveling life.

"Look, dude," he tried to comfort me. "At least it can't get any worse."

But he was wrong, things got worse, for both of us.

Leopoldo and Claudia lost their job at the bulb factory. It had taken Leopoldo less than a week to begin complaining that his back hurt from leaning over the conveyor belt all day. Then he started limiting his workweek to Saturdays and Sundays, based on the theory that the clueless boss would think he was a go-getter and overlook his fraudulent time cards for the other five days of the week. When this didn't work out, Leopoldo began griping about how he was being exploited. My mother supported his charges of exploitation because she noticed the nefarious timing of the raids by *La Migra*. Immigration officials came like clockwork to haul off half the workforce the day before payday. Finally Leopoldo denounced the boss in front of the whole processing plant: "You exploit the workers! You are motherfucker!" And they were both fired on the spot.

A few days later we were evicted. The landowner came up from Seattle to tell us he was selling his timber rights to a logging company. The whole forest would be clear-cut. The cabins would be razed, and nothing would remain but a wasteland of stumps. We needed to get out ASAP.

Maybe some good could come out of this, I thought. Maybe we could rent a house in Mount Vernon, complete with lights and a television and, dare I dream, a toilet. But Claudia's face was taut with worst-case scenarios. "Now that I'm married I can't qualify for Welfare. We've got no jobs, no money, no car. What are we doing to do?" All these problems made Leopoldo thirsty, and he went outside for a warm beer and a joint.

Our savior came in the unexpected form of Crazy John, who stopped by with his girlfriend Erica to tell us they were moving out to Camano Island, off the coast of Snohomish County. His family had some raw land out there, he told us, and he and Erica were going to build a home together. Leopoldo's eyes swiveled up from his smoldering blunt with opportunistic curiosity. My mother's face softened, and she raised her eyes in thanksgiving. When Crazy John heard that we were being displaced by Capitalistic Earth-rapers coming to murder the trees that he once called friends, he naturally invited us to come along with him. "It's the least I can do, Claudia, after all those months you let me sleep naked in your car."

We piled into Erica's powder-blue AMC Gremlin like preschoolers on their way to the zoo. Crazy John, nominally sitting in the front passenger seat, filled up my entire field of vision. Erica had him lift his leg every time she wanted to shift gears. Her brown hair was worn in a perfectly even bowl cut, which gave her the appearance of a medieval monk. She was never without pink bubble gum and a Pepsi, and cracked anal sex jokes for most of the hour-long ride to Camano Island. My mother gesticulated excitedly the whole way, talking at Crazy John and Erica about the Spirits and intentional community and about how we were going to start a new civilization together on the land.

"Look, Joshey, look!" Claudia was pointing animatedly at a wall of temperate rainforest. "Look at those trees!" I *was* looking at those trees and it was not good news. Forget electricity and television, there wasn't even a structure out here, not even a mailbox. Upon closer inspection, there wasn't even a clearing in which to build a structure. But Leopoldo and Claudia saw potential. They squinted their eyes and waved at various patches of trees and walked back to the car holding hands.

"Is Leopoldo coming with us?" I asked when we'd returned to Janicki Road to throw our belongings into cardboard boxes. I knew he was, but asked the question anyway, wanting some assurance that things would somehow be better when we were squatting in the woods out on the island.

"Of course he is, Joshey. He's going to build us a pyramid to live in, like in ancient Egypt. And you are going to have your own room. But, in exchange, you're going to have to be more responsible when we get there. You know how your friend Eli is always volunteering to help out, to clean up? Well, you're going to have to be more like Eli."

The day before we moved to Camano, I wandered down to Eli's house one last time to say good-bye. His house was empty and windswept. A few articles of clothing and some kitchen utensils littered the floor, but the place was abandoned. Their neighbor told me they had evacuated in a panic a few nights back, just ahead of a DEA raid. The doors were open, and I found a family of raccoons squatting in my friend's room. Everything was wet and hopeless. Out back was a little warehouse where Richard had kept a flock of sticky green pot plants, striving to reach blinding grow-lights above. It was abandoned now, nothing but empty shelves and a layer of crackling glass on the floor. I began rummaging through a set of little drawers, looking for some clue that would explain why everything was falling apart. Instead I found dozens of tiny plastic bags. All empty, save one. This one held a pair of shriveled stems. I didn't know why, but I knew they were shrooms. I couldn't remember whether they were poisonous or psychedelic or both. But it didn't matter. I chewed both of them. Bitter, soapy. But nothing happened.

I made it halfway up the trail toward home before the shrooms hit. Then I felt compelled to lie down in a mud puddle and further examine two white rocks glittering in the gravel. They were like Stonehenge, only more ancient. And here *I* was to be a part of this important place. I rearranged the sparkling white obelisks, and they were joined on all sides by a dozen more shiny white standing stones, piling themselves up into cairns and henges. Memorials for the dead, monuments for the living. I orchestrated the construction of a great primitive temple where all were free to pray to the Sun and Moon, the Stars and the Heavens. This was to be the last ceremony of the peoples and then we would all be drowned and gone. I rolled onto my back, and the oval green leaves above shimmered and flashed, tinkling with a thousand bells, capturing all that was beautiful, all that was fragile, before the nuclear winter enveloped us all. And I slept. And I woke, shivering, soaked through with muddy water and nauseated. I staggered up to the cabin and slept in my little loft one last time.

THIRTEEN

The Fall of Carthage

My blade flashed back and forth in the shadows, biting at the darkness with decreasing enthusiasm. "My machete arm's sore," I complained.

"Don't think of it as work, Josh," Claudia encouraged me. "Think of it as an adventure."

"But my arm still hurts."

"Think of it as founding a new community."

Claudia and I spent the whole day hacking a passable trail into the untamed land on Camano Island. Leopoldo couldn't join us because he was hitchhiking into Stanwood, on the mainland, to buy handsaws, nails, beer, and the other things he would need to build us a pyramid. At nightfall, we sat down in the wet moss, panting and sweaty. The machetes were smeared with green slime and dinged up. We'd cleared a path maybe twenty feet into the forest. A thousand more feet waited for us. Then we could begin felling trees to create a clearing on which we could construct a shelter. After a few days of this, my right arm was numb, and I was plagued with mosquito bites.

On my first trip into Stanwood my feet led me directly to the pay phone outside of Safeway to call Uncle Tony collect. It was my only way out. He agreed to pay for my Greyhound bus ticket down to San Francisco for a visit, but he wouldn't agree to let me live with him. Claudia saw me off at the Greyhound station in Mount Vernon and, after I spent a couple of days sitting next to a narcoleptic Korean War veteran, the bus rolled into San Francisco.

Tony's apartment above the bar was unchanged. The white crown molding I had gazed up at as a little kid, worrying about nuclear war, was still crumbling above me. The green chair in the corner hadn't moved an inch, and Tony's prayer book still lay open to the Gayatri Mantra. The apartment was an island in time, the only constancy and certainty left in my world.

Tony made chorizo for himself and quesadillas for me.

"Why can't I live with you?" I asked again.

"Because Claudey sent you down for a visit, not to stay."

"She won't mind. And Leopoldo would be happy. He says I'm lazy and just in the way all the time."

"Let's call Claudey."

"We don't have a phone, remember? We don't even have an address anymore."

"Well, I have a month of vacation saved, so let's enjoy the rest of our two weeks in the City and then we'll go up to Expo '86 in Vancouver like we planned, OK?"

"Or, we could just stay here and not go back to Washington."

"Where would you stay, Mr. Josh?"

"Here, with you."

"I have to work."

"Big deal. I'd just wait for you to get home. I'm used to taking care of myself."

"All night, every night while I'm mopping up the State building, you'd be here by yourself in the apartment?"

"Sure."

"What about school?"

"What about it? I'm not even going to school now."

"No, Josh. It can't be that bad."

"It is."

The next day we went out to see Monty Python's *Life of Brian* at the Red Vic, a repertory theater with couches and tofu burgers. The comedy distracted me from my impending return to the barbarian north.

All evening I did impressions of the farcical Judean zealots complaining about all the good things the Romans had done for them. "It's funny on two levels," explained Uncle Tony, "because of the irony of their discontent, but also because it was true. That's really what the Romans would do. They'd come in first under a white flag. As simple merchants wanting to trade. Then they brought in roads, then settlers, then public works and temples, then armies for protection. The next thing you knew, you had to pay them taxes, bow down before their gods, and sacrifice all the freedoms that made your people special. That's what they called the Roman Peace. It was peace as long as you did everything they told you to do."

"The Romans were like Leopoldo," I decided. "He came to us as a refugee, all innocent. Then he moved in. The next thing you know he makes Claudia drop out of school. She loses her Welfare and her job, and now we don't even have a house."

"I know," said Tony.

"And, he threw out my painting of the train after Claudia said it captured the spirit of the railroad. He was jealous that she liked it."

"Really?"

"Yes, and then he took my guitar. And he even renamed Benji."

"Your dog?"

"Yeah."

"What did he name her?"

"Chisquiarisquistisquis."

"What? Chorizo?"

"Chisquiarisquistisquis."

"That," said Tony solemnly, "may be his greatest mistake."

We both laughed. In the familiar apartment, above the bar on Sixteenth and Sanchez, the things I was complaining about seemed impossible and far away.

After a couple of weeks, my brief furlough in Tony's city of refuge had come to an end. Tony was taking me back to the field of battle. But first we had a week planned at the World's Fair in Vancouver, British Columbia.

At the Douglas Border Crossing, two uniformed Canada Customs agents boarded our idling Greyhound bus. The dark interior enveloped them in a pall of diesel fumes, cigarette smoke, and sour human breath. The agents grimaced and removed their reflective sunglasses, blinking in the unnatural darkness. Scanning from side to side, they made their way down the aisle, surveying the rows of would-be border crossers. It was the standard collection of American tourists coming north for the World's Fair with a few seasonal berry pickers thrown into the mix. But near the back of the bus, the agents stopped to scrutinize something out of the ordinary.

They considered the big brown fellow and the little white boy a suspicious duo. The big fellow had long black hair and wore steel-toed black boots and a black bomber jacket. He didn't have a passport or a driver's license. He was trying to get over the border with some sort of California identity card that bore the name Antonio Rodriguez. But despite the Spanish name and the incongruous long black beard, he looked like an Indian to them. A Nez Perce or an Okanagan, maybe. The little white boy with the curly brown hair and blue eyes didn't have any ID at all. The two agents looked at each other. This wasn't going to happen. Not on their watch.

They pulled Uncle Tony and me off the bus like a couple of wanted fugitives. We were hustled through a vacant parking lot toward a cluster of buildings. By the time we were ushered into the lobby of the customs building we were completely enveloped in a sea of khakied figures. The current of the crowd veered me to the left, and suddenly Uncle Tony was no longer beside me.

"Hey!" I stopped. "Tony!?" I called out, pushing against the tide of bustling agents.

"Ja-ash!?" I heard Tony calling back to me from around the corner, a touch of concern in his voice. A hand pushed down against my shoulder and a strange meaty face topped with a crew cut filled my field of vision: "Sir, we need . . ."

I interrupted him: "Get out of my face." I twisted out of his grasp and snaked my way back through the eddy of moving khaki figures. Out of the swirl of motion, Tony loomed ahead, fixed in place like an immovable pillar clad in black. His long black hair and black beard guarded his round brown face. I ran to his side. Tony bent to one knee and brought me in for a hug.

"What the hell's going on?" I asked.

One of the agents from the bus leaned down to me: "Sir, please come with us."

"No way."

The agent joined our huddle on one knee. In a gentler, almost pleading tone: "Sir, we'd like to just ask ya a couple a questions. OK?" His singsong Canadian accent was detectable and silly enough to make him seem less menacing. "Just around here, OK?" he said, pointing down the hall. "Then, we'll bring ya right back to your big friend here, okeydoke?"

Tony looked me in the eyes and nodded: "Mr. Josh, you will be *fine*. I will be right here waiting for you."

"OK," I agreed. The agent put his hand on my shoulder again. "Don't touch me," I said. He stepped ahead of me, and I followed his military gait down the hall to a bare room inhabited only by a small metal table and three black chairs. At the doorway we were joined by another agent. They sat me down on one side of the table and then seated themselves across from me. I felt like the suspect in a detective movie. Who do they think I am? I asked myself. Some perpetrator running cocaine and Chinese prostitutes over the border? I'm a ten-year-old kid, jackasses.

The meaty-faced one began asking me questions while his pudgy, pasty-faced partner appeared to be filling out a form of some kind.

"Sir, what's your name?"

"Me?" No one had ever called me "sir" before.

"Yes."

"Josh."

"What's your full name?"

"Joshua."

"What's your family name?"

"I don't have one."

"Ya don't have a family name?"

"No."

"You're just called Joshua?"

"No, I have a last name."

"Yes, sir, that's what we're looking for."

"Reed. But that's not a family name."

"What do you mean, sir?"

"I mean I'm the only one who has that name."

"What's your father's name?"

"Claude Palmer, but he's not legally my father."

"Um, OK. Who's legally your father?"

"No one."

"Uh, OK, sir. What's your mother's name?"

"Claudia . . . Suárez, now."

"Suárez?"

"Yeah. That's her husband's name."

"OK, and sir, what was her name before that? Reed?"

"No, it was Rhys."

"Rhys?"

"Yeah, but that was the name of her husband from before I was born. He was a Black Panther, but he kind of wasn't black. He was half Carib Indian and half Jewish."

"Wait, sir. So her maiden name was Reed?"

"No, she was Domas, but that was shortened from Domashevitsky."

"Sir, where did Reed come from?"

"That was her pen name at this poetry workshop in the 1970s. It was after this Communist writer, John Reed, who wrote about the Russian Revolution and a line in this book called the Talmud that says it's better to be like a reed than a tree."

There was a long silence, and the two men stared at me, both blinking in confusion.

"Look, sir. We're going round and round here. Do you know Antonio Rodriguez, your traveling companion—the big fellow with the long black hair and the like?"

"Yeah, that's Tony."

"So do ya know him, sir?"

"Yeah, that's what I just said."

"Well, ya didn't say that, sir. Ya said, 'That's Tony,' not that you knew him."

"Yeah, I know him."

"I see. Now we're getting somewhere. And how do you know him, sir?"

"He's my uncle."

This was very surprising to the customs agents. "*Really*? So, is he your mother's brother?"

"No."

"Your father's brother?"

"No."

"Is he married to one of your aunties?"

"My *aunties*? No, he's not married to anyone."

"So how are you related to him then?"

"He's my uncle."

"Sir, you've just admitted he's not your uncle."

"I didn't admit anything. I *just* said he's my uncle."

"Sir, look here, now. We know he's not related to you. That's clear enough. Not by blood. Not by marriage. So he's *not* your uncle."

Holy crap! I thought. One of my mother's prophecies was finally coming true. I really was being harassed by the police. She'd always prepared me for the day they'd come for me. The FBI, the CIA, the System. They would detain and arrest and beat me for being different, for being a subversive. But it was all wrong. I was being interrogated by the *Canadians*! Canada was supposed to be the place you escaped to. The land beneath the North Star, where fugitive slaves and draft dodgers went to be free. But it was the Canadians who were treating me like a criminal for being different. And then I felt something new and strange. A guilty pride in my own country. My mother had raised me to hate America, but I was feeling what could only be described as patriotism.

I spoke now with the stars and stripes at my back. "He *is* my uncle. I'm from *America*, see? It's a free country. In *America* you can have whoever the fuck you want as your uncle."

"Sir, language!"

"I can talk however I want."

"Sir, did Rodriguez tell you to say that?"

"What?"

"Did Rodriguez tell you to say he was your 'uncle'? Did he threaten you? Or your family? Did he hurt you? Your mother doesn't know where you are, does she?"

I finally got it. They weren't after me. They were after Tony. They thought Uncle Tony was kidnapping me. It took me a while to process this because I couldn't imagine a face, a person more familiar to me than Tony. He was such a fixture in my life that I'd always assumed we looked related somehow. And then panic overcame me. Tony was all I had left, and now they were trying to take him away from me.

"Do you guys think I'm being kidnapped!? I'm not being kidnapped!"

"Well, sir, that's your word, not ours."

"Well I'm not being kidnapped. Can I go now?"

"No, sir."

"You know what, you guys are idiots."

"Sir!?"

"No, let me tell you, *sir*. This is really totally fucking ironic. Tony—that guy out there—was the one who was actually kidnapped as a kid. *Tony*. And now, he's like the most responsible person I've got. He's basically like my father. Now, it would be real nice, I'm sure, to just call my mother to straighten this out. But we can't because we don't have a phone because she and her husband, Leopoldo, are in the forest building a *pyramid*. Yeah, like ancient Egypt. And I don't have to be stripping bark or hacking branches right now because this is supposed to be my one fun thing this summer. To go with *Uncle* Tony to Expo '86 in Vancouver. Tony came all the way up from San Francisco to take me. He spent all his money on tickets and everything, and now you're asking me retarded questions in some closet like I'm a criminal. *I* didn't do anything wrong. *Tony* didn't do anything wrong. Just let us go!" I crossed my arms and started to cry as I imagined leaping across the table and tearing into them.

They walked me back down the hall. I could sense them quivering in their khaki uniforms with indignation and frustration. Tony was sitting where I'd left him, reading a book. On the coffee table in front of him were piled high his volumes of Heidegger, Schopenhauer, and the Bhagavad Gita. It was his subtle way of telling them that they could detain him for another three months for all he cared. He'd have plenty to read. Amid glares and stiff "sirs," I was formally released back to Tony's custody. We walked out into the sunlight, and Tony looked down at me and smiled. "Now wasn't that easy?" He always said that. Because it was never easy.

The Customs agents didn't have the mettle to arrest us, but that didn't mean they had to let us over the border. We were formally denied entry into the country, and ejected onto a traffic island in the netherworld between nation states. Tony's nonrefundable Expo tickets were now totally worthless and his Greyhound bus tickets led to nowhere.

"What a rip-off!" I yelled back at Canada.

They were highway robbers! And worse. They'd stolen my last liberty of the summer. Now I had nothing left to look forward to. Nothing was left between me and my return to servitude on Camano Island.

"Fucking bastards!" I yelled.

Oddly enough, the United States Canada Peace Anniversary Association had elected to celebrate the world's longest peaceful border by riveting an engraved stone and aluminum standing ashtray onto our traffic island. Now it was the embodiment for all that was wrong in my life. I spit and swore at the ashtray: "Fuck you!" Then I began kicking it over and over. Kick, spin, kick. Tony sat on the bench reading, making an effort not to notice me. In the middle of my next spin, I saw a bristling Customs agent crossing the street from Canada. I kicked harder, perfecting the form of my roundhouse the way Leopoldo had shown me.

"Sir! Hey! That's public property, sir!"

I kept kicking, like a kung fu professional in the dojo.

"Sir!"

I stopped and turned to address the moustachioed face of authority.

"Fuck you! You don't like it!? Well, this is what happens when you fuck with people's lives!"

The face shook with impotent rage and crossed back into Canada.

Tony spoke into the intervening silence. "Josh, come here."

"No."

"Please, sit down for a second." He patted the bench next to him. "You know who my hero was when I was a kid?" I didn't know, which was strange because I thought I knew everything there was to know about him.

"Hold on," I said. Who was it? Who could have been his role model when he was little, kidnapped from his family, and raised by an abusive Cuban lady? I unclenched my fists and sat down to think about it. It couldn't have been Arjuna, or some Hindu character, because he wouldn't have been exposed to them yet. Someone from TV probably, since there were no friendly faces in his childhood. Who were those old-time tough guys?

"Was it John Wayne?" I guessed.

"Nope."

"Dick Tracy?"

"Nope. Give up?"

"Yeah."

"Bugs Bunny."

"No it wasn't." He was trying to be funny.

"It was. Bugs Bunny was my hero. He still is. You could stick a shotgun in his face. You could throw him in boiling water. You could try to kill him any number of ways. But he never lost his cool. He never let them see him angry. If you go around, Josh, giving in to your anger and being violent, you're going to scare people. And eventually you're going to hurt someone, and then they'll lock you up, or worse. Just because you're being bullied doesn't mean you get to pass it on."

I wanted to tell him to shut up, but I knew I wouldn't get a rise out of him. He'd just go back to reading his stupid book.

Eventually a southbound bus came across the border, and we left the 49th parallel to recover from the biggest threat to American-Canadian relations since the War of 1812. We'd only covered a few miles before we realized we had nowhere to go. Claudia wasn't due to pick us up at the bus station in Mount Vernon for another week, and we had no way to contact her.

We climbed off the bus in the city of Bellingham, where we wandered around the suburban streets, counting down to the end of the week. In the evening at our hotel we played chess and quizzed each other on the Roman names for Greek gods. It was an old game. When I was little Tony told me the Greek myths as bedtime stories.

It was his turn. "Ares."

He'd given me an easy one. "Mars," I said.

"Hestia," I volleyed back.

Tony thought about it. "You got me, Joshey, what is it?"

"Her Roman name was Vesta. She was the goddess of the hearth."

"Good one."

"Why do the Greek gods have Roman names anyway?" I'd never thought to ask before. "I mean, why didn't the Romans have their own gods?"

"Because the Romans were nothing but *thugs*." Tony's face filled with emotion. "Everyone thinks of Rome as this magnificent empire—buildings, science, art—but everything they had they stole from the Etruscans, the Samnites, the Greeks. The only thing they came up with themselves, the only thing they were good at, was violence. They figured out how to put together these unstoppable armies and they destroyed anyone that wouldn't bow down to them." Rome was reminding me of Leopoldo again. "When they destroyed Carthage, they even tore up the paving stones. Then they salted the Earth to make sure nothing would ever grow there again."

"I feel like my life is Carthage," I said.

Tony's face soured. "Don't worry, Mr. Josh. I'll talk to Claudia."

"She won't listen to you."

"She doesn't have to listen to *me*. She just has to listen to reason. No one has a right to treat her like that. To treat you like that. She knows that. She's a *feminist*, Mr. Josh."

"It doesn't matter. She won't hear you," I said. "She's been conquered."

Tony heard me, how serious I was, and lapsed into silence. "Well, if that's true," he said slowly, "at least you'll always have me."

We had reunion rituals, my mother and I. Time-honored traditions dating back to the summer she'd left me for Mexico. When we saw each other again, we jumped up and down. We smiled until it hurt and hugged each other hard enough to make up for lost time. Then she was supposed to notice how much I'd grown, how much taller I was, what a crazy haircut someone had given me. The tradition ended on the steps to the ramshackle bus station in Mount Vernon. Uncle Tony had given her plenty to comment on. I had a shiny corporate haircut, a brand-new Casio wristwatch, a faux leather jacket, and a blue book bag filled with dreams of school for the fall. But if she noticed she didn't say anything. She was wearing muddy velour pants and a filthy yellow tank top, stained with sweat and drizzles of sap. She'd left the machete in the car and was eager to get back to it.

"Claudia, notice anything different about me?"

"You look like a city slicker."

She greeted Tony with perfunctory efficiency and warned him that his week with us couldn't be a vacation. "We've got a lot of work to do before the rains come. Leopoldo is already worried about the two hours I'm wasting picking you guys up."

"So he's already mad?" My voice carried a note of exaggerated distress. I was playing it up for Tony.

"No, I wouldn't say he's mad," Claudia patiently explained. "In fact I wouldn't say he has any negative feelings at all. I think he's just curious, Josh. Really trying to understand why you'd leave right when the hard work began. We've been busting our asses, Josh, and I guess I'm a little curious too."

Leopoldo had won the game before it even started. He'd obviously been working on my mother all month, and now I was cast in stone as the lazy, ungrateful child. We crossed over the Skagit River without speaking. Tony chipped at the icy silence from time to time with "Ooh, look, Claudey, cows!" but no one was laughing.

When we arrived, Leopoldo was too busy hauling logs to say hello to us. He'd yoked himself with a chain to a fat length of spruce and was furrowing the forest floor in a painful progression of inches. His bare torso flexed mightily against the shiny silver links of chain. His face contorted with grimaces and growls, and he slowly, triumphantly dragged the large chunk of tree out of the circle of stumps, my mother running around uselessly behind him the whole time. This impressive feat accomplished, he made the time to come over and meet Uncle Tony. They were an odd mismatch, these two men. Uncle Tony towered far above Leopoldo, looking like he'd been plucked from the Eastern Philosophy section of a bookstore in North Beach and accidentally dropped into a rainforest with Bruce Lee's Mayan cousin. Tony carried a jacket and newspaper under his right arm, and a black umbrella hung from his left wrist. Leopoldo shimmered with sweat and sized Tony up like an opponent going into the next cage match. Then he offered Tony a crushing handshake and spoke in rapid-fire Spanish. Tony was slow and rusty in his childhood tongue. Leopoldo took advantage of it, never letting Tony slip back into English. Then it was back to work.

Tony and I were tasked with finding more rocks for the fire pit. After an hour of climbing through bushes we found ourselves lost. "Can't we just stop and ask for directions?" asked Uncle Tony. He was joking. We were shown the way home by a thunderous crashing in the distant canopy where Leopoldo was bringing a tree down. When we climbed back into the little clearing, Uncle Tony sang out: "Oh, Josh, where's the bathroom?" This time he wasn't joking. I pointed to a large stand of ferns, and Tony cringed the same way he did when he forgot to put sweetener in his coffee. He disappeared into the bushes with two rolls of toilet paper, a gallon of water, and a bottle of soap. He came back an hour later declaring he was never going to go to the bathroom again.

We still didn't have a big enough clearing to hold the great pyramid Leopoldo was going to build, but we had enough room for Claudia's planned art studio. The ground remained studded with stumps, but Leopoldo had concluded they were impossible to pull up, so we would simply integrate them into the building design. "Stumps as foundations!" Claudia loved the idea. She was animated by the new buildings that would soon rise from the forest floor. She twirled her fingers where her kiln would sit and waved at the imaginary corner for the nonexistent potter's wheel. We talked our way, mother and son, further into the forest, leaving the men by the campfire to roast soy dogs with Crazy John and Erica.

We talked about the coming fall, and Claudia agreed that I could give school a try again if I were willing to risk the public middle school in Stanwood. I told her I was more than willing. I was eager! But she was hardly listening, still smiling to herself as if enjoying a most wonderful dream. Then she shared with me the full ballad of Leopoldo, chanting on and on about him with stories I'd never heard before. She told me about Leopoldo's days in the dormant volcano with the FMLN. His time in the jungle when the Revolution was near collapse. His nights of agony and survival in the torture chambers. About the pretty girl he'd rescued from the death squads and about how he'd reluctantly agreed to be her lover when she'd insisted. How they'd fallen in love and how the death squads had raped her and torn her body apart one rainy night. And there were things she couldn't tell me: Leopoldo's nom de guerre, the secrets of his escape from El Salvador, the identities of government officials who'd risked and even lost their lives to ensure that Leopoldo survived. She was in love with him in a new way now.

She didn't say it, but I could see she was drinking in Leopoldo through every pore. She was lost and gone. He'd taken her from me.

That night we slept on plastic sheets laid against the forest floor. Tony crinkled back and forth and sighed loudly into the darkness. Leopoldo was up before dawn, hacking branches down over our heads. And he spent the rest of the day agitating against Tony, pulling Claudia aside to discuss each new problem with this strange man I'd brought into camp. Claudia became the herald of their mutual displeasure, and she wasn't afraid to let Tony know what he'd done wrong. He'd never once offered to help chop down trees or haul logs. What he had been given to do, the simple task of collecting rocks for the fire pit, he'd failed at. Instead of volunteering to sharpen the saw blades or strip bark from the logs, he'd been spotted sitting on a stump, reading a book. Who did he think he was? Reading a book while everyone else was working? What kind of a role model was he trying to be?

Tony took it all in without saying a word in his own defense. Instead he sought redemption by peeling an entire sack of potatoes. But that wasn't enough. I overheard Leopoldo complaining to Claudia the next morning. "I can tell by the way he speaks Spanish that he is Mexican." *Mexican*. The dreaded word hung in the air, and then Leopoldo connected the dots. "He remind me of one Mexican I know, same long fingers, he move the same. He was a knife fighter, and he try to take my woman. Why you think he is here, Claudia, why?"

The time for the showdown had arrived. Leopoldo screwed up his face tight and swaggered over to the stump where Uncle Tony was still hunched over his potato peeler, trying to be useful.

"Why you come here?" Leopoldo addressed him in English. "Huh? You buy all the fancy clothes for the boy. You make to embarrass me? Because we are poors? You know I cannot buy him these. You watch, but you no work." His fists were clenched now. His red tank top clung to his rising chest. "I know why you come. You come for to take my woman. To San Francisco. But she already make up her mind. She choose me. She no want you here no more. We making a family here. Now you have to go."

Tony stood up very slowly. He carefully put the potato peeler down on the stump. Leopoldo took a step back and readied himself for the fight. But Tony walked away silently and gathered up his jacket, umbrella, and black duffel bag from the plastic sheeting. When he came back his head was bowed and he spoke in soft tones. "Leopoldo, *con permiso*," he began, and asked permission to speak with my mother alone in private. Leopoldo thought this over and finally nodded his head yes. "Come on, Claudey," Tony nodded to my mother, "let's talk." They walked out of the circle of stumps, Tony shuffling, head down, Claudia marching behind him, her jaw fixed tight.

Leopoldo paced back and forth behind me. I pretended to wipe the mud off of my shoes with an old T-shirt, leaning forward to pick up scraps of conversation. Claudia's voice ratcheted louder with each rebuttal. She was throwing it back at him. She didn't know what *he* was thinking, didn't know what planet *he* was living on. Uncle Tony didn't raise his voice until the very end. He concluded with: "Then you *are* crazy, aren't you, Claudia!?"

We drove Uncle Tony back to the bus station in a devastated silence. Tony stared out the window at the cows through a cloud of despair. Claudia gripped the wheel from behind a steely mask. I sat in back with mute tears flowing down my face. I'd stopped sobbing by the time we'd loaded Tony's duffel bag into the car, and my heaving and wailing had subsided by the time we crossed over onto the mainland. I was left with a jagged swelling in my throat and a heaviness in my chest.

At the bus station, Tony bent down onto one knee to give me a good-bye hug. His eyes were puffy.

"Am I ever gonna see you again!?" I cried out, wanting him to make it all better somehow.

"I don't know . . . Josh," he choked out. Then he was sobbing, and we just held each other crying, a strange island of defeat in a bustling crowd of people jostling their way toward opportunities elsewhere. Tony walked away from me slowly, his head held down in permanent sorrow. I waited for him to turn back one last time, but he didn't. He disappeared onto the bus and was gone.

I cried the whole return trip to the island. When we climbed back into the circle of stumps, Leopoldo was in a great mood. He was a big smile, enjoying a cigarette in a patch of sunlight. He put me in a headlock and then gripped me around the shoulder. "Look, Josh. I cut down a big tree."

The next day my mother wrote in her dream journal:

Tony went home yesterday both genuinely distressed and enjoying his sense of self-pity and innocent suffering . . . Poor little Josh—it seems that heartbreak + premature separation has been the theme of his life all this year . . . I felt that I was rescuing him from a dangerous state of trance and that his terrible pain was akin to drug withdrawal—have the strong conviction that he will become less and less eager to share unreality with Uncle T. . . . Josh was shaken apart—but seemed in the process to have broken free of his slick city shell . . . he emerged the loving and sensitive child I have so sorely missed. Leopoldo said, "It feels like we got you back again" and Josh cuddled into him with a great sigh of relief.

What she mistook for a sigh of relief was actually a groan of surrender. The walls of my life had been razed to the ground. The earth had been sown with salt.

FOURTEEN

If a Tree Falls . . .

On September 2, 1986, I awoke in the predawn darkness, damp, flecked with tree needles, but eager for the day. I was eleven years old and it was the first day of middle school. Not home-school, not some meditation school. A real school, well lit and warm. Full of books and certainty and opportunities to shine. Tony had told me that if I worked hard enough I could be a lawyer or a doctor or anything I wanted. School was my chance at a better life.

I hadn't slept well, partly because of the anxiety that came before the first day of school, and partly because of the "bed" itself. We were sleeping on the forest floor on wooden pallets salvaged from the dumpsters behind Thrifty Foods. Our communal "bed" was lined with flattened cardboard and topped with an old tattered tarp. The ribs of the wooden pallet dug into my hips and shoulders all night. When I turned over, the whole thing rocked, threatening to wake up Leopoldo, which would have thrown him into a rage. In the middle of the night some nocturnal creature had come sniffing through our campsite. A raccoon? A badger? Something bigger? Whatever it was, it came so close I could hear it crinkling the tarp as it probed Leopoldo's side of the "bed." After that it was hard to fall back asleep.

I was already dressed. I'd slept in my school clothes, afraid that I wouldn't be able to find them in the misty darkness. Claudia had found the camel sweater and brown slacks I was wearing at the Salvation Army, likely donated by the estate of some small dead professor. She had patched up the holes in the elbows and one knee with a blue paisley fabric. They were the best clothes I had.

I rinsed my fingers clean with water poured from a reused plastic milk jug. First the right hand and then the left, leaning forward with my legs spread wide to avoid getting my pants wet or splattered with mud. I rinsed out my mouth next, gargling the icy water and swallowing it. My gums ached from the coldness and my tongue clung to the stale taste of leached plastic. I poured out more water into the palm of my hand and rubbed around my eyes. I ran my wet fingers through my greasy hair, combing out bits of forest debris. I hadn't had a real shower in weeks and didn't own a toothbrush, a hairbrush, or a mirror.

My morning grooming completed, I retrieved my blue plastic book bag from under the tarp and began making my way across the campsite. The glow of morning was now filtering down through the forest canopy but a heavy mist still clung to the ground. As I reached the perimeter of our little clearing, I looked back to see the outline of my mother squatting to pee at the base of a spruce tree. I didn't turn back to say good-bye. I had a schedule to keep. I had paced out the path to the road in the preceding days and knew it should take me about seven minutes. But that was assuming full daylight, and I didn't have much extra time budgeted in case I got lost or got stuck in a patch of stinging nettles. As it was, I made it to the octagonal cabin where Crazy John lived with little trouble and followed his well-beaten path straight to the road.

I emerged from the wall of forest right where I wanted to be—directly across from the DEER XING sign. The black silhouette of the crossing deer had a bullet hole in its head. This was the spot, I'd been told, where the school bus to the mainland would stop.

A group of kids was already congregated around the sign. They were staring at me as I stepped out from under the shelter of the forest canopy. I must have looked like a wild animal. The oldest kid—a big, solid girl with acne—stepped defensively in front of the others. I hopped over the little drainage ditch and crossed the road.

"Is this where the bus stops?" I called out. I extended my hand as I approached. "I'm Josh," I said, introducing myself with my best smile. No response. "I'm starting sixth grade."

"Where did you come from!?" the big girl spat back. She stepped toward me, her hands raised in front of her. She was wearing black jeans and a black ski jacket. Her hair was dark brown, cut close to the top of her head but incongruously billowing out in long curls from the back. She looked to be fourteen or fifteen years old.

I didn't know how I should answer her question. I clearly couldn't tell her the truth. But how much of my story did I need to lie about? I smiled and gestured casually back at the woods across the road: "Oh, we're building a house out here. You know, just got the land, just getting started." I nodded, trying to pretend like I was a normal kid, a new neighbor on the Island from somewhere normal.

The big girl didn't seem to buy it. Her fists balled up. The other kids crowded around just behind her, staring at me. One of them was clearly her little sister. She had the same square blocky face but without the acne. The other two were siblings. They both had tapered, equine faces anchored by prominent buck teeth and were wearing acid-washed blue jeans and fleece-lined denim jackets. Their blond hair was feathered up in graceful swoops. They looked so clean.

The big girl's little sister pointed at me and shrieked: "A spider! He's got a spider!"

I followed her gaze to my chest, where a big brown hairy spider was strolling over onto my left arm. I flicked the spider off quickly but saw that my sweater was speckled with little twigs and tendrils of moss and lichen. I began brushing myself off matter-of-factly and looked up with a grin as if to say: "Whoopsy! Don't know how that got there."

The big girl stepped forward and shoved me hard with both hands.

"Get out of here! You're not supposed to be here!" She kept after me, driving me back several steps with each shove. She was strong and dwarfed me in size. She shoved me again. The shoulder of the roadway had turned to gravel, and I almost lost my balance as I slipped on the loose rocks. The bus stop was receding into the distance. I finally pushed back at her, yelling: "Cut it out! Leave me alone."

Her face screwed into a vicious scowl and she began throwing punches at me. One glanced off the side of my face. The next punch landed square in my chest and paralyzed me for a moment. I gasped for breath. She grabbed my shoulders and pulled me down into her bosom—she smelled like fresh soap—and then she drove her knee up into my belly. I hugged myself defensively, doubling over. She charged at me hard from the left and knocked me off my feet. My right shoulder hit the gravel, and the side of my face slid along the ground. The dirt was dry and chalky. She shoved me with her foot, and I slid down into the little gravel ditch that ran along the edge of the roadway.

The strap of my book bag broke in the fall and a cascade of pens, pencils, and notepads tumbled into the trickle of water at the bottom of the ditch. I began sobbing. Before Leopoldo had sent him back to San Francisco, Uncle Tony had spent the last of his money buying me the book bag and school supplies at Pay-N-Pak. We'd picked them out carefully to prepare me for the new year. I scrambled around on hands and knees gathering up these little scholastic talismans. The pens and pencils I fished out could be dried, but the notepads where already turning to pulp, the blue lines of the paper bleeding into uselessness. On my knees, I looked up at the big girl, holding the mortally wounded remains of my hopes for the year in my lap.

"Look what you did!" I choked out. "You fucking bitch!" I screamed at her—a line I'd learned from Leopoldo.

Looking down at me, the big girl tightened her lips and jutted her jaw forward. She jumped down into the ditch and kicked me in the shoulder and again in the side, and then scrambled back out. She walked back toward the bus stop, apparently finished with me.

Squatting in the ditch, I tried to regain my composure. I knew I shouldn't let the other kids see me cry. I took a few deep breaths and then busied myself resuscitating my book bag. I'd packed that bag so precisely, wanting everything to be perfect for my first day of school. Now it was all ruined. I dried my school supplies as best I could on my pant legs, leaving wet streaks across my thighs. The two halves of the strap from my book bag hung impotent and unusable. The hard plastic buckle that had held them together was broken into pieces. I tied the two halves together, pulling the soft plastic straps tightly into a double knot.

My work completed, I climbed out of the ditch and dusted myself off. The big girl was standing, arms crossed, at the line where gravel turned to asphalt. I got it. That was her line of demarcation. I was now about fifty feet from the bus stop where the other kids were gathered, but I wasn't going to attempt a border crossing with the big girl standing sentinel. I'd have to wait her out.

The bus came growling around the corner behind me and passed within a foot of where I was standing on the narrow shoulder. Faded yellow, riddled with rivets. The bus stopped up ahead of the sign and the doors opened. Thick clouds of black diesel smoke chugged up from the exhaust pipe. The other kids ran forward. But the big girl wasn't budging. She just stood there, arms crossed, guarding the border. I watched as the other kids disappeared up into the bus, but she still didn't move. Out the back window a line of faces blankly witnessed our standoff. The bus honked. I tensed, leaning forward, book bag slung over my shoulder, waiting for her to turn. She still didn't move. I stared at her, pawing at the gravel with impatient feet. She stared back impassively. The engine growled. The black smoke kept chugging upward. Then the big girl turned suddenly and began running for the bus doors.

The second she leaned into her turn, I launched after her, sprinting toward my ticket to school and beyond. I *knew* she was going to tell the bus driver to leave without me. She wanted the doors of the bus to close in my face and leave me choking on smoke. I was sure of it, but I couldn't let that happen. I churned across the gravel and leapt onto the asphalt, running, pumping with my arms, the book bag slapping against my back.

When I came alongside the bus, I felt my shoulder lighten as the book bag strap gave way again. The bag skidded along the ground, spraying pens and pencils in its wake. I stopped and kneeled to pick up the bag, frantically sweeping up school supplies, scraping my fingers across the blacktop in a frenzy. The school bus honked twice in quick, annoyed succession. I scooped up my jumbled belongings and looked up. Every window of the bus was filled with laughing, howling children.

I stumbled up the steps of the bus. A sea of jeering faces greeted me inside. The kids in the back were rising up, straining to get a good look at me. The bus lurched forward, and I stumbled, grabbing onto a green vinyl seatback to keep my balance. The air was buzzing with whispers and snorts. I kept my eyes down, working my way back row by row, looking for a seat. But they were all full. Kids slid to the aisle-edge of the row to keep me from sitting by them. Feet stuck out to trip me, kicking at my shins.

A pudgy porcine face—all teeth and nostrils—suddenly popped into my field of vision, screaming: "Freak!" He'd found the word they were all looking for, and soon a steady chant of "Freak! Freak! Freak!" rained down on me. Finally, mercifully, a vacant seat appeared toward the back of the bus, and I slid wearily into it.

Snap! I felt a sharp sting across the back of my neck. I jerked forward, startled, and covered the back of my neck with my hands. *Snap!* The sting again, this time along my knuckles. I slipped down off the seat, as low to the floor as I could go, and looked up to see the cause of my new torment. He was a huge kid—probably a high-schooler—with a comically red face. He had a buzz-cut on top but sported long blond curls that billowed down onto his shoulders. Who were these short-on-top/long-in-back barbarians?

He flicked a thick middle finger off the pad of his thumb. "I'm Kjell and I'm going to do this to you all day long," he vowed in a death-metal growl. I stayed wedged between seats, squatting on the floor for as long as I could, but my legs began to cramp up. I pensively hoisted myself back up onto the seat. Kjell seemed not to notice me. I looked out the window and saw forest giving way to rolling grasslands. *Snap!* Kjell snapped me on the back of the neck again. He laughed in deep chest tones. I spent the rest of the bus ride with my hands clasped tightly to the back of my neck. From time to time Kjell would snap me on the back of my hands or on the top of my head. I bobbed my head evasively while trying to look at distant points out the window to avoid vomiting from motion sickness. The bus bounced and swayed. The air was thick with the stench of diesel.

The kids around me were yelling and laughing loudly. Some of this was directed at me, but most of it seemed to be just the way these simian life forms communicated. They were yelling about what fun they'd had over the summer, about who had grown boobs, and who was a big faggot. The bus eventually crossed the bridge onto the mainland, and a town began to develop on the left side of the highway. The yelling seemed to get louder and louder the closer we got to school. Until we stopped to pick up a couple of Mexican kids, and then the bus fell silent for the rest of the ride.

When the bus finally released us into the loading zone at Stanwood Middle School, I was jostled from side to side and absorbed into a stream of students surging forward into the sprawling campus. This was a real school. People were flowing in all directions under covered walkways leading to multiple buildings. I felt safe in the crowd. If they couldn't focus on me for more than a moment they'd leave me alone. Up some stairs and through the hallways I skittered, head down.

I found my homeroom and slid into my desk just as the bell rang. Our teacher, Mrs. King, greeted us: "Good morning class! Are you ready to learn?" I nodded vigorously. This was where I was meant to be. I sat at the edge of my seat like a sprinter in his starting blocks. I raised my hand every time I knew the answer, which, except for math, was most of the time. I raised it so many times the teacher stopped calling on me, and the boys behind me began fake-coughing "Faggot!" into their hands. I didn't care. These idiots could brutalize me all they wanted on the bus, but in the classroom I would outshine them all.

When the bell rang, Mrs. King caught my eye and beckoned me over with a scoop of her hand. "Come talk to me," she said, as though she needed me to keep her company through the loneliness of recess. She pulled up a chair next to her own for me, and we talked like a couple of friends. Mrs. King had a smooth and youthful face framed by perfectly round, brown curls. She looked directly into my eyes when she was listening to me, and her lips leapt up into little smiles whenever she spoke. She asked where I'd gone to school before, and I told her about being home-schooled and about my brief time in a New Age school where I'd learned to write poems and interpret dreams. She had me read a passage from a book and read from a handwritten page. She then asked me to do a couple of math problems.

Our conversation fell silent. Mrs. King clasped her hands shut and placed them on her lap. She leaned forward, seeking out my eyes, and told me she thought I was very bright. But, I was years behind in math. I'd have to go to remedial math. And probably remedial English too, but only because I couldn't read or write in cursive. It felt like she'd slapped me across the face. My temples swelled, and I fought back tears. "Remedial" was for bullies who couldn't find the United States on a map of North America. Couldn't she see how smart I was? Mrs. King's eyes opened to their full aperture. She wasn't smiling now. She bent her head to one side, viewing me from a new perspective. She unclasped her hands and, smiling again, volunteered to stay after school to tutor me in cursive: "Like I said, I think you're really bright, Josh. If you'll agree to stay and learn cursive, I'll agree to stay and teach it to you."

"I can't," I apologized. "I have to take the bus home. Not really home, but where we're staying."

"Can't your mom pick you up late?"

"Yes, she could've, but she can't now because we don't have a car anymore. Well, we do have a car *some*where but this guy Leopoldo crashed it."

Mrs. King straightened her neck and narrowed her gaze. "Well, let's call your mom and talk about this," she concluded.

I looked down at the floor, tracing the linoleum patterns with my eyes. I rubbed my shoulder. "We can't call her because we don't have a phone, Mrs. King."

Her face hardened. "Well, I don't know if there's anything we can do, then." With that, she let me go out to catch the remainder of recess.

In the schoolyard, I sat by myself on a bench, staring at the patch on my knee. If Mrs. King couldn't see me for the gifted student I really was, no one could. School had failed me. Or, more likely, I'd failed at school. Either way, it wasn't worth the struggle to get here. This *remedial* school wasn't going to make my life better.

A girl from my class named Erin came and sat down next to me. She wore thick pancake makeup and had orange bangs that stood straight up through the magical power of hair spray. Erin looked at me with pity and shook her head. "Did you even wash your face this morning?" She made eye contact with me, searching my soul to understand why I was choosing to be so gross. Her eyes drifted to the right side of my face and seemed to stop at my ear. She grimaced. "Oh my God. I'm not even going to say it," she told me. "It'd be too mean."

I looked past her, pretending I didn't care. Pretending I didn't want to punch her in her made-up face. Pretending I didn't want to punch *myself* in the face.

Erin excused herself to talk to some of the popular girls over by the monkey bars. I slipped away to the bathroom, which was dark and cavernous and reeked of bleach. I scrutinized myself in the mirror over the sink. The right side of my face was streaked with dirt. My right ear was pocked with black dots. My neck was flaking little rolls of dead skin. My lower lip was swollen and red on the right side. I washed my face as best I could in the cold water at the sink but there was no soap. I scrubbed at my cheek and my neck with the rough, pulpy brown paper towels and began to gingerly pick off the little bits of grit that were embedded in my ear. I didn't get far before a group of eighth-graders came in and announced to no one in particular: "All faggots out!" I assured myself I wasn't a faggot but wisely fled the bathroom anyway.

In the hall between periods, I struggled with the combination lock on my yellow locker. There was something enticing about having one little place in the world that was all my own. But as the bell rang, I gave up trying to open it. What was the point? I was never going to come back to school to use it. I stood with my back to the lockers, staring up at the asbestos ceiling tiles. A group of boys hustled by on the way to class. One of them turned his head to stare at me, a wry smile developing on his face.

"You guys, go ahead. I'll catch up," he said. "I gotta take care of something."

He stopped right in front of me. I lowered my head to look at him. He had spiky blond hair and wore a baggy gray sweatshirt. His face was clean and clear, and when he spoke I could see the flash of a retainer in his mouth.

"What are you looking at, fag!?" He was trying to sound tough.

I opened my mouth but knew there was nothing I could say. I saw his right upper-cut coming and shielded my belly, taking most of the force of the punch on the back of one arm. But then he kneed me in the groin, and I sank to the floor. He hurried off to rejoin his friends. The churning nausea didn't last that long, but I didn't have the will to get up. Who was this kid? The reason he left his friends, the reason he was late for class, the thing he had to "take care of," was stopping to knee me in the balls?

On the bus back to Camano Island, Kjell found me again, even though I was hunkered down in the middle of the bus. He snapped at the back of my neck whenever I sat up. It was too much: Kjell, the yelling, the sickening turns in the road. A dark heaviness in my gut pulled me into despair. I massaged my temples, trying to use the astral projection techniques my mother had shown me to rise above it all. But I couldn't focus long enough to get into a meditative trance. I was going to throw up. I felt the waves of nausea beginning to climb up into my chest.

But then, out the window, the black deer with the bullet hole in its head floated into view. I lunged out of my crouching position and scrambled to get off the bus before the big girl. She tried to trip me up as I passed her seat, kicking at my knees. I stumbled but didn't fall. I leapt off the bus, gasping for air, and ran across the road and into the forest before she could come after me. From the underbrush I watched, panting, as the bus moved off. The big girl stared defiantly at the wall of forest and shouted: "Sissy!" Then she and her sister and friends walked up the road and disappeared around the corner where, no doubt, their driveways led to warm, clean houses and milk and cookies and television.

I began crying as I made my way back through the forest to the clearing where we were squatting. The tarp covering our "bed" was littered with branches and evergreen needles. Tools and empty water jugs were scattered around the pile of boxes that contained our worldly possessions. My mother was gone. She had probably hitchhiked into town to pick up supplies. Leopoldo was on the other side of the clearing, out of sight, sawing at the base of some tree with his bow saw. I was still sobbing as I set my haggard blue book bag down on the ground and began rummaging through a black milk crate for something to eat. I found a jar of pickles and wandered a few hundred feet deeper into the forest.

Eventually I sat down on one of Leopoldo's fallen logs, where I stopped crying but still convulsed a little involuntarily. School was no longer an option. I wasn't going to get up and go through all of that again. For what? For aches and bruises and humiliation? I'd departed in the morning with nothing but my intelligence. And now my stupid remedial self didn't have anything left.

A sharp crack rang out of the forest in front of me. High above me the canopy rustled and snapped. The soft light silhouetting the feathery sprays of the massive cedar across the clearing began to shimmer down the length of the tree. The tree was moving. It was falling. At me! The tree was rumbling now as it came. I didn't feel anything, not even fear. I just didn't care. Why get up and move? Who would miss me? My mother? Leopoldo? He wanted me dead. The kids at school would be cheering for the tree.

The cedar tree's long branches were cracking and exploding as they collided with other trees on the way down toward me. From somewhere a raven cawed in panic. But I sat still. The cedar tree now hurtled down at me, blocking out the light above and casting a shadow over me. In its wake, brilliant light fingers of God came pouring through the canopy. And, in that moment, I saw very clearly a young man laughing. He was tanned, with a close-cropped beard. Head thrown back, black eyes shining. His black curly hair dancing in the wind. He was cloaked in a white prayer shawl under a blue desert sky. This visionary man was the future, the son I might have some day if I could find the strength to struggle through these troubles.

The ends of branches were beginning to strike the ground ahead of me like spears. Everything was popping and exploding. Forest debris swirled around me, surging in the wind that heralded the tree fall. I slid off the log and began running, bobbing and weaving, ducking under branches and leaping over logs. I was screaming in fright, but also with exhilaration.

I would make it through this and have a child. *My* childhood might be hopeless but I could make someone *else's* wonderful. I would give my kid running water—showers and baths and toilets, electricity, a safe warm home, toys, new clothes, and a good school. I would model his childhood on the opposite of mine. I would never beat him or abandon him. I would never have sex in front of him or give him drugs. He would never know alcohol or violence. I would train my son to be upright and strong, to stand in defense of the weak against bullies.

I was flying through the forest, dodging falling shadows and braving a gauntlet of branches and sprays that whipped down around me. As the massive cedar tree made landfall at my heels, I hurled myself into the lee of a large stump. The ground shook with a tremendous rumble. Branches, bark, and dirt rained down around me. The air filled with secondary crashes and cracks as the tree finished falling in the forest. In front of me was the edge of the clearing. I could see the blue glint of my book bag skewered by a jagged branch.

The landscape had shifted but I was all right. The undaunted, uplifting words of Robert Nesta Marley, came to me then like prophecy:

The stone that the builder refuse
Will always be the head cornerstone.

I stood up and dusted myself off for the millionth time that day. Just then, Crazy John came bursting out of the foliage, shirtless, his wiry red hair standing out at strange angles. "Are you OK?" he bellowed at me, his eyes wild with concern.

"Yeah. I'm OK," I said. He calmed himself down with deep breaths and stared at me. I smiled back and said: "Well, this will make a great story some day!"

"This'll make a great story right now," Crazy John said, his outstretched arm displaying for me the beauty of the lush green forest around me. He farted with a swish of his hips and turned back into the foliage from whence he'd come, cawing like a raven.

I knelt and began freeing my book bag from the branch that was pinning it down. I needed that bag. I had to go to school the next day.

FIFTEEN

Rainfall

Leopoldo was in a race against the rain, and I knew he was going to lose. He knew it too. We'd both lived in Washington long enough to know that he had a month, at most, before the rains started and never stopped. A month to build a solid foundation, erect sturdy walls, and lay down a waterproof roof. A month to protect us from the elements. But Leopoldo was still chopping down trees.

Claudia was oblivious to the obvious outcome. Even as the skies began to darken, she was still talking about the pyramid and her imaginary art studio and her pretend pottery shed. Leopoldo knew she would catch on eventually, so he did his best to blame me for his impending failure. I was worthless, he said. But this worked to my advantage because it meant I could keep going to school. If I were as bad as he said, then I was doing him a favor by getting out of his way.

Leopoldo resented me for going to the "fancy school" and complained to Claudia: "Josh think he too good for hard work now." In the evenings, he tried to punish me for my elitist ambitions. He put me to work hacking branches from fallen logs or hand-planing boards out of wet timber. Only nightfall saved me from a forest full of chores.

Sitting around the fire at night, Claudia debriefed me on my day, curious to see what I was learning in school, what lies they were trying to feed me. Leopoldo snapped at us for talking too loudly or for talking in a tone of voice he found to be disrespectful. Watching me write an essay about what I did over the summer, he detected my vulnerability: homework. School wasn't just on school time. Some of it was on *his* time. Leopoldo called me away from the fire. He had his hands full fixing a saw blade and he needed his flashlight. I rifled through the milk crate of tools and patted down the bed, but the flashlight was nowhere to be found. I suspected he'd hidden it. It took me half an hour, but I finally located it wedged between a bag of clay and a rotting melon. When I brought him the flashlight, he threw it into the mud and told me I was too late. I took my place on my log by the fire and returned to my essay. But he wasn't done. Leopoldo pushed me onto the ground and rolled my seat into the flames. He said we needed it to keep the fire going overnight. I joined Claudia by the wheelbarrow of bricks Crazy John had hauled back into the clearing and together we constructed a brick bench by the fire. Leopoldo descended on us in a frenzy of frustration. "No, no! Those bricks for the fire!" He dismantled our seat from under us and cast the bricks into the ash around the fire pit. I sat cross-legged in the dirt and finished my essay, the light from the fire flickering across the page.

But my essay would never get handed in. The next night, he mistook my draft essay for scrap paper and threw it into the fire. "What are you thinking!?" I yelled at him, but he put a finger in my face and told me, "You better show to me some *respect*. I working and you sloppy, throwing around the papers. What *you* are thinking!?" And so it went.

With time running out and the skies starting to darken, Leopoldo swerved into an arrangement to end work on the pyramid and achieve failure with honor. He borrowed Erica's AMC Gremlin and, on his way home from the bar, he crashed it into a telephone pole. When his hangover had subsided and the damages had been tallied, Leopoldo declared his back unfit for further service. Not that he didn't try. He heroically scraped the bow saw against the last remaining spruce tree in the clearing, but the pain was too great. He lamented, and we agreed, that he would've finished the pyramid but for his debilitating injury. When the heavy rains came there was no one to blame but Fate.

The outdoor kitchen was washed away. The ground turned to soup, and the moss dripped like a thousand oversaturated sponges. We scrambled around in the mud without a plan, wringing out our blankets and wrapping our disintegrating cardboard boxes in slimy plastic garbage bags. A dozen rotting trees lay dead at our feet, but we still had no shelter. I stepped onto the school bus the next day soaked to the bone and slick with grime. The bullies couldn't get enough of me. When I climbed back through the jungle at the end of the day, Claudia had finally lost her uncanny optimism. She and Leopoldo had hitched a ride to the scrap yard in Burlington and returned with a roll of salvaged plastic sheeting and a pile of dirty lumber and crumbling particleboard. They hammered this collection together, and the result was a patchwork lean-to nailed onto a large tree stump.

The lean-to on the stump where Claudia, Leopoldo, and I spent the fall and part of the winter of 1986. Its leaking ceiling was five feet high at its tallest.

Somehow this was home.

The incessant rain shrank our world into that damp bedraggled square—seven feet by seven feet, at most—floating above the slime like an ark of despondency. This left room for nothing more than a family bed of soggy foam mattresses and a thin strip of bare particleboard that became our makeshift kitchen. It took half an hour to bring water to boil on our battered green camping stove, and the rice was half-cooked and chewy when it was served. Our bread was nothing but a collection of little scraps once all the mold had been cut away.

After dinner, the adults filled up our small space with venom, spitting at each other in front of me without inhibition, as if I were just another stream of water dripping from the ceiling. I sat at the foot of the bed, hunched over my math packet. Math was the hardest since I had never really learned it before. Without knowing my multiplication tables, each problem took half an hour. The kerosene lamp wedged between my feet began sputtering, and a new leak opened up over my head. We were out of buckets and bowls, so I threw an old blanket down to soak up the water and slid down the bed to a drier spot. I hummed loudly to myself to drown out their screaming.

Leopoldo suddenly decided the argument was over, yelling: "He *is* showing off! Why he doing school here? You no tell me what *I* know! You no tell me what *I* can do! You shut up or I give you *what else*!" I didn't need to turn around to know his hand was raised in the air. I braced myself for impact like I was a passenger in his car. But only silence ensued. A thick punitive silence, from both sides, as they rigidly lay their bodies at opposite sides of the bed. And then: "Josh, turn off the light!"

I looked up at the collage of wall, glistening with rivulets of water in the glow of the lamp. He had me now. The sun was setting early. It was too dark for homework without the lamp and there was nowhere else to go. "Josh!" I blew out the lamp, and carefully positioned myself on the bed between the plastic buckets and metal bowls. They steadily splashed and pinged as I tried to fall asleep.

The next day Mrs. King gave me a minus on my math homework. She wrote: *Incomplete. Try harder, Josh!*

The only way around Leopoldo's light embargo was to get up earlier. But even then, not enough morning sunlight filtered into the lean-to, so I took to sitting on a wet stump with a cruddy blue tarp pulled over my head. At just the right angle, the light filtered in, but the raindrops did not. Soaked and groggy, I scratched at the damp pages on my lap with a mechanical pencil, trying not to tear the fragile paper. I still didn't finish my homework most days, but it didn't matter. It wasn't about completion anymore. Homework was an act of defiance, a way of showing myself I still had a measure of control over my life.

One morning I awoke shivering and choking. The air was thinner than usual and carried a new chill. Winter was on its way. New leaks had sprung from above in the night. I was soaked to my core and coughing. I couldn't breathe right. The cold, the wetness, the mildew and mold—it all conspired to obstruct my airways with impenetrable congestion. I sat up and blew against the barricades in my sinuses to no effect. Claudia and Leopoldo were curled up together under an old fur-lined parka. Leopoldo's hand was still closed over the neck of a wine bottle.

Outside I stamped around in the mud and rain, trying to rally myself for the thousand-yard trek through the rainforest to the bus stop. Even with my impenetrably clogged nostrils I could tell that I stank. My hair was unspeakably greasy, but I didn't have the fortitude to stand naked in the freezing rain with a bottle of shampoo. I barely had the fortitude to stand up.

This was rock bottom. I knew that now, and it was somehow inspiring. I couldn't imagine it getting any worse. It just couldn't. In a month or less the snows would come. Sure, it would be colder, but the roof would stop leaking. That would be an improvement. Or maybe this gnarly congestion would progress into a serious illness, and then they'd have to hospitalize me. That would be an improvement, too. From here, from this place and this point in time, there was nowhere to go but up.

Unexpectedly, it was Crazy John who would start us on our way. On Camano Island, Leopoldo and my mother both acknowledged the strange irony of being taken in by a crazy man, but Leopoldo wasn't about to question free rent, and my mother had always believed that crazy was only one step away from enlightened. Crazy John looked on silently as Leopoldo chopped down tree after tree and alternated between loving and beating my mother.

All the while, Crazy John was diligently working on his octagonal structure by the road. By the time the rains came, he'd built a cozy little cabin for himself and Erica to share. They were all set for the winter with a tight roof and a propane stove and lamps. He'd even built a little covered shoe rack where you could store your muddy boots before going inside. "That John. He make to embarrass me," Leopoldo complained to my mother.

When Crazy John came knocking at the decomposing door of our lean-to to ask us for help paying the property taxes, Leopoldo shoved a finger in his face: "This you *trick*!? You tell us free rent, then we work so hard on the land, and now it *your* land? And now we have to pay to *you* the rent!?"

"No," Crazy John said calmly. "It's still my family's land and you're still welcome to live here as long as you want. But they sent me the property tax bill because it doesn't seem fair for them to pay it since they're not living here. And it seems fair for you to pay half of it because you are living here."

"You fuck us!"

Crazy John walked away into the rain. Leopoldo muttered about him all evening. "He crazy if he think we paying this!" Leopoldo was hot now, fueling himself with green bottles of malt liquor until he couldn't stand it anymore. "I go talk with him."

He rattled around in our kitchen crates outside, and I fell into a deep, disturbing dream. At some point in the night Leopoldo stumbled through the mud, following Crazy John's footprints back toward his octagonal cabin.

Shouting and shrieking broke my sleep. I could hear Erica screeching in terror. Claudia scrambled down the bed. "You stay here, Joshey!" She stomped her boots on, and one foot busted through the soggy particleboard floor. I dismissed it all as another bad dream and went back to sleep.

In the morning, I found Leopoldo sitting at the end of the bed vomiting into the green rainwater bucket. When he turned around to wince at me, his face was slate gray. He looked like a corpse. "What I *do* to them?" he moaned. Leopoldo remembered crashing through Crazy John's door the night before, but then the details slipped into a haze. Did he have a knife? Did he put the knife to Erica's throat? She was pregnant. "Claudia," he choked out, "you tell them I sorry."

Claudia trudged through the mud with Leopoldo's message, but *sorry* wasn't enough. She came back in defeat, her head down, the neglected hood of her jacket full of rainwater. Crazy John and Erica were scared for their lives and the life of their unborn child. Leopoldo had threatened to kill them, boasting that he had murdered white people before and wasn't afraid to do it again. "Look at me!" he had demanded. "To kill is for me a sport. When I aiming to kill, I always make the goal." By some miracle, Leopoldo hadn't pulled a knife on them, but they weren't taking any more chances. We had until noon to get out or Crazy John was going to call the cops.

We struggled through the mud and rain, gathering our most prized possessions. Then we slogged toward the trail, stopping to let Leopoldo vomit every few feet. We filed past Crazy John's octagon in a desperate little procession. He stood on the front porch of his cabin, stone-faced, his arms crossed against his chest. As I passed, lugging a crate of my poetry journals, I looked up at Crazy John's face, trying to catch his eyes. He wouldn't look at me. It was too awkward. I recognized the averting of the eyes. It was what normal people did. And then I realized that he wasn't crazy anymore. Now it was our turn.

SIXTEEN

A Kind of Normal

The Stanwood library opened its doors to me without question. Mercifully warm and clean, it was a shelter from the rain and the echoes of Erica screaming in the night. I washed my face in the white sink and took refuge in a book about the Golem of Prague. There I stayed for hours until Claudia's insistent whisper pulled me back. She was brimming with excitement. "Joshey, I found the perfect place! Right here in Stanwood!"

A home in town! I pictured a two-story house with a yard and a climbing tree. Maybe a driveway with a basketball hoop. But my image of perfection evaporated as we pulled out of the library parking lot. We weren't climbing the hill to where the nice houses looked happily down onto the world. We were looping around into the little barrio at the edge of west Stanwood, where the migrant workers subsisted, their laundry hanging outside in the rain like advertisements for poverty. We pulled off of the paved street and inched down a muddy alley until we came to a stop in the gravel parking lot of the old Masonic Lodge.

"Look, Joshey! Our own place." Claudia was pointing across the alley at a little ground-floor unit that jutted out like a stubby toe from a pile of shabby blue apartments.

"Oh no," I said.

"What 'oh no'? It's perfect."

We began unloading our soggy cardboard boxes, and Claudia grinned at our good fortune, repeating: "Perfect!"

Perfect was a relative term. The apartment was surrounded by muddy alleys and shared a tiny patch of grass with eight Mexican families living in a fourplex. The electric heating was on the fritz, a family of shaggy gray sewer rats ruled over a corner of the kitchen, and the bathroom stank like a Superfund site. But Claudia had a point. We were no longer living on a stump.

Compared to the stump, or compared to anywhere since San Francisco for that matter, we were doing all right. We had running water and electricity for the first time in four years, and we didn't need to hitchhike anymore. Claudia had found a job taking care of an elderly Norwegian lady named Inga who lived only a couple of blocks away. We were walking distance to the library and a store. And, most importantly, I was only half a mile from school.

I celebrated my eleventh birthday with a long, hot shower, scrubbing the filth and sap out of my hair and changing into dry, clean clothes. I was drenched in rainwater by the time I made it to homeroom, but I was still clean.

"Oh, we are going to have fun together," promised Mrs. King when I told her that I had moved close enough to stay after school for tutoring.

"I have a shower now," I told her.

"I didn't notice," she lied. Then she spent the next three weeks showing me how to write in cursive and unveiling the mysteries of the multiplication tables.

"So the tables are just memorization?"

"It's just memorization."

"I'm good at remembering things."

"Yes, you are. The key is to remember the good things."

All that was new in Stanwood was good. But, of course, we brought the old with us. Still struggling to explain his near-killing of Crazy John and Erica, Leopoldo maundered around the new apartment like Dr. Jekyll waking to memories of Mr. Hyde. Gone were the days of blaming his violence on flashbacks from El Salvador. Now Claudia confessed to me that Leopoldo had a drinking problem. He had a sickness called alcoholism. "The good news, Joshey, is it's treatable, but it will require a lot of love and support from us to help him through it."

My mother told me she had invited Leopoldo to join us in Stanwood only because he promised to be on good behavior. If he messed up again he would have to move out. It took him a month before he did, but by then it was too late for us to kick him out. He had an immigration hearing coming up, and he needed our family to be living happily together under one roof to avoid his deportation back to El Salvador, where the death squads were presumably still waiting for him.

After such an ad hoc existence in the wilderness, I took comfort in the predictable certainties of life in town. The lights were bright and they were easy to turn on and off. The water flowed freely—hot when you wanted it, cold when you didn't care. School was a regular routine: get up, shower, walk to school, survive, walk home. Even my home life fell into a grim sort of normalcy.

Three nights a week Claudia stayed with Inga. When she came home, we'd catch up over rice and tofu, and Leopoldo would sulk about one thing or another until his complaints became rumbling preludes to brutality. When the tension in the room became unbearable, I'd run for cover. I had my own room now, and I'd diligently lock my flimsy hollow-core door and hide under the blankets until the storm had passed.

The mornings after the storm, I'd awake to quiet. To absolute stillness. And I'd wonder whether it had all, perhaps, been another bad dream in a long series of them. And I'd go out to discover that it had been real. Claudia would have already cleaned up the apartment as best she could. And now she'd be reclining in the brown chair, holding ice or raw steak to her head and face. The full array of salves and herbal ointments would be jumbled out on the table. Her face would be swollen, shining in reddish lumps. Sometimes she carried blackened eyes, welts, cuts, and burns—cigarette and otherwise.

I'd get to work at once, helping her patch up. Sometimes we'd boil comfrey and measure out witch hazel for poultices to dress her wounds. These were my chances to be mature, to tend to my mother lovingly. I reacted with sympathy when she winced and sighed with satisfaction when she was soothed. I'd remark, "Oh, Claudia," at each injury, and she would reassure me through busted and swollen lips, "It's OK, I'll be just fine, Joshey." Sometimes I'd pretend to focus my imaginary third eye on sending healing energy to her the way she'd taught me.

When Leopoldo finally woke, the man who'd caused all this carnage was on his best behavior. He would be soft, moving slowly and tenderly. His face carried nothing but care and empathy for my mother. He'd speak quietly and sweetly. He'd shuffle around the room, halfheartedly straightening up. He was, after all, stoically nursing his own pains: a pounding headache from the hangover, swollen fingers, sometimes nasty gashes from having punched out a window or smashed through the sheetrock.

More than anything, he was sorry.

"Aw, baby, I'm so sorry." Or, "Honey, my heart. It is a breaking to see you like what I done."

Claudia remained impassive, emotionally distant.

Then came the promises.

"I make to you a promise that I will heal for myself. That I'm going to drop this drinking forevers."

And then came the visions for a brighter tomorrow.

Leopoldo would get a real job, and we'd be able to save up for a real place. A clean place without rats dying on the living room floor. He'd tell her: "I don't care about none of that macho shit no more."

And then, slowly, my mother would let him back in. She thawed and she warmed. And by the end of the day, it would be like old times. Like back at the beginning of the relationship when he was a refugee and they were falling in love. Maybe this was going to be the man to build a family around after all. Maybe he really was going to be a father for me. We'd go out to eat in the Viking Village, and we'd walk together, talking and laughing. And Leopoldo would clown around and make jokes. And he'd pick me up and carry me on his shoulders. And he and Claudia would walk arm in arm across the parking lot to the Scandia Bakery for coffee and a Norwegian flatbread called *lefse*. And Leopoldo would be smiling. Even with the bruises, swellings, and cuts, doctored with salves, and masked with cosmetics, Claudia would be smiling too.

And then it would start all over again.

That winter brought wild storms howling in off of the Puget Sound, followed suddenly by calm and open skies. Like the alternating rhythms of rain and sun, I accepted the rounds of violence and reconciliation in my home as normal. Not ideal, not pleasant, but reliable and certain. The steady cadence of Leopoldo and Claudia marching together as husband and wife.

Home was bearable in times of peace, but in times of war I sought political asylum at the Stanwood library. There I began cruising the Dewey Decimal System for meaning and inspiration. But I didn't just leap into the beige metal stacks with my eyes closed. I had a destination in mind—the neighborhood of call number 296. *Judaism*. Whatever that was.

My research was the fulfillment of a prophecy made back on Cultus Mountain, before the advent of Leopoldo. Climbing the trail one evening we passed the cabin of a neighbor named Ray and noticed it glowing through the darkening mist. Ray rarely ventured up from Seattle, so we stopped in to say hello. Ray looked like a fisherman from the back of a *National Geographic* map of Crete and exhibited an appropriately Mediterranean hospitality. He welcomed us in with one of those thick Back East accents that vaguely reminded me of Grandma Harriette.

He was originally from New York, he told us, and wanted to know where we were from.

"The Bay Area," replied Claudia.

"No way," Ray said. "I don't believe you."

"Why not?"

"You're Jews, right? Ain't no *lantzmen* from San Francisco."

Claudia laughed. "Yeah, we are Jews. How did you know?"

"Your kid's got a rabbi's nose."

They laughed and spoke of ancient times. Places and people east of the Mississippi. Chicken soup and strange holidays. Ray's whole body shook when he laughed, and he concluded his story with: "So I bet I was the only Italian kid in Brooklyn who had not one, but *two* bar mitzvahs."

Claudia and I stepped back into the mist, and a faint light of recognition flared in my mind. We weren't totally alone in this universe. There was a name for us. A name for why Grandma Harriette said "Who really knew?" when I asked her where we were from. A name for being Russian, Lithuanian, and German, but cringing at the memory of the Russians, Lithuanians, and Germans. The name explained why my grandfather was blacklisted by McCarthy and forced to drag his family from place to place. And this same name must be the reason we continued to wander, searching for a promised land, while we avoided Christians, read books, and gesticulated wildly with our hands. A name that explained it all. But I'd forgotten what it was.

"Claudia, what was that thing he said we were?"

"What thing?"

"There was something he knew we were. Because of my nose."

"Oh, Jews?"

"Yeah. What is that?"

"I never told you we were Jewish?"

"No. What is it?"

"Jews, you know. Like Einstein, Freud, Marx."

Being my mother's son, I knew who those men were. But I didn't see the connection. "Like we're related to them?"

"Sort of." And then she gave me a very Jewish answer: "You know, Joshey, I don't exactly know what it means to be Jewish. We'll have to go to the library and look it up."

I was in the library now, riding the reading room through space and time, discovering that I was part of something. Something profound. I was the descendant of an ancient tribe that had emerged from the mists of prehistory to introduce the world to God, to write the Bible, and to shine unto the nations like a beacon of righteousness. We had been scattered to the wind, driven to the four corners of the Earth. Oppressed and demeaned time and time again, yet we wandered on, excelling in isolation wherever we went. We didn't need to be normal like everyone else; we were Jews. When the library closed, I walked through the darkness, an only child no more. Now I knew I descended from the seed of Jacob, and somewhere out there were a million of my nameless brethren, clinging to diasporic rocks just like me, but thriving nonetheless.

"I was flipping through the pages," I whispered to my mother in the rank, lutefisky darkness of Inga's sitting room. "And there was a drawing of Maimonides. He looked just like me, but with a beard and a turban. The same face, the same rabbi's nose."

"He spoke to you across the generations," Claudia assured me.

"Yeah . . . he did," I agreed with her for once.

My mother whispered to me about our family. My great-great-grandmother Rivka was a folk healer in the forests of Russia. My great-grandmother Eta called the mounted police Cossacks and threw her body in front of the Nazi ships unloading in Boston Harbor in 1939. And then Claudia told me that somewhere out there I might have a half brother. When she was a teenager she'd dated a Colombian Marxist revolutionary and had gotten pregnant. She'd given the baby up for adoption in New Jersey and had never seen him again. It was 1987 now, so that would make him twenty-three. My mother shook her head and shrugged. It was all part of an old world she'd forgotten about so long ago.

But it was a brand-new world for me. I lay in bed that night still immersed in my voyage of self-discovery. Though I sojourned at the very end of the Earth, the blood of Abraham still coursed through my veins. And beyond the horizon, in the wilds of far-off New Jersey, that same blood might course through the veins of a brother as well. Maybe someday this brother would find me, grasp me by the arm, and pull me up out of this broken world where screaming and smashing were considered normal. Maybe I'd finally go home, wherever that was.

The buzzing of the mechanical bell dismissed the last day of sixth grade, and I trudged home half-satisfied with myself. I'd finished my first year of real school with a 4.0 grade average and had managed to make a couple of friends. But I still felt like an alien and was getting my ass kicked by bullies at least once a week. Now it was summer, and I took to wandering the dusty neighborhood on my new used BMX. But my days of cruising on my bicycle were cut short by a rock to the head. I crashed into a bush and rolled onto my back. What hit me? A bird? Two teenagers were peering down at me, laughing. They picked up my bicycle and began wheeling it away.

"Hey," I yelped after them.

Now someone was standing next to me. A dark brown kid in a white tank top. "*Oye, pendejos*, give him back his bike," he called after the bicycle thieves. They slowed to a stop. "Give it!" the kid called again. They looked at each other but then continued slinking off with my bike. "Oh, well. That's some BS, right there," the kid said, and he gave me a hand up.

"I'm Ervi."

"Early?"

"Ervi, like Ernesto."

Ervi Sánchez was an inch shorter than me but talked and walked like a man. His eleven-year-old face was pocked and pitted as though he'd already gone through a rough adolescence back when he was three. Ervi was the savvy, cynical anomaly that slipped out in the middle of his seven bubbly cheerful siblings.

"You gotta walk like this, man," he schooled me, cycling his bare shoulders back and forth. "That shows the dudes you're in charge. And you gotta wear a tank top to show off your guns for the honeys." He was all about the honeys. And deals. "You have to meet people. Make connections. Then you can be the middle man, and make the deals."

"What deals?" I asked. "Drug deals?"

"No, homie. *Deals*, just *deals*, man." He didn't know exactly what he was talking about, but he was sick of his parochial, hardworking family. "They think all there is to do is work. I hate them."

I loved them. Ervi's parents, four sisters, three brothers, and various other kin overflowed a small two-story house at the edge of town. His father was a little man but he paraded around the house slowly like a Mexican cowboy on market day. His mother was permanently affixed to the kitchen, where an endless train of savory dishes passed from her hands. Ervi's father and siblings worked all day every day. The little kids tended a garden out back with their mother. The older kids toiled in the spinach fields with their father. The only exceptions were Ervi, who wandered around town with me, making connections and talking up the honeys, and his oldest sister, Rosa, who worked in the packaging plant at Twin City Foods. When Rosa discarded her hairnet at the front door, her raven hair leapt free and swirled around her copper face, inlaid with green eyes and pouty lips. Catching sight of me standing awkwardly next to Ervi, she sashayed over and placed her hand on my shoulder. With a toss of her gleaming hair she sweetly asked Ervi: "Is this the white boy I ordered?" And then to me: "Why did you take so long?" She was smiling seductively, staring right into my eyes. Everyone was laughing. "Ah, finally, the *gringo* of my dreams," she sighed lustily in Spanish, and pressed me to her bosom.

No matter what I was doing, I tried my hardest to plant myself in Ervi's living room at 6:00 p.m. on weekdays to provide his sister the comic relief she desired. Her hair tosses and chesty hugs became more exaggerated in time. Everyone enjoyed the act, but no one more than I, even though it caused a strange tightness in my pants.

Back at home, the boredom of being alone in the apartment was punctuated with explosive visits by Leopoldo, who had left to pick cherries and apples in Yakima in Eastern Washington. The agricultural work, he said, was tantamount to slavery. He did such a good job of re-creating that sense of oppression for us that I informally sought asylum with Ervi's family. They didn't ask any questions when I became a regular in their dinner lineup. His mother just smiled and chatted with me in Spanish as she slid an extra bowl of rice and beans my way.

Dinnertime was sacred for the Sánchezes, and they gathered together around a collection of connecting card tables to share stories and interrupt one another with rapid-fire jokes that I didn't quite understand. After dinner, the family got down to the business of playing a card game called Lotería that combined the artistry of tarot and the lyrical auctioneering of an open-air market in Guadalajara. What was not to love? I tried to play one round but was immediately shocked when Ervi's brother called out "El Nigger" for the little black man with the cane who appeared on one of the cards.

"Hey," I called back instinctively. "That's racist." That was apparently hilarious, and the whole table burst into laughter.

"That's what the card says." Ervi's brother grinned.

"No it doesn't. It says . . . *El Negrito*."

"Yeah, it's the same thing."

"No, it's not. That's a really insulting word."

"How's that worse than *little black man*?"

"It's just different. You can't say it." Ervi's parents watched our verbal ping pong with amused interest, but Ervi had had enough.

"Come on, homes. This game is for sad old *abuelitas* in Mexico. This is *America*, man. We should be out there making deals." I deferred the N-word fight to another day and followed Ervi down to the corner store, where we talked up some hair-sprayed girls in the parking lot.

When the last traces of dinner had been scrubbed away, Ervi's parents slept on a fold-out couch in the living room. All the girls slept in one room upstairs, and the boys in the other. Ervi unfolded a spare cot for me, and I lay staring into the blackness, listening to him and his brothers breathe quietly into the dream world. They were probably even poorer than me, but happier. I wrestled with that irony and then succumbed to sleep myself.

Ervi slept over at my place exactly once. We woke on one of those rare mornings when Leopoldo and Claudia were both home. Ervi watched in silence as our breakfast ritual unfolded. Leopoldo, still drunk from the night before, pushed my mother around in the kitchen and cursed at her in Spanish. When he looked over to see me and Ervi staring at him, he accused us of being *maricónes*, and turned to my mother to tell her: "If Josh is going to be a gay, I'll be his first one."

"That's just my mom's husband," I apologized as we walked quickly away from my apartment. Ervi didn't say a word, but his mother invited me along with them to a family reunion up north the next day. More than a dozen of us impossibly squeezed into an old white van, and Rosa made a big show of pretending to sit on my lap. I told her it was fine to sit there. "You're so strong," she stage-whispered seductively and then called my bluff. I gladly traded forty-five minutes of inhaling her floral shampoo for the loss of all feeling in my lower extremities.

The extended Sánchez family filled an entire field outside of Burlington, and needed two accordion bands, multiple barbecues, and a row of porta-potties to provide for the whole group. As the lone gringo in the field, I felt like all eyes were on me. My out-of-placeness peaked when my turn finally came in the dinner line. For some inexplicable reason, a whole cow head, complete with eyes and horns, was being peeled of its flesh on the serving table in front of me. "What part do you want?" the smiling man in the cowboy hat asked me in Spanish. I pointed to a pink, fleshy part of the cheek, and he plunged his oversized fork into it. After I escaped from the serving area, I slid my cow cheek onto Ervi's plate. He was too busy talking to his cousins to notice.

Listening to the cousins rap about the *chicas* in Spanish, I realized that I knew a *mamacita* was a hot girl, in general, while a *guera* was a hot white-looking girl. And *guey* was literally a "castrated bull" but was used to mean *dude, asshole,* or a pause word like *uh* or *um,* depending on the context. My fluency in Spanish had reached a new level. And so had my fluency in the language of Leopoldo. I could read him now, using his face as a weather vane for how the day was going to unfold. A deep yawn meant he was playful. A rub of his lips together meant he would try to sedate himself with marijuana before resorting to booze. A flex of the upper lip meant he was manufacturing an excuse to fight. And a sulking brow meant it was only a matter of time before he began beating my mother.

Watching Ervi and his cousins laugh over their lunches of cow meat, I suddenly realized how ironic it was that we were vegetarians. Claudia passionately believed that violence against animals was barbaric, yet violence against her was perfectly acceptable. I slid the cow cheek back to my plate and took a bite of the forbidden flesh. Better to be the adopted son of this playful carnivorous migrant family than return home to my violent vegetarians.

That night I finally mustered the courage to be the caller in the Sánchez family game of Lotería. The third card I threw down was the black man with the cane. "El Africano Americano," I called out, and the table erupted with laughter and applause.

Summer drifted along until one day all of the spinach had been picked. At the edge of town the fields stood bare in lonely furrows. I stood on the cracked sidewalk in front of the *Casa Sánchez*. The house was dark and empty. They were gone. On my door I found a note from Ervi saying: "See you next year. Keep making deals."

Seventh grade began, and apparently all the apples and cherries in Eastern Washington had been picked as well because Leopoldo was back with a vengeance. He filled up the house with a new high-intensity rage that threatened to overload every one of my circuits. If only there was some way of grounding his energy. Or of jolting him out of his furious stupor. If he wouldn't listen to reason, maybe he'd pay attention to absurdity. One night I came out of my room in a turban fashioned from a black turtleneck and sang "Ali Baba's Camel" by the Bonzo Dog Doo-Dah Band. I pranced around, kicking and faux camel-riding with such dedication that Leopoldo's drunken fist seized-up in midair. He stumbled around, pointing and laughing at me, and when I ran out of lyrics I improvised with gibberish words, bouncing around like an old vaudeville puppet. When Leopoldo began to tire of that routine, I tapped around the room, grinning with ingratiating absurdity like the butler from the old Bojangles movie I saw at the library. It worked. I danced us up a night of peace.

Another night I emerged into the middle of an escalating argument with an empty macaroni box strapped to my face. I sucked air through a hole in the plastic siding, peered through a broken pair of my mother's glasses, and walked in slow motion under a suit of pillows and duct tape. I was an astronaut. I moonwalked in long strides and radioed dramatic and garbled transmissions back to Houston. Another successful intervention. But I soon ran out of routines, and Leopoldo lost interest in my increasingly repetitive distractions.

We were back to the alcoholic cycle of horror and honeymoon, and I fled to the library again. But the long stacks of books didn't captivate me anymore. I'd exhausted the fiction section, and was tired of *reading* about Judaism. I wanted to *practice* it. But the twenty-two inscrutable letters of the ancient Hebrew alphabet stood in my way. It took me an hour to crudely sound out the shortest prayer in the book, and that was for drinking wine, which was the last thing I needed more of in my life.

On Sunday afternoons, a group of elderly Christian ladies met in the backroom of the library to discuss nuclear disarmament and friendship with Russia. They called themselves the Stanwood/Camano People for Peace and were delighted to have an unthinkably young new recruit. One of the ladies invited me to attend Our Savior's Lutheran Church, where I was drafted to be the first *real Jew* to play the role of "Jewish Shepherd" in their Christmas pageant. I attended Lutheran Sunday school for a few months before parting ways due to theological differences and the teaching that you had to unconditionally obey your parents.

"Even your stepfather?" I asked.

"Even your stepfather," answered the Sunday school teacher.

"Even if he hits you?"

"Yes."

"Even if he hits your mom?"

"Yes."

One evening back at the library, I spotted a yellow casting call on the bulletin board for the Camwood Players, a community theater group. Their production was *Keep the Home Fires Burning*, a comedy about the power of

Christmas. I tried out for the part of the Yuletide Yahoo, who was supposed to be a cross between Puck and Harpo Marx. Because the character had no lines, my audition was a series of pantomimed emotions, comedic dance, and pratfalls.

"I got the part! I got the part!" I announced to my mother as I jumped around Inga's house.

"Tell the boy to go feed the horse," said Inga from under a cloud of dementia.

"Joshey, I *knew* you'd get it," said Claudia, hustling me out the back door before Inga's tyrannical daughter fired her for bringing her kid to work again.

I had first taken to the stage as the Scarecrow from *The Wizard of Oz* back in Shingletown. When I heard the applause after I finished screeching the last notes of "If I Only Had a Brain," I knew I'd found my calling. Standing in the spotlight, a hundred faces fixed on me, wanting me to entertain them, to carry them deeper into a fantasy world where tensions escalated dramatically and then burst into happy endings. When I was on stage the audience was mine. I deserved and received their undivided attention. No one could ignore me. No one could upstage me.

As the Yuletide Yahoo, I wore a red jumpsuit and, on cue, had the power of honking a magical horn that froze the other players and cleared the stage for my antics. I dinosaur-walked, grimaced, and spun myself silly. I puffed out my chest and strutted. I stumbled, fell, and picked myself back up again. And when the audience couldn't laugh anymore, I honked my horn again and let the conventional actors continue their spoken words. On closing night, I wowed the crowd in the first act, working myself into a prolific sweat. I toweled off backstage and then ducked out a side door to get some fresh air before my next entrance. I had exactly seven minutes. I sat on the steps for a minute, panting, and then foolishly walked down to the sidewalk. A group of boys from my class in middle school passed by, punching each other as they walked home from Video Farm.

"Dude, is that Josh?"

I turned to run back up the steps, but it was too late.

"What a faggot!"

One of them caught me in a headlock, and the others began kicking at my groin.

"You look like a *freak*!" They had caught me wearing a red jumpsuit and court jester hat, and could hardly contain themselves.

"Kick his ass!" they goaded each other.

My turn as the Yuletide Yahoo.

"Stop," I choked out. "I'm in a play . . . have to get back."

They didn't hear me or didn't care. I pried at the arms around my neck and curled my legs up to protect my nether regions. The whole time I was counting in my head. Four minutes. Three minutes.

I decided they would be done with me sooner if I stopped resisting. I took a deep breath and went limp. They landed some good solid kicks in my belly and one in the groin. Two minutes. They pushed my head into a cedar hedge, trying to shove me all the way through. And then something else caught their attention and they left me crumpled up on the sidewalk. One minute.

I sprinted back up through the side door and burst onto the stage on cue. I limped and dragged myself around at first, letting the audience believe I'd been clobbered by unseen forces backstage. But then I erupted into a frenzied primal dance, the kind of physical celebration early man must have used to communicate a great triumph over superior forces. I swung around the stage and ended my set with a series of headlong clumsy flips that would have made Buster Keaton proud. The audience clapped and howled.

"Wow, Josh," said the director after the show. "That was great! It was nothing like what we practiced in rehearsal, but you really pushed yourself to the limit. In fact, it looks like you gave yourself a black eye."

"I did, but the show must go on, right!?"

"Yes, the show must go on."

SEVENTEEN

Men Don't Cry

Snow fell, and it was too cold to wander around outside anymore. Claudia was sleeping at Inga's most nights now, and the old lady's daughter had set a strict policy of no Josh in the workplace. At the same time, my beloved library announced it was closing earlier for the winter. There was nowhere left to go but home.

This felt like more than a conspiracy of circumstances. Fate itself was telling me that I couldn't hide from my stepfather forever and was marching me back to reenlist under the command of Comandante Leopoldo. My stepfather came home to find me reading in the living room.

"Why you are here?"

"The library's closed," I apologized.

Leopoldo took charge at once. My standing orders were to have dinner waiting for him on the table when he came home from work, or wherever it was he went during the day. My culinary skills were limited to pasta, rice, and sandwiches, and Leopoldo told me I was a "bullshit cook" of even these simple dishes. I had done it all wrong, he told me. The food was terrible. But, by the end of his critical tirade, I noticed he'd eaten everything on his plate and demanded seconds.

After dinner he would take to the couch for refreshment. On the bad days this meant drinking beers and accusing me of nefarious crimes like ratting him out to my mother after I'd seen him shoplifting again. He would stab at me with his calloused finger and indict me: "You being mafia with me! This bullshit, Josh, bullshit." I would usually receive a sentence of push-ups.

On the good days, he converted his paycheck into marijuana. The herb made Leopoldo so pleasant that I began hoping he would spend all of our money on it. As the smooth smoke slowly slid out of his nostrils, he would tell me happy stories from back home. Stories about the time he made a hot woman's pussy dripping wet on the bus by rubbing on a secret pressure point between her thumb and forefinger. Or about the time his friend El Flaco took a dump off the back of a moving truck onto the windshield of a passing Mercedes. These stories left me feeling a little nauseated, but I could tell they were his attempts at acting fatherly.

Sometimes Leopoldo wouldn't come home for a day or two. Claudia told me he was probably out "whoring" with his new friend Carlos. On those days I had the apartment all to myself and would initially feel a surge of freedom. I could do anything I wanted! But this gave way to boredom and loneliness, and I found that I inexplicably preferred Leopoldo's company to his absence. I had developed a strange dependency on him. He wasn't a father exactly—more like an older brother who was psychotic most of the time. The rest of the time, he was something like fun.

Leopoldo must have felt some brotherly impulse too. He began to open up to me, telling me that his father used to beat him and his mother mercilessly. But when his mother remarried, her new husband taught him how to defend himself and be a man. Now Leopoldo was going to teach *me* how to fight. And, so our push-up and sit-up regimen began anew. "Get down, *cabrón*, get that butt down, *hijo de puta*." *Asshole, son of a whore!* He brushed off his kung fu moves for me and promised to teach me how to box. I was terrible, of course. A total disappointment, not worth wasting his time on, but it was the thought that counted.

If I was too weak to box properly, Leopoldo decided the least he could do was teach me how to wrestle. Several weeks of rug burns followed. Leopoldo never let me pin him but, when he was feeling generous, he would award me points for a clever hit. When he was less inclined he would throw me around violently, blurring the line between horsing around and a beatdown. Sometimes he would put me into headlocks until I couldn't breathe or punch me on my shoulders until my arms went dead. Once he threw me into the side of a table and bruised my ribs. Another time he grabbed me by the testicles and brought me to my knees in tears. "Mens don't cry," he warned me, "only pussies cry." When I "chose" to be a pussy by crying, he stormed out of the house and was gone for the night.

I tried to interest Leopoldo in nonviolent activities, but it wasn't easy. Whenever I read to him or tried to tell him about the things I was learning in school, he told me I was showing off, trying to embarrass him. I had more luck with chess and checkers. In El Salvador, he told me, he'd been a chess master, so I challenged him to a game. He knew how to use his knights well and had a few good moves, but I beat him handily. I assumed he had let me win the way Uncle Tony used to. But Leopoldo threw the board on the ground and told me I had cheated. When we switched to checkers, he gloated to discover he could kick my ass across the board. So, checkers it was. Night after night I let him double- and triple-jump me, and he was often so satisfied with beating me on the checkerboard that he didn't need to take me down in the wrestling ring. Given the alternative, I was more than happy to let him win.

One day I found a black T-shirt at the Salvation Army, emblazoned with sparkling pot plants and the phrase A TOUCH OF GRASS. Leopoldo understood the pun and thought it was the funniest thing he'd seen since El Flaco took a dump on that fancy Mercedes. By transposing *class* and *grass*, the shirt was uproariously upending the Capitalist class system. Leopoldo had to have it. He could have just taken the shirt from me but, instead, he offered to trade me for his sacred red tank top, the one with the Native American warrior silhouette on it. The tank top had been given to him as a parting gift by the shaman who had trained him in California, and now Leopoldo was giving it to me. He bowed when he gave it to me, and I felt like a karate student receiving his master's black belt. The next day, Leopoldo proudly reported back that he had worn the TOUCH OF GRASS T-shirt to work at Twin City Foods, and the manager was scandalized beyond words when she saw it. For my part, I couldn't bring myself to wear the special red tank top. I'd seen Leopoldo beat my mother too many times while wearing it. I folded it carefully and tucked it into my drawer underneath my plastic samurai sword.

Another morning I awoke with an unfamiliar feeling of paternal affection. It was one of the rare quiet mornings when my mother was home from Inga's and we weren't recovering from an alcohol-induced home-wrecking the night before. I didn't love Leopoldo, but I was legitimately happy to have him around. I didn't quite know how to express this appreciation—if I were too sappy, he'd call me a faggot; too subtle, and he wouldn't get it. So I lied. Over a breakfast of rice and tofu, I told them I had dreamt that Leopoldo was a reincarnation of Lao Tse, the ancient Chinese philosopher who founded Taoism. From now on I was going to call him Lao as a sign of respect. Leopoldo nodded humbly, accepting the wisdom of the dream world, and Claudia looked like she was going to cry at the cosmic beauty of it all. She wrote in her dream journal: *L's impact on J has been extremely positive. The 2 are affectionate and playful with one another. L also has a serious concern w preparing J for manhood.*

Leopoldo's next alcoholic rage was less destructive than usual, and his repentance the morning after was more heartfelt. "I feel like he's spiritually purer this time," I told my mother. "But he's said he's going to quit drinking so many times before, I don't know what to think."

"Josh, you just have to love him. That's what'll cure him," Claudia promised me. "Think about him with love. He really loves *you*, you know. Don't worry, he's going to get better."

Across the room, Leopoldo was frowning at himself and at my mother's bruised face. How could he have done such a thing to his woman? He promised us he'd finally commit to one of those twelve-step programs. He'd become a new man.

We came in for a group hug and told each other that we were all in this together. As we cleared the apartment of debris from the night before, our cleaning felt charged with symbolism. We were purging the cycle of violence from our family. Leopoldo nodded approvingly as I picked up the empty beer cans strewn around the house. But he stopped me when I began pouring the green bottles of Mickey's Fine Malt Liquor down the sink. "Josh, don't waste that. I want to give to my friend Augusto." His concern for needless waste expressed itself again when he saw Claudia throwing out the makeup she used to cover her bruises and black eyes. "You shouldn't throw that away."

"Why?"

"You might need it."

"Why? You know I don't wear makeup."

"You just might need it. That's all."

A few days later, Leopoldo brought home a box of wine, since that didn't count as alcohol. And he insisted that he and Claudia drink *together*, like husband and wife, matching each other mug for mug. My mother went silent, clenching her jaw in anticipation of the inevitable. But then some dark idea flashed across her face, and she reached for the chipped mug of cheap wine. "*This* is what you want? *This*!?" She drained the mug and then went for another, and another.

Leopoldo seemed delighted. "What you want to say to me!?" He encouraged her. "Tell me! Tell me what you want to say!"

My mother slurred her words: "You're emotionally four years old! The age you were when your mother abandoned you. Well, *I'm* not your mother. *I* didn't abandon you. I've stuck by you, and what do I get? You listen to me, you make your sexist homophobic jokes, then you hit me. And around it goes. And what about poor little Josh!? We keep promising him again and again a real father. And look at you!" I was hiding in my room, freaked out by my mother's addition to the list of drunkards in my life. She was screaming now. "You're an asshole!" Dishes were smashing against the wall like heavy artillery. She was shrieking.

"Josh! Josh!" Leopoldo was pounding on my door, half-laughing, half-screaming. "Josh, come out here!" I didn't move, so he smashed through the door, his fist driving right through the wood paneling like he was the Hulk. "Josh, come see your mother." He grabbed me by the back of the neck and pushed me out in front of him like a human shield. "She a crazy bitch!" He was laughing, sharing a joke with me.

I ducked as a green plate shattered on the wall over my head. "Look, Josh. See your mother?" Claudia's face was bright red and her eyes were wild and watery behind her glasses. She was shaking another green plate in her hand like a deadly frisbee. Leopoldo grabbed my hair and shoved me toward her. "Claudia! I bring the boy. He see how *you* crazy. You really *loca, más loca que yo*. When you drink, you crazier than me." He seemed to be enjoying her rage. It proved that she was no better than he. When he finally punched her in the face in front of me, he did it calmly, almost mercifully, as if he were showing me how to put down a lame horse.

The next week we went to Seattle to meet with Dale Ramerman, Leopoldo's immigration attorney, to prepare for his first INS hearing. The attorney asked me if I was willing to testify that their marriage was not set up to circumvent immigration laws. I stared back at him and solemnly swore: "I'll do whatever you need me to do. Everything I can possibly do to help Leopoldo's case."

The attorney nodded and said: "Good."

Leopoldo went misty-eyed for a moment and put his hand on my shoulder to let me know he was proud of me. We brothers had to stand up for one another.

It was, perhaps, that brotherly bond that caused Leopoldo to yell, "Josh!" through the hollow walls a few nights later. From my mother's caterwauling I was pretty sure they were having sex, but maybe they were done now. I knocked on the door to their room, and Leopoldo called out: "Josh, come in here!"

Leopoldo's naked backside was rising and falling on the bed in a series of slow push-ups. His back glistened, and his hairless butt was flexing up and down. My mother's white shins were propped up on either side of him. I shivered at the sight of them having sex, as if I had just brushed up against an electric fence. I must have heard wrong. "Josh!" he called out again. "I show you how to make love to a woman." I stayed where I stood, still not sure that I had heard right. "Josh, come climb on my back. Come!" He was saying the words I thought he was saying. He was telling me to come climb on his back. This was, of course, unthinkable, like punching a baby in the face. But what did I know? I felt my active brain shut down, and a kind of haze slipped over me, as though I'd taken a big hit off of a bong or stayed up all night suffering through a never-ending drum circle. "Climb on my back, Josh!" It took me a hundred thousand steps to get to the bed, but I marched forward on autopilot and climbed onto Leopoldo's back. His skin was hot and greasy. His muscles were thick and undulating like a machine. Leopoldo bucked beneath me in long, slow gyrations. I couldn't think it, I couldn't let my mind grip on to it, but somewhere down there was my mother. What was supposed to happen now? When was this gruesome piggyback ride over? Could I leave? No, he wanted something from me.

"Wheee," I said, like a sarcastic teenager pretending to enjoy the thrill of a toddler swing. Suddenly, over his shoulder, I caught a glimpse of my mother's face, eyes closed, expressionless. Wires were crossing in my brain, and I felt the sudden need to curl up and die. I jumped off of him and ran from the room, down the hall, and out the front door.

I sprinted down the alley, oblivious to the dirt and gravel I was kicking up with my bare feet. I fled down the darkened streets until I collapsed in the wet field behind the Lutheran church. The cold dew leapt through my pajamas, and I was suddenly shivering, my feet howling with dozens of cuts. I was panting. "I'm going to throw up now," I told myself. "I feel sick and I won't be better until I vomit this out of me." But I didn't throw up. I couldn't. I just sat there shivering, holding my arms across my chest. Avoiding that flash of my mother's face, trying to spin away from it, trying to go back in time so that I would never enter that room. I was polluted somehow and needed to vomit. "What's wrong with me? Why can't I throw up?" I was sick . . . and *they* were sick. Sick beyond measure.

Everything had changed. I would never be able to look at their faces again without seeing a little of that sickness in their eyes.

EIGHTEEN

Bankruptcy

When I received her undivided attention, Claudia had a way of staring deeply into my eyes, as if she were scanning my inner soul. Maybe it was just her instinct to stare directly into people's souls, or maybe she had picked up the technique in psychic circles. I didn't know, but I couldn't look her in the eyes anymore. That searching, wide-eyed gaze was unbearable. I wanted to hold up a mirror and say: "What do you see in there? Pretty messed up, huh?" But I wasn't that mean.

My mother pretended nothing had happened, and I did my best to pretend too, darting my eyes around the perimeter of her face when we spoke about the television I wanted her to buy. Our move to Stanwood had brought with it the blessing of electricity, and I had dared to dream that the blessing of television might soon follow. But Claudia was not about to give corporate America an audience in our living room for their brainwashing lies. Didn't I know that television would ruin my mind?

But now it was different. My seventh-grade teacher had assigned watching the nightly news as homework for our current events unit.

"It's homework, Claudia," I pleaded, staring down at the floor. "I *have* to watch TV."

She wouldn't throw down fifty bucks for a used television of our own, but she reluctantly agreed to let me sneak into Inga's house after the old lady and her adult daughter were asleep. There I could watch the eleven o'clock news under Claudia's vigilant supervision. I stared at the strange glowing screen hesitantly at first, like a novice snake charmer, ready to jump away when I felt the first sting of brainwashing. From time to time, I averted my eyes from the screen to exercise my mind, reciting famous quotations from memory to test myself for brain damage. After a couple of nights, I dismissed my mother's concerns as paranoia; television was harmless. Although I had to admit that the moving color pictures gave me a new perspective on certain news stories. The Midwestern drought that Claudia had dismissed as a corporate scam to gain more farm subsidies sure looked like a bona fide disaster to me. And, despite his evil policies, Reagan actually moved and talked like a nice old man, not a demon loosely draped in human skin.

But the most startling difference was my take on the intifada. This was an issue that kept me awake at night. How was I supposed to take pride in being Jewish with genocide being committed in my name? But now the intifada was being televised. Instead of a still, grainy picture of a Palestinian boy holding his leg in pain, I was presented with broad pans of hundreds of men hurling rocks and Molotov cocktails at almost impossibly restrained Israeli soldiers. I peered in to look at their skin color. Claudia had characterized this conflict as a redux of the Civil Rights Movement, except this time around the dark-skinned oppressed minority wasn't just being denied its basic human rights and dignity, it was also being targeted for extermination. But that wasn't what it looked like on camera. When presented with my thoughts on the issue, Claudia assured me my conclusions were all the result of selective editing and government manipulation of the media. But I wasn't so sure.

Claudia's grip on my worldview began to erode in front of the television, and it disintegrated completely a week later at Video Farm, the popular video store and arcade where I had taken to loitering after school. They showed previews on the television up front, and you never knew when they might start projecting a free movie on the big screen in back. On the day in question I found Erin, one of the popular girls, eating Twizzlers next to the poster for *Dirty Dancing.*

"Hey, Erin," I said casually.

"Hi, Josh." This was a pleasant surprise. We were assigned partners in home economics, but I didn't expect her to acknowledge me in public. She was smiling at me. "They said they'll show *The Princess Bride* in back if I set up the chairs."

"That's rad," I said. "Do you need help?"

"Yes! You can carry that stack of chairs. It's too heavy for me." I started unstacking the chairs, but Erin interrupted me: "What are you doing? Take the whole stack."

"If it was too heavy for you, it'll be too heavy for me," I reasoned.

"No it won't. You're a boy."

"What's that got to do with anything?"

"Hello!? Boys are bigger and stronger than girls."

Oh, that's what she meant. Poor, sweet clueless Erin. I looked at her with her massive hair-sprayed bangs and makeup and frilly white shorts. She was such the victim of societal brainwashing that she didn't even understand the basics of feminism. It was time for me to set her straight.

"Boys are *not* bigger and stronger," I lectured her. "That's just a sexist myth that's been taught to you your whole life. Anything a man can do, a woman can do. Men and women are exactly the same, except for their you-know-whats. You've been programmed to think that boys are *supposed* to play sports and girls are *supposed* to be weak, but that's all a lie."

"No it's not. Boys *are* bigger and stronger than girls. Duh! Think about it. Think of all the men you know. Now think of all the women you know. *Most* men are bigger and stronger than *most* women."

I humored her and embarked on her little mental exercise. Skimming through a list in my head of everyone I knew, I realized the men were stronger in every case. She was right. I grudgingly conceded the point and then hauled the entire stack of chairs into the back by myself. I didn't focus on a single frame of *The Princess Bride*. Men *were* bigger and stronger. It wasn't a sexist construct. It was biology. How could I have been so blind?

If my mother had been *so* wrong about this, what else had she gotten wrong? What else was a lie? Maybe the Israelis were actually decent people trying to make the best of a complicated situation. And if this were true, maybe the same could be said for America. Maybe the police and the government and the corporations—everyone I'd been taught to hate and fear—maybe they were all fundamentally good people, trying to do their best in complex times. And what if black and brown people weren't morally superior to white people? What if we were all just individuals who should be judged by the content of our character? Wasn't that what Dr. King had been talking about anyway? And, if that was the case, maybe your politics shouldn't define your moral worth. Maybe you could be an über-Republican but still be a good person. And, maybe, just maybe, you could believe in the Revolution and the People and still be a terrible person.

I walked back, thinking about the river of ideas I'd been swimming in my whole life. All of the life choices my mother had made, all of the deprivations I had suffered—were they all premised on delusions? What the hell!? The river had started to evaporate around me at Video Farm and had run dry by the time I reached home. The walls of my room were plastered with protest posters I'd picked up over the years, and I looked at them now with new eyes.

Me, at age twelve, gaining perspective in the boughs of a tree.

First, I tore down ISRAEL OUT OF PALESTINE! And then I tore down U.S. OUT OF NORTH AMERICA! And then I ripped at my political wallpaper with the zeal of a recently deprogrammed cult survivor until all that remained was one anti-nuclear war poster. Then I tore that down too. Who knew? Maybe you *could* hug your child with nuclear arms.

With the fog of Claudia's dogmas suddenly lifted, I felt like a window had been opened in my mind. I was breathing fresh air for the first time in my life. At the same time, fear of the Immigration and Naturalization Service began to inhabit our home like sinister vapors. They were hovering around us, just out of sight, watching and listening, judging our every action. With the wave of some papers the INS could break up our family and send Leopoldo to his death on that sizzling tarmac in San Salvador. Now the vapors were taking shape. Our attorney told us that the INS would begin conducting interviews in a month. They wanted assurance that the love between Leopoldo and Claudia was real and not some cooked up sham.

The impending interviews didn't humble Leopoldo the way I thought they would. If anything they seemed to embolden him, adding a new level of cockiness to his dictatorial rule. He forbade my mother from socializing and required explanations for every errand she made. He took to referring to her as *Janucha*. When she asked what it meant, he laughed: "It's a very bad word. I won't even to translate it." Claudia opened her dream journal one morning to find that Leopoldo had drawn himself walking a pussycat on a leash, saying, *Mira, Cabrona—Look, Bitch.*

My leash was shortened as well. After dinner, I had to sit in the armchair until Leopoldo gave me permission to go to my room, ostensibly to ensure that I was digesting my food properly before lying down. When I made mistakes, which was often, he made me do push-ups. He'd count my mistakes all evening. I dropped a grain of rice on the floor—"That's one." I left a bit of grit on a plate after washing the dishes—"That's two." At five mistakes, I owed him ten push-ups. I developed a nervous eye tic, and I began to fantasize about him dying. Not so much me killing him, but an act of God. A car crash or an industrial accident. Maybe a lightning bolt. Pressure was building, and I knew something had to give.

The day before the INS interview, I found Leopoldo and Claudia sitting at the kitchen table, rehearsing their lines.

"Leopoldo, what side of the bed do I sleep on?"

"Left."

"What do we do for birthdays?"

"Have a party and go out to eat."

"What's your pet name for me?"

"What you mean *pet*?"

"Don't worry about it. The answer is *honey*."

"OK. Honey."

I sat down next to them and finished falsifying entries in my journal. In sixth grade Mrs. King had told me to keep a daily journal to practice my penmanship. Now Claudia wanted to offer it up as proof that Leopoldo was really living with us. The lawyer loved the idea but was worried about the gaps in time when Leopoldo had gone to Eastern Washington to pick fruit. Claudia asked me to rewrite those parts of the journal to gloss over the weeks of separation, and I had done it. But knowing that my journal was going to be submitted into evidence compelled me to make a lot of other changes as well. *Leopoldo threw me into the table and bruised my ribs* became *I was clumsy and bumped into the table and bruised my ribs.*

I was lying. Claudia was also lying. She wrote a letter to the INS describing Leopoldo as: "A Central American Indian in tune with traditions of natural healing. I've seen him work three different cures, including healing a deep cut of mine with the ash of burnt newspaper."

And Leopoldo lied too. In fact, over the next few days, we discovered that Leopoldo was nothing but lies. When we first met him, he was a refugee in deep mourning. He'd just received a letter from his mother in El Salvador, announcing devastating news. His young son had been tragically gunned down and killed in a cross fire. I remembered—right before he had sex with my mother the first time—Leopoldo had been waving the letter around and crying: "He dead! He dead!" Now we discovered that his son wasn't quite dead. According to the translator at the law office who had sifted through all of Leopoldo's boxes of correspondence, the letter was *not* from Leopoldo's mother. It was from his *wife* in El Salvador. And the boy hadn't been *murdered.* He'd just been *sick.* He was very much alive now and doing well. In front of the lawyer, Leopoldo concocted a long story about how he must have originally misread the letter, but not even Claudia believed him. He'd apparently been writing to the kid for years.

Most astoundingly, there was no documentation whatsoever to support his claim that he'd been a guerrilla in the FMLN. It *was* clear, however, that he'd been a draftee in the US-backed Salvadoran army. He'd apparently served with distinction and appeared to have received an honorary discharge. Leopoldo explained that he'd joined the rebels *after* the army, but the time line they had put together for his Immigration filing was running out of room for a second military career. To bolster his credibility, he finally revealed the secret code name the FMLN had given him. It was Leo. I'd never served in a rebel cell, but even I knew code names weren't just abbreviations of your real name.

During a break in the interview preparations, I found Leopoldo up front, flirting with one of the legal secretaries who was also married to a Salvadoran. "I followed Archbishop Romero," he told her with a straight face. "I been always part of the peace movement. No matter how bad it get, there's no excuse for the violence."

It was all lies. I couldn't believe it. I didn't want to believe it. The truth made me and my mother the biggest suckers of all time. We had been bilked out of years of our lives. The whole thing, all that time, it was just a big con game—a stunning scam. I couldn't even bring myself to be angry. I just felt totally ripped off.

We exited I-5 toward Stanwood, and the streetlights flickered across the side of Leopoldo's face. He didn't look scary in this light. He looked like a clown. Seated next to him was my mother. She looked like one too. A couple of clowns in a tragic circus.

But as bad as Leopoldo was, I couldn't help but wonder: Was I any better?

"Where the *fuck* you go to!?" Leopoldo had called after me a few months back. "I no say you can go!"

I closed the door gently behind me and ran down the alley. When I saw that he wasn't chasing me, I rounded the corner slowly and swaggered down the block. A new family was moving into the house where the pack of Dobermans used to be, and I wanted them to see me strut. But they didn't notice me. They were too busy unloading the stuffed parrots and the crate of Creedence Clearwater Revival albums from the back of a black van.

"Hey, what's up," I said to the fat kid with the camouflage headband. "I'm Josh."

"Hey, I'm Andy. Some people call me Mandy, not like a girl's name, but like *Manly Andy*—Mandy."

"Mandy?"

"Or Andy. Whatever you want." Mandy was fiddling with a pair of plastic nunchucks. He was dressed like a commando but built like a marshmallow.

"You moving in?" I asked.

"Yeah, we were living in the trailer park but *my* dad married *their* mom," he said, pointing at the three blond kids shuttling rag rugs and lava lamps into the house. "We're kinda like the Brady Bunch."

I didn't know who the Brady Bunch were but figured they were some notorious family of outlaws from TV. "Cool," I said. "I live around the corner with my mom and stepdad. He murdered a lot of people in El Salvador."

"Cool," said Mandy. "Very cool."

Despite his warlike attire, Mandy turned out to be kind of a dud. He preferred action movies to actual action and was too afraid of imagined snakes to take the shortcut through the field behind the church. I left Mandy to veg out on the couch and became fast friends with his stepbrother Jim. Jim was a year older than me, and at night we dressed in black and prowled around the neighborhood like ninjas.

I'd found my newest adoptive family and spent every waking hour with the Brady Bunch. Jim's mother drank heavily and cut hair for money on their front porch. Mandy's father smoked weed alone in the black van after dinner and had a bumper sticker that said THERE ARE MANY WAYS TO SAY I LOVE YOU & F*ING IS ONE OF THEM. Jim's youngest sister was eight, but she still sucked her thumb and dragged a security blanket around with her. I didn't pay her any attention, focusing instead on the older sister, Rachel.

Rachel was a year younger than me. She had a sweet face but it was interrupted by oversized teeth whenever she dared to smile. She had a crush on me. I could tell by the way she blushed when I told her she looked pretty. When she followed me from room to room, I pretended not to notice, and I ignored her when she spun around to show me her rudimentary knowledge of ballet. Rachel had so many questions for me, but I was too cool to answer them. "Tell me about New York, Josh! What was it like?" She'd keep at it, begging for details, and finally I would notice her, gazing down at her like a rock star deigning to acknowledge the shrieking groupie in the first row. Then I'd begin concocting stories for her, and she'd inhale them like opium, her head nodding, her eyebrows rising. Sometimes all she could say in response was "*Wow.*" Who could blame her? I was very impressive, or at least I pretended I was.

She might know a little ballet, but I'd studied at a Russian ballet school in New York City. She loved to go square dancing with her mom, but I'd taken first place in the junior square-dance competition at the Kansas State Fair. She loved Madonna, but my dad had played bass in Madonna's backup band. I'd even hung out with her a couple of times at parties in New York. She was pretty short in real life, I told Rachel, and had a surprisingly husky voice. Madonna smoked nothing but clove cigarettes. And lest Rachel begin to doubt my manliness, I told her I'd once killed a man. I was dating a girl three years older than me back in California. Her stepdad used to come to her room and beat her with a belt. I didn't think that was right, and one day I confronted her stepdad with a pistol. He lunged at me, and I shot him between the eyes. After a night in juvenile hall they let me go, calling it self-defense. The stepdad's family had vowed revenge against me, and now I was in the witness relocation program here in Stanwood. I'd done all of these things before I was twelve.

They were lies, but they were easy. I kept dishing them out, and Rachel kept eating them up. She asked a lot of follow-up questions, but they were no problem. I'd spent a summer living with my father on the Lower East Side so I was well equipped with all the little observations I needed to build a fantasy world amidst bohemian celebrities in the Big Apple. I'd read Madonna's interview in *Penthouse,* so I knew intimate details about her life. And I'd read more books than Rachel's family put together, so I had no end of inspirational source material to draw from.

Rachel also required some proof, of course. I couldn't just say I was a ballet dancer or a square-dance champion without getting up from my chair. But I'd learned the art of false identity from a sensei of fraud. Leopoldo could claim to be a black belt in kung fu or a chess master because he made it clear that these things didn't matter to him. They were mere playthings he'd put down already. If you made a big deal about his alleged mastery of a specialized martial art or an ancient game of skill, he told you that you were acting like an excitable child. Leopoldo would show off a few moves and nothing more. If that wasn't enough to convince you, then forget you. Leave him alone and stop wasting his time. This routine was somehow very convincing, and I practiced it on Rachel. I rose from my chair wearily, stretched dramatically, gave her a few spectacular arcs of my hand through the air, and pointed at the window with my toe. That was master ballet, take it or leave it. Square dancing was a little harder because I had no idea what it even looked like. It was some sort of *yee-haw* cowboy dance. So I shuffled around muscularly in a circle and that was championship-level square dancing. And it worked. Rachel shook her head in wonder at my humble displays of greatness.

Successfully sliding my deceit down her gullible throat gave me a charge of power and control, but it also left me with a nagging nausea in my belly. But I didn't let my guilt stop me. I kept on feeding her lies.

We weren't boyfriend and girlfriend exactly, but we took long walks together, and she told me boring secrets she'd never told anyone else. One Sunday she made a picnic for us, and we ate her sandwiches together in the middle school playground. For dessert we sipped from juice boxes, and I told funny stories to make her laugh. Rachel grinned impishly and suddenly sprayed me in the face with her juice box. My eyes stung. That little bitch! I grabbed Rachel by the hair and yanked her toward me. I slapped her in the face and then slipped behind her and put her in a headlock.

"I'm sorry, I'm sorry," she cried.

"You better be sorry," I spit at her. I held her tightly.

"I'm sorry," she cried again.

I was calm now. "You do *not* disrespect me like that." She nodded, and I let her go. When she stopped crying, we walked back toward home, holding hands for the first time.

The weekend after Leopoldo was exposed as a fraud, Rachel's mother invited me to go with them to the mudflats on Camano Island. We slid on our bellies all day across miles of briny mud. We laughed at the sinfulness of being so dirty. At the end of the day, our grime-streaked bodies ached all over. But it was a good ache, the way a soldier must feel after walking through a battle unscathed. While the rest of the Brady Bunch made a fire on the beach, Jim and I toweled off up at the car.

"Check it out," he said. "I got my M-16 out of storage." He was holding a black military assault rifle out in front of him. It bore the unmistakable ribbed hand guard and square handle that defined the American infantryman in the Vietnam War.

"Whoa," I said. The gun invoked a dissonant blend of lust and fear. "Is it real?" I asked.

"Nah," said Jim. "It's just a BB gun."

"Can I hold it?"

"Sure," said Jim. "This is how you cock it." He pulled back a lever along the chamber with an exhilaratingly ominous mechanical snap.

The rifle nestled perfectly against my shoulder. It was born to be held in my arms. I crouched down in the bushes and swept the barrel back and forth along my field of fire. The muddy delta, the jumbled rocks, the jungly weeds—I could have been in Vietnam. But when I tried to imagine clusters of Vietcong to shoot at, I kept seeing Leopoldo's crouching form in front of me. His sneering face, his scraggly-ass goatee, his red headband. I imagined drilling him right through the head. And then, through my sights, there was Rachel laughing down by the bonfire with her big horsey teeth. Could a BB even travel that far? I lowered the sights to her shoulder and pressed the trigger. Through the little iron circle I saw her face collapse in tears. She was clutching at her arm. Then her crying was carried on the wind.

"Oh, shit, Jim. I think I just shot Rachel!"

"Where?"

"On the arm."

"You fucker! Now my mom's going to take the M-16 away from me again."

I handed the rifle back to Jim and walked down to the bonfire like a condemned man. I was the worst person in the world. I would've preferred to die by the side of the trail but knew I had no choice but to face my victim. By the time I reached her, Rachel had stopped crying but was still sniffling. I apologized over and over, and Jim hissed at her until she agreed not to tell their mother.

We rode back to Stanwood from the mudflats in silence. My hand was limp in Rachel's clutch, and I bowed my head in shame. As I thought it over, it was suddenly clear to me what was happening. I was becoming a little con-man, molded in Leopoldo's image. And I knew this meant he was winning somehow.

When we got out of the car, I pulled Rachel aside and confessed it all to her. Everything I'd told her was a lie. Everything. I couldn't dance. I'd never met Madonna. I'd never had a girlfriend. And the only person I'd ever shot was her. Rachel's face pulled itself apart, and she cried, worse than when I'd shot her.

"Why, Josh? Why did you lie to me?" she asked in tearful gasps.

"I don't know." I shrugged.

"I hate you! I never want to see you again."

"I'm sorry," I said numbly and turned away from her.

When I came through the door of the apartment, Leopoldo was waiting for me. "Where the *fuck* you been!?"

"I shot a girl," I said, and closed the shattered door to my room behind me. He didn't come after me. Maybe he was too confused by my answer. Or maybe he was proud of me.

NINETEEN

The Revolution

Leopoldo was shouting, but no one was listening anymore. The ground was shifting under his feet. It wasn't an earthquake, not yet, but the mud was pulling at his boots, and he was steadily slipping down the slope.

Claudia had lost her ever-talkative tendencies and would lapse into silence for hours at a time. She moved around the apartment like a ghost. She wasn't defying him, but she was depriving him of her company. I wasn't defying him either, but I was coming close. I was flexing, testing the strength of my opponent in little ways. I dragged my feet when Leopoldo demanded urgency and asked sarcastic questions when he ordered me around. It was clear to me now that a showdown was coming. Leopoldo was not going to leave voluntarily. I would have to force him out.

The problem was when. Things were too intolerable to wait much longer, but I knew I couldn't trigger the inevitable confrontation until the time was right. And, from where I stood, no time seemed ideal to go up against an ex-military commando who enjoyed fighting. He was a liar, but he was still lethal. So I kept my head down and probed for weaknesses and opportunities, like an unarmed scout scurrying through the silent landscape in search of the perfect battlefield. When the day of battle came, I would be ready.

As Leopoldo felt his hold over us slipping, he resorted to drink more than ever. His alcoholic binges became ever more destructive and raged on well into the morning. When I came home in the afternoon I would find him stumbling about in a pit of wreckage, incoherently apologetic. These were the moments when he was at his weakest, but I couldn't fight him then. This was Leopoldo the pitiful alcoholic fool. And that wasn't the man I wanted to stand up to. I wanted to take on Leopoldo the abusive bully, when he was at his strongest. Yet that was when I was most afraid of him.

Spring unexpectedly delivered a week of rainless skies, and I spent every afternoon shooting baskets down at the hoop behind the church. The open air lifted a measure of heaviness from my chest, and I stood at the free-throw line carefully lining up my shot. My ball clanged off the rim and rolled out of sight into the church parking lot.

A moment later my ball reemerged in the hands of Byron Smith, a weasel-faced eighth-grader I'd seen hanging around with the heavy metal kids. He was accompanied by a long-haired teenager I'd never seen before. They were both grinning.

"You wanna fight?" the teenager offered me hopefully. My dog, Benji, barked in warning, but I stood my ground.

"No, give me my ball back."

"How about we fight for the ball?" They were on the court now and kept coming closer.

"No, I just want my ball back and then I'll go home." This was not what he wanted to hear. His pasty face was in mine now, and he poked me in the chest. He had rings on his fingers.

"How 'bout you fight my friend Byron here, or I do this to your little faggoty dog!? You ever seen one of these?" He pulled out a black Chinese throwing star from his denim jacket and stabbed it into my ball. Byron flinched, and the ball gasped and wilted.

"Fucking jerks!" I protested. "That was my ball."

"What'd you call me!? Huh!?" He was back in my face.

I could've run, but once they'd popped my ball and threatened to kill Benji that was no longer an option. And although Byron was older, he was about my size. I glared at Byron's bucktoothed grin and wet spiky hair and felt confident I could hold my own. I nodded, as if to say *OK, I'll fight you.* Byron came at me in a flurry of fists, punching me in the face three or four times before I could even raise my hands. I was on the ground, blood in my mouth, blood pouring out of my nose.

"Get up, faggot! Get up!" the teenager was hollering down at me. "Get up!"

I pulled myself onto my feet and drove into Byron's midsection. We rolled around on the blacktop, and I crushed him in my arms with all my strength. He struggled to free himself, but I could feel that I was stronger. And then I was on top of him, punching and smashing at his face.

"And Byron's down," the teenager announced. "Oh no! . . . The Ref gets involved!"

A sudden boot to the back of the head sent me into blackness for a moment.

When I came to, I was on my side, feet kicking me in the ribs, back, shins, butt. Then a heel to the temple, and my skull creaked.

Somewhere a voice announced: "And the faggot goes down by TKO in the second round!" And then laughter trailed off around the corner.

I limped home, spitting blood, crying, and swearing oaths of revenge. My face was swollen and numb, my lips were cracked, and my nose refused to stop bleeding. When I came in the door, Leopoldo greeted me with: "Why you gone so long!?"

"Two boys beat me up," I howled at him.

"Why you cry like a pussy?"

I tried to pull myself together, but couldn't stop shaking. Claudia came home from Inga's just then. "Oh my God, Joshey, what happened!?" she shrieked, grabbing at my face as though I were dying.

"Two boys beat me up." I was crying again.

She turned to Leopoldo: "Do something! What are you going to do!?"

"What can I do?" he shrugged.

"We could go *find* them," I growled. "They're probably on their way to Video Farm. You could have a little 'talk' with them."

But I knew it was no use. He never stood up for me. When I told my mother I was getting bullied by the big girl back on Camano Island, I actually felt sorry for the girl as I watched Claudia dispatch Leopoldo ahead of me down the trail. What was he going to do to her? Thrash her? Or just scare her so bad she would piss her acid-washed jeans? But he did nothing. He just shrugged his shoulders and reported back: "She say Josh use very bad words." The girl gave me an extra special pummeling that day for telling on her.

And now it was the same thing. "What can I do? If two boys fight you, you fight back to them. Here." Leopoldo reached under the sink and gave me a wet, broken mop handle. "You carry this in you pants. If they come to you, hit them." The scrap of wood was a joke.

This man had killed people, sought out fights with the police, and beaten his wife with impunity. All he was good at was violence, but he couldn't raise a finger to protect me? What use was he? He was nothing, totally worthless. I shook my head in disgust and went to the bathroom to clean the blood off my face. Looking at my battered image in the mirror, I didn't see a victim looking back at me. Under the blood, I was nearly a man, with a shadow of a moustache and a solid jawline. Battle-bruised but tough. Flashes of the fight flickered through my head, and I realized that I'd fought back for the first time. I'd thrown punches. I'd tackled Byron Smith and taken him down. And I would have beaten him too if his friend hadn't kicked me in the head.

I had the will to fight.

A couple of days later, Leopoldo stood over me as I swept the kitchen floor. "You complain about sweep the floor? When I was a boy, you know what I get for my birthday?" he barked at me. "My father, him threw the cake to the floor and say 'Happy birthday, motherfucker!' "

"Yeah, but I bet he stood up for you if you were getting beaten by bullies."

"What you say to me!? Go to you room!"

I dropped the broom and marched off to my room. As I passed the door to his bedroom, I pictured his face in front of me and punched at the door with everything I had. Pain sizzled through my knuckles. I'd busted a hole in the door. Leopoldo was on me like a storm.

"What you do?" He shook me by the collar. "What you do!?" He threw me to the ground and crouched over me, a finger in my face. "You . . . no . . . disrespect to me." I'd gone too far. He was going to kill me.

"It was an accident," I said meekly. "I'm sorry."

Leopoldo slammed the front door behind him, and I locked myself in the bathroom to bandage my swollen knuckles. I was still scared of him.

In her dream journal, Claudia wrote: *I worry about Josh—having to repress what would seem a natural anger . . . and then hitting his hand on the back of L's door (accidentally). Did he inherit his mother's tendency towards masochism as a solution to inexpressible anger?*

Leopoldo didn't come home that night. He used his one phone call to tell us he was in jail. He had gotten into a fight with the police and kicked a cop. They were making a whole big deal about it.

"Should we go visit him?" I asked.

"We can't." Claudia's face looked funny. "He forgot to tell us what jail he was calling from." She was almost smiling. "Looks like it's just you and me for a couple of days."

Just us. It felt like it had been years since it was just the two of us. Claudia started laughing. "I can't believe it, Josh. After all we've given up for him. I dropped out of school for him, and we wound up living on a stump. Now we're living in this dump with the rats. The whole time he was promising you he'd be a real father. His self-destructiveness is appalling. Here he is at the edge of legal entry to America after a year and a half of court fights and he destroys his chances by kicking a policeman."

"Do you think they'll really send him back to El Salvador?"

"Maybe."

"Do you really think they'll shoot him at the airport like he says?"

"I don't know. You know . . . I don't know if I even care anymore."

They didn't send him back to El Salvador. They sent him home to enroll in a twelve-step program. But I gained something in the process. I had my mother back.

Leopoldo was no longer a hero of the Revolution in her eyes. It was one thing for her to be beaten by a freedom fighter suffering from memories of oppression, but quite another to be battered by an alcoholic veteran of a US puppet army. It shouldn't have mattered, but it did. His spell had been lifted, and Claudia was starting to see clearly again.

I began sneaking over to Inga's every night, after the old lady had gone to bed, to spend time with Claudia. We were friends again, my mother and me, like old times. And now we were plotting a conspiracy. It was so unthinkable that we whispered, even though Leopoldo was a block away. Could we leave him? And, more importantly, where could we go? Wouldn't he find us? Leopoldo had done such an effective job of limiting Claudia's social life that she didn't have any friends of her own. The only people he didn't know about were back in San Francisco.

Claudia refused to even consider asking Uncle Tony if we could come live in his one-bedroom apartment. The last thing she wanted was to share her bedroom with another man. But she agreed that Claude's family might be the solution. His parents owned a big house in the Castro, and they might be willing to let us take refuge with them until we could get back on our feet. Claudia wrote letters to Claude and his family, and I rushed home from school every day to get to the mailbox before Leopoldo. We finally received a letter back from Claude's father, and I opened it with trembling hands. His reply was "No." He was having some health issues, and it wasn't a good time to have a kid around. His daughter, Claude's twin sister, had added a note saying: "We do <u>not</u> owe you <u>anything</u>!"

There was nowhere to go.

When Leopoldo got home, I slipped past him out the door. "Where you go!?" he demanded to know. I slammed the door behind me and walked into the night. What would Leopoldo do? I thought to myself. If he were me, what would he do? It was obvious. He would kill his stepfather.

Down at Bob's Market, I ran into one of Ervi's cousins in the back of the store by the six-packs of beer. He was about twenty and wore his flannel shirt open with only the top button fastened, like a Mexican gangster. He told me Ervi might be coming back to the area in a month or two once spinach season started. I sat with him on the curb while he put back his beers and, when the moment seemed right, I asked him if he knew where I could get a gun.

"How much money you got?"

"How much do I need?"

"At least two hundred."

"I've got about eighty-five saved up."

"Come back when you got two hundred, and we'll talk."

I went to bed that night doing math in my head. I was 42.5 percent of the way to a solution. A mere $115 separated me from a gun. My friend Dorothy had told me she could get me a summer job sorting vegetables on the conveyor belts at Twin City Foods. I'd be making five bucks an hour there. At that rate, I'd have all the money I needed in three days of work, maybe four, depending on what Ervi's cousin had to offer.

Maybe it would be a rifle. I'd fired long guns before, so that was a plus. But it would be hard to maneuver and fire indoors. I would have to lure Leopoldo outside somehow, and outdoors people were liable to see me shoot him, so that was a minus. A pistol would be better. I could conceal it and get up close to him, inside the apartment. But I had never fired one before. They looked complicated in the movies. I'd have to practice.

If I was going to do it, I had to do it right. Leopoldo had survived being shot before. He even had the scars to prove it. Or did he? How did I know what a bullet scar really looked like? Everything else he said seemed to be a lie. Maybe he wasn't as tough as he appeared.

The week before, I was a quarter of the way through *The Godfather* at Video Farm when I began having a sense of déjà vu. Wait a second, I said to myself. I already knew this plotline from somewhere. They duct-tape a pistol to the back of a toilet in a restaurant and the protagonist steps into a waiting car after shooting a mob boss and a policeman in cold blood. Where did I know this from? Oh, yeah. Leopoldo told me he had executed the Mafioso and the chief of police in San Salvador for the FMLN in the same way. He must have seen the movie too and simply expropriated the scene into his autobiography. Something about his bullshit infuriated me worse than his battering.

I dreamt powerful dreams about guns that night. Bullets clicked into magazines and revolving chambers whirled through the dream world. A deep voice reassured me that guns were "the great equalizers," and I knew this to be true. They tore through muscle as easy as air, and they let the little man take down the big man with the simple pull of a trigger. "Josh, get the fuck over to here!" I heard Leopoldo yell in my dream. I turned on him and drew, and *pow*! Over and over. Each time smoother than the last, until I awoke with a confident smile.

Claudia was home from Inga's when Leopoldo came through the door, breathless. He'd been at his friend Augusto's place and seen on the news that there had been a major meltdown at a nuclear plant in North Carolina. Claudia started to panic, but I flipped on the radio and scanned the news channels. Nothing. Not a word. "Yeah, I don't think so," I said.

Claudia and I flipped through the atlas together. "Look at how close North Carolina is to DC," I reasoned. "There would have to be something on the radio."

"You no believe me!? I hear it with my own ears and eyes."

"You're wrong," I said.

Leopoldo went on and on, telling us about the meltdown in Spanish, my mother translating the words I couldn't understand into English. The pumps stopped working, the coolant failed, the reactor exploded. The "good reporter" was trying to let the people know but the "bad guy" from the company was trying to stop her.

"The *good* reporter?" I snorted. "It must have been a movie."

"No, Josh. You no listening."

"Did the news report have a car chase in it?"

"Yes."

My mother shook her head and closed the atlas. I turned off the radio. "You are such a joke," I said.

Leopoldo narrowed his eyes. "You say I'm a liar?"

I didn't answer him. The time wasn't right.

"You disrespect me, maybe, Josh? Claudia told me you got some complaints about me. That you no tell me 'cause you afraid of me? What you gotta say?"

I wasn't going to take the bait. "I'm not saying anything to you because I *am* afraid of you." Ironically, in that moment, I realized that I was finally no longer afraid of him.

"I no hit you. What you have to say?" Claudia was at his side now, with her hands folded in front of her. She thought she was making some kind of peace.

This was neither the time nor the place. This was *not* the battlefield of my choosing. But, then again, why should I back down? He wanted to know what I had to say. Fuck him! I rose to my feet and yelled: "I *do* disrespect you! Everything you touch, you destroy! You ruined our lives! And all you do is take! You're a monster! You're scum!"

"*¿Qué es esto?*" He didn't know the word *scum* and turned to my mother for translation.

She pulled at the air, trying her best: *"Es un tipo de planta muy pequeña en el agua." It's a type of small plant in the water.* She wasn't capturing the point properly, so I continued.

"You're less than scum. *Abajo de* scum! You're nothing without us! You hear me!? You're nothing!"

Leopoldo stepped forward and punched me in the mouth, almost casually. I was twelve years old, old enough now. I went sailing backward into the couch, but jumped back onto my feet. My upper lip was cut and bleeding, but it felt good. This wasn't the battlefield of my choosing, but I would make it mine. I was ready to fight.

I bounced on my toes and weaved my head back and forth like a boxer. Leopoldo stood stone still, eyeing me apprehensively. He was stronger and tougher, but I could see it in his eyes: He was scared of *me*. He was a bully, and he enjoyed punching people who wouldn't hit back. He wasn't a fighter.

But I was. I was animated by an unquenchable fire. Power and strength and hatred coursed through my veins. He could knock me down as many times as he wanted, but I'd keep getting back up. I'd come at him again and again until he went down. It was him or me now. If he didn't leave I would kill him. With my bare hands if I had to.

I raised my right hand in a fist and pointed at the door with my left. "Get out! Get out!" I screamed at him. "Get out right now!"

Leopoldo's face flickered with a mixture of anger and surprise, his jaw tightening, his eyebrows rising. A ripple of curiosity passed behind his eyes, as if he didn't recognize the man/boy before him.

We stood there facing one another, frozen in time. The boy in the white T-shirt with the oversized nose and big eyes bounced in anticipation, his fists shaking with rage. A first line of thick hair darkened the boy's upper lip, and the lip was swollen and bleeding. The blood tasted hot and metallic, and the boy was no longer afraid of the man across from him. The man stood still, a red bandana pinning down his dull black hair, betrayed now by a single strand of white. The man's face was gray and taut, perched over a muscular frame achy from misuse. His fingers opened and closed, unsure of themselves.

We stood there not saying a thousand different things, and then a slackening of Leopoldo's jaw and a tightening of his eyes signaled something. He was tired. Leopoldo turned suddenly and stomped out of the apartment, slamming the door behind him.

I was still shaking my fists, ready to fight, until I saw my mother's eyes. They looked alive and angry, as if a porcelain mask had just been shattered off of her face. "We have to get out of here!" she was repeating to herself. Claudia had found her way back to sanity. Somehow it was alright for him to beat the hell out of her. But not to hit me. Not her boy.

Claudia locked the door and began working the phone, calling the few people she could think of that Leopoldo didn't know. One of the elderly Quaker women from People for Peace referred her to her friend Susan, another Quaker, who seemed to quickly grasp the urgency of our situation. As the sun began to set, we ran relays to our old green Toyota Corona with armloads of everything worth keeping. We moved skittishly, like bank robbers racing the clock. He might show up at any minute.

But he didn't show, and we took shelter in the basement of Susan's house outside of town. I paced back and forth, still expecting Leopoldo to come through the door and finish our fight. But silence and stillness prevailed, and I finally sat down and smiled. I'd won.

That night, my mother and I debated whether I should keep attending school for the last few weeks of seventh grade. What if he found me? I decided to assume the risk. I cared about my grades too much, and I was convinced that Leopoldo had never paid enough attention to even know where I went to school. And, on some level, I secretly hoped that he would come for me so I could stab him in the throat. I finished the year riding the bus with Susan's children. None of the kids on the bus tried to pick on me, which was a good thing because I had a butcher knife in my backpack.

On the first day of summer, Claudia whooped at me: "We finally found it!"

"It?"

"Community! The intentional community we've been looking for all these years." Her eyes were glowing, and she was gesticulating excitedly with her hands. "It's called Walker Creek."

She told me she'd been bagging up bulk brewer's yeast at the food co-op in Mount Vernon when she received a message from the Spirits. They were going to guide us into the promised land. Just then a woman with a mane of fiery red hair glided by. She was talking loudly about how they needed just one more family for their commune out by Big Lake. We were that family.

In August of 1988, Claudia and I piled ourselves into a decommissioned yellow school bus and drove out into the foothills of the Cascades to start a new life. We slept in the bus at night and cleared trees by day. With hard work, we managed to raise a waterproof roof over our heads before the rains came. And then we kept building. Every day, a little more, until we had constructed a new world for ourselves.

EPILOGUE

The Promised Land

The day after the roof went up at Walker Creek, I boarded a train to San Francisco. It was nighttime when I stepped onto the platform in Oakland. Uncle Tony emerged from the darkness to give me a hug. "Now wasn't that easy?" he said.

That summer he started taking me to punk rock shows on Gilman Street in Berkeley. The music was angry and tore at my ears. It was just what I needed, and I threw myself with abandon into the gladiatorial pit of slam dancers. I was hit from all sides and thrown back and forth. But I hit back just as hard, driving my shoulder into the man next to me until he went down. And then I helped him back up. Under the strange rules of chivalry in the punk community, if you went down everyone around you stopped to pick you up.

"How old are you?" screamed a curious punk with a mohawk and multiple facial piercings.

"Twelve," I screamed back.

"That's fucking awesome that your parents let you do this!"

"I don't have parents!" I screamed back.

"That's even fucking awesomer!"

One night Uncle Tony and I stood outside of a Circle Jerks concert to cool off. A skinhead ran out of the club and into the street in front of us, where he was immediately struck by a car.

"Somebody call an ambulance!" yelled Uncle Tony as we stepped off the curb to come to his assistance. But before we could get to him, the skinhead jumped back up, pounded himself on the chest, and roared.

"That's what I'm fucking talking about!" I yelled at him.

"Fuck yeah!" he yelled, and we ran back into the club together, colliding into everyone in our path. After what I had been through, I felt like I had been struck by a car too. The secret was to keep dancing.

When I came back to Washington at the end of the summer I had a shaved head, black clothing adorned with skeletons, and a skateboard under my arm. Claudia didn't recognize me when she met me at the Amtrak station in Seattle. I'd grown taller than she was, and she said I looked scary.

"Good," I said. "I *am* scary."

I returned to Stanwood Middle School for eighth grade. Over the summer I'd grown from one of the shortest kids in the class to one of the tallest. I carried my skateboard with me wherever I went and toted around a backpack full of weapons. For the first time in my life no one tried to mess with me.

By the end of the year, my hair had grown back, and I had outgrown my black clothing. I didn't need the punk rock anymore. My hunger to smash and destroy had been sated, and now I wanted to get back to building myself a rewarding future. A future with comfort and certainty, away from the precipice of constant risk. I knew the path out of our subsistence lifestyle led through college. By the glow of the candles I renewed my commitment to academic success each night, calculating cosines and reading Melville in the flickering light. I kept up my study of all things Jewish too, convinced that Judaism was my only path out of spiritual poverty. And I returned to the stage, making second homes for myself in the drama departments at the high school and the local community college. In the summers I drove heavy equipment in the Skagit Valley pea fields on the twelve-hour night shift. The massive pod strippers shook the Earth, rendered me temporarily deaf, but brought in enough extra income to keep our car running.

I stayed focused on the future, but I also stayed armed, assembling a massive arsenal of weapons, including a semi-automatic M14 rifle with a ten-round clip that I bought at the Barter Fair in Okanogan, throwing knives, survival knives, boot knives, bayonets, machetes, and a host of BB and pellet guns.

The obsession with weapons and, increasingly, all things military was not just my reaction to feeling powerless at the hands of Leopoldo. It was also a symptom of generational rebellion and in it I was not alone. I had the good fortune to come of age at Walker Creek with two boys my own age: Quan and Mason. We three, and others like us, instinctively gravitated toward militarism because it was the opposite of everything our parents stood for. If they were going to lecture us about love and peace and organic salad, we were going to embrace blood and war and K-rations. Together we formed the Walker Creek Community Defense Force and the Walker Valley Rangers, paramilitary groups that drew on our fellow *counter*-counter-cultural brethren. We were mostly just for pretend—weekend war games—but some of our incursions into off-road vehicle parks and a nearby Boy Scout camp crossed a line. I was arrested a couple of times and narrowly avoided juvenile hall. Still, a hard core of us clung together, sending ourselves on patrols farther and farther into the wilderness for days at a time.

After a while I realized our forest patrols weren't about playing war anymore. They allowed us to experience camaraderie in the face of adversity. We were pushing ourselves to the limits to prove that we were men. These were coming-of-age rituals, and we savored the beauty of the wilderness surrounding Walker Creek. Lush little valleys of temperate rainforest and misty evergreen mountainsides that took our breath away. In the raw, untamed wilderness, I experienced the mysticism of King David's 104th Psalm and felt God breathing, renewing the majesty of creation with every breath.

I had stumbled onto monotheism on my own as a young child, and now I began to look at the world through the lens of the Torah. I recognized myself in young Moses wandering through the wilderness, preparing to reconnect with his people. One day, as the sun was setting on our camp at the summit of a hill, I found myself reading the poetry of Yehuda Halevi aloud into the gathering darkness, a rifle sprawled across my lap. I realized that the poetry would sound just as good without the rifle, maybe better.

So Judaism became my rebellion. I had come to believe that everything that animated my mother was painfully contrived. Her 1970s Wiccan spirituality, her Marxist political perspective, her anarchist Utopia. These were all fabricated fads as outdated as their human creators. I craved authenticity. A tradition with roots that sunk all the way back into the mists of prehistory. I found what I was looking for in the ancient spirituality of the Land of Israel. It was the one and only original, and I would accept no imitations, additions, or substitutions.

As my mother began to anticipate my theological progression into Orthodoxy, she cautioned me: "You realize that you're subscribing to a rule-based, patriarchal religion?" I hadn't thought about it that way before, but it made perfect sense. For a kid who grew up without rules and without a father, could there be anything better?

My years at the Walker Creek commune gave me dignity and peace of mind, but were a struggle nonetheless. We were completely off the grid—no running water, no electricity, no refrigeration, no toilet. Between the ages of twelve and seventeen, I was the man of the house, and I spent much of my time chopping wood, hauling water, and generally fighting to survive the elements. Walker Creek was a politically conscious, agrarian, consensus-based community in the mountains. Our landmates were refugees recovering from the nearby Love Family commune, and were sick of charismatic leaders and empty platitudes. For my mother, Walker Creek was something like the Utopia she had been searching for her entire life, but for me it was never more than a temporary place of refuge. The *actual* Promised Land had become my promised land.

My ticket out of Walker Creek came in the form of a full scholarship to Oberlin College. I didn't know one college from another, but Oberlin's brochure boldly asked: "Think one person can change the world?" I couldn't tell if the slogan was meant to be inspirational or ironic, but either way, it appealed to me. In the middle of the cornfields of Ohio, I threw myself into world-changing discussions that lasted through the night. I met young people from all walks of life who actually read books and cared about issues the way I did. I graduated with a triple major in Judaic/Near-Eastern Studies, Politics, and Environmental Studies, but felt that my education was not complete without learning more about my heritage.

I'd started teaching myself to read and write Hebrew when I was in middle school and, by the time I stepped off the plane in Israel, I spoke it well enough to tell my cabdriver: "After two thousand years I've come home!"

He responded: "Welcome home, brother!"

Everyone responded that way, and I fell in love with the land and the people of Israel. I studied at Ben-Gurion University in the Negev Desert for a year and then learned at yeshivas in the ancient holy cities of Jerusalem and Tsfat. Poring over ancient texts in the Galilee—chanting and dancing, fasting and praying—Judaism was all I'd hoped it would be.

Below the house of study in Tsfat, I built a home for myself out of an old cave at the edge of a catacomb complex. I was finding strength and peace on my spiritual quest, but I knew I wasn't ready to stay long-term. Sequestering myself in the house of study felt too much like I was running away from reality. From my cave on the mountainside, I applied to law school back in the United States. From what I had seen, lawyers were the exemplars of success in America, and were uniquely qualified to shepherd the poor and powerless through the chaos of the legal system. I wanted to be such a person.

When I was accepted at Berkeley Law, I packed my bags with sublime memories of Israel and new excitement for America. I had been raised to believe that America was the Evil Empire, an oppressive Babylon of deceit and greed. But now that I had traveled through Central America, Europe, North Africa, and Israel, I knew that no one could top America for freedom and opportunity. Where else could an urchin raised on a tree stump find the gates of a top law school open to him? And where else could I finally achieve that sense of normalcy I'd always dreamed of?

When I came to Berkeley, I brought Uncle Tony with me to the campus and walked him to Sproul Plaza. "Well, Tony, this is it," I said. But he didn't respond. When I was in Israel Tony had suffered a nervous breakdown, lost his job, and become homeless for a time. I later learned that he'd struggled with alcoholism for years. "Tony, I'm a student here now, just like you always said." I didn't see any recognition on his face. He was partially deaf, and the antipsychotic drugs were visibly shackling his mind. "How ironic is this?" I told him. "I finally fulfill your dream and you're not here to see it."

Tony turned to me slowly and, in his thick drugged voice, said: "Now, wasn't that easy?"

Three years later I brought him with me to my law school graduation. When I came off the stage with my diploma in hand I thought he'd repeat his catchphrase. But he didn't. He just smiled and said: "We did it."

I graduated from law school with every blessing I could have asked for: my life partner and wife, Leah, a house in trendy North Berkeley, and a job as a high-paid attorney at a top corporate law firm. Over time, I was also blessed with three delightful daughters. I had finally overcome the adversity of my childhood, burying the many hardships of my past under the bounty of the American Dream.

Given these many blessings, I did my best to give back, regularly taking advantage of pro bono opportunities to advocate for the less fortunate. One of these projects—the case of Deborah Peagler—changed my life. Deborah was only fifteen years old when she was taken from her home in South Central Los Angeles by a pimp and drug dealer who systematically and brutally abused her for six years. The police failed to protect her, and when she finally ran away from him, the pimp tracked her down and tried to bring her back. He was stopped by friends of Deborah's mother who strangled him to death with an extension cord. The 1982 killing was investigated by Operation Hardcore, a shadowy group of Los Angeles prosecutors who called themselves the Gunslingers and boasted a 100 percent conviction rate. These prosecutors suppressed key information and, relying on perjured testimony and false evidence, sought the death penalty against Deborah, alleging that she had had her "boyfriend" killed for life insurance proceeds.

By the time I took Deborah's case in 2002 she had already served twenty years of a life sentence. What followed was a seven-year grueling crusade that consumed a third of my waking hours and garnered nationwide media coverage. By the time we won Deborah her release, we had removed an office of a thousand prosecutors from the case for disqualifying conflicts of interest and called into question the ethics and efficacy of the entire criminal justice system. Our struggle to free Deborah Peagler was captured in the film *Crime After Crime*, but what the film didn't reveal was the deep personal satisfaction and sense of closure I received from helping to liberate an unjustly incarcerated survivor of domestic violence like Deborah.

When I took Deborah's case, I had been suppressing my memories of the Leopoldo years, and my willingness to represent her didn't have any conscious connection to my own experiences with domestic violence. But the nature of the representation soon exposed the parallels to my life, and my personal story became the focus of many media inquiries. I began telling people I took Deborah's case "for my mother." Deborah's plight was similar to Claudia's. The key difference was that Leopoldo didn't find us when we ran away. Deborah's batterer did, and he ended up dead. But only in writing this book did I discover that I also took Deborah's case for an even more personal reason. To prove to my ten-year-old self that I finally had the strength and the courage to protect someone from abuse.

Domestic violence is an unstable injustice. Once it is unleashed, you never know what damage it will cause. Some batterers abuse their families for years, and they get away with it, leaving the victims to pass it on to the next generation in an ongoing cycle of violence. While other batterers, like Deborah's, get a dose of what they've been giving and end up strangled to death. Leopoldo's fate was awkwardly somewhere in between. I finally stood up to him, but never got the chance to kill him. Although it pains me to admit it, it took me decades to see this as a good thing.

On our first night sleeping in the school bus on the commune at Walker Creek, I asked Claudia: "What if he finds us out here?"

"Don't worry," she said reassuringly. "I talked to Aviathar about our situation and he agreed that if Leopoldo finds us, he'll shoot him on sight, right through the head."

I slept well that night. Aviathar, the de facto patriarch of the commune, was my friend Quan's stepdad. He was tough and protective when he had to be, and inspiring and supportive the rest of the time. He became like a father to me and, if it hadn't been for his mentorship and positive role-modeling, I might have turned into a different kind of man.

But in the days that followed, I realized I didn't want Aviathar to protect us. I wanted to protect us myself. For the first year, I lived with the daily fear that Leopoldo would track us down and began training for the day of confrontation—lifting weights, doing push-ups and sit-ups, hacking at the air with machetes, and firing into Leopoldo-shaped targets. As the months went by, I stopped fearing the confrontation and began hoping for it, finally praying for the day he'd come stumbling into my sights.

But he didn't find us, and we never saw him again. The last we heard of him, he was being served with divorce papers while in jail for yet another assault on a police officer. Maybe they finally deported him, and he was executed on the tarmac in San Salvador like he told us he would be. It's remotely possible that he reformed his ways and became a righteous man. But I imagine that he's still alive somewhere, up to his old routine, beating the woman in his life and then apologizing and pressing raw meat to her face to bring down the swelling.

Until I began writing this book, my mother and I never discussed the abuse. We never even uttered the name *Leopoldo*. When we referred to that man, we called him Dickface, a term for him we still use. In the years that followed, I inserted an emotional distance between myself and my mother. Her marriage to Leopoldo was too much of a betrayal. I couldn't trust her anymore, and I implicitly forbade her from dating men again. When I was sixteen, a scrawny ice-climbing instructor named Willie showed up in her bed. I spent a couple of long nights sitting next to their slumbering forms, wrestling with whether or not I should drag him out into the snow and kick the shit out of him. I didn't. But I would have if he had so much as raised his voice at her.

As an adult, I pushed Leopoldo far from my mind. Although, every now and again I'd see a crime thriller from the 1970s, and halfway through the movie I'd realize that I already knew key parts of the plot because I'd heard them repackaged as part of Leopoldo's life story. In those moments, I would still feel pangs of illogical regret that I never had the chance for one last confrontation.

Claudia and me finally free from Leopoldo, Stanwood, Washington, 1988.

This finally changed when I found myself in the world's largest maximum-security prison for women, as Deborah's attorney. She was a new client then, and we were going down a list of questions. I asked her what her batterer would typically do when he was done whipping her. She told me that he would gently tend to her wounds with witch hazel, doctoring the red welts on her brown skin. He kept steaks in the fridge to heal her, she told me. The meat brought down the swelling. I stopped writing, and we both looked into the distance past the bars on the window.

And she said: "Isn't it funny how raw meat heals raw meat?"

I agreed that it was funny.

After a pause, she started thanking me again for taking her case. "I was a stranger to you," she said. "You didn't even know me and yet here you are."

"Here I am," I said. "I feel like I've known you for a long time."

After a silence, she said: "All I ever wanted was for him to leave me alone. That's all I wanted. But he came after us. He found us. You have to believe me. I didn't want him dead."

I believed her. I believed that, unlike me, this "convicted killer" never wanted her batterer dead. And there—in the prison—I was finally thankful that Leopoldo never did find me, waiting for him.

For years, all Claudia would say about the Leopoldo era was: "He didn't kill us. He made us stronger." For better or for worse she was right.

Claudia's Communist Jewish parents raised her with strange views of the world. One was that the world was binary. You were either on the side of the People or on the side of the Corporations. There was no in-between. Heroes of the People could beat their wives without tarnishing their goodness, and corporate executives could treat their families with abounding respect without meriting any. Another worldview was that violence in the home was just an inherited quirk of personality, not a moral failing. Grandma Harriette was abusive to Claudia as her mother had been before her, and her mother before her, and her father before her, all the way back to a pogrom in the Old Country where Great-Great-Great-Grandfather Avram Gedalia's parents were murdered in front of him. Claudia was also raised to believe that the Revolution could happen tomorrow. This was some strange translation of the Jewish messianic ideal transfigured into Marxist rhetoric. But it stressed that at any moment the entire paradigm we live in might suddenly shift. Therefore life planning and career building were naive wastes of time.

To a large extent, these beliefs shattered when Leopoldo's regime came crashing down. He may well have been on the side of the People, yet Claudia realized he was an evil man. Domestic violence wasn't a quirk, it was a deep moral failing. And the Revolution wasn't happening tomorrow nor, most likely, the day after.

In the years that followed, Claudia modified Timothy Leary's famous phrase "Turn on, tune in, drop out" by adding "and crawl back." After our escape from Leopoldo, we grew up together, my mother and me. When I went to college, she went to college. When I started a career, she started a career. After graduating from Western Washington University with a degree in journalism, she went on to work for seventeen years as an award-winning local journalist and another five years as an investigator for public interest law firms.

When I found my way back to Judaism, so did Claudia. Today she identifies as part of a Jewish community, and her granddaughters call her *Savta*, the Hebrew word for grandmother.

Despite her participation in mainstream society, my mother didn't completely abandon the world of the Spirits. She still relies on ESP more than most and is still waiting for the day when science catches up with our third eyes. Claudia eventually moved away from Walker Creek to be closer to my family in the Bay Area, but she still can't bring herself to live anywhere without an open forest nearby to slip into should the need arise.

She has recently taken up political mural-painting again, but she is also volunteering as a domestic violence counselor. To some degree she still walks in an awkward gray area, participating in the counter-culture and in mainstream society without being entirely comfortable in either.

People sometimes ask me: If you could do your childhood all over again, would you grow up in the cushy suburbs you always dreamed of? And I always give a complicated answer. As a father, I have done everything in my power to give my children the stable, secure, and comfortable childhood I never had. But I also recognize that while my early life was difficult, I received an unconventional and powerful education that taught me self-reliance, righteousness, and empathy like no other. In the end, I would rather slog back down those trails at my mother's side again. There are many ways to judge a mother, but I think the best way is to look at the man her son grew up to be.

When my mother saw *Crime After Crime* in the theater, including the scene of me saying that Deborah Peagler was a metaphoric extension of my own mother, her comment was: "I never knew it affected you that much."

"Of course it did," I said.

"But it was only for a few years."

I didn't know how to respond. This book was my response. Writing it reopened old, imperfectly healed wounds but helped to heal them properly. As part of my interviews with my mother about the Leopoldo years, she e-mailed me her translations of the Spanish love songs he used to play for her. And she added this note:

> *Listening to these again, I recall how it felt to dance to them. How sweet it felt. But what should be a memory of love is now a memory of having been used in a con game. That's a pain that remains with me while the bruises have long since healed. That and the regret for the lost energy, the lost dreams, the lost years, when I could have found real love or accomplished something worthwhile with all my efforts.*
>
> *And the horrible loss of the last years of your childhood. I'm so sorry.*

I cried when I read the end of her message. After twenty-five years, it was the apology I'd been waiting for. It was short, but it was the beginning.

If I do nothing further in my life, may it always be said about me that I never owed that kind of apology to my three daughters. The cycle of violence ended with me.

ACKNOWLEDGMENTS

Joshua gets all the credit for fitting the battle, but he had thousands of friends help him tear down the walls of Jericho. I am profoundly grateful to the many people who helped me build this book on the foundations of my past.

The idea for the book was conceived and nurtured by my wife, Leah. I'd been writing fiction for years, circulating my stories past her before diligently filing them away in a drawer. "They're good," she would say, "but you need to write about your childhood first. The truth is so much more interesting than the stuff in the drawer. Seriously, who else lived in an ice cream truck?" This book was Leah's project for me and, once I found the courage to tell the dark parts of the story, she encouraged me, supported me, and edited me every step of the way.

The courage to write this book was given to me by Deborah Peagler in a maximum security prison for women. While working on Deborah's case, Elizabeth Fernandez of the *San Francisco Chronicle* wanted to write an article about my personal motivation for championing the rights of battered women. I'd never talked publicly about the Leopoldo years, and the thought of resurrecting those disturbing memories and advertising them in the newspaper seemed too much to bear. But Deborah turned me around. "Joshua, you told me telling *my* story would inspire people to help stop the cycles of violence. If it's true for me, it's gotta be true for you." She was right, of course, and I agreed to do the story.

The irrepressible Josie Lehrer enlisted me for her innovative theatrical production, the *Men's Story Project,* designed to challenge society's conceptions of masculinity. Telling my story in my own words onstage was an emotionally raw experience, but the positive response I received was overwhelming. In the following months, I continued to write and perform short pieces about my childhood at spoken word events produced by my wife, and the vision for this book began to take shape in my mind.

When my dear friend Yoav Potash premiered *Crime After Crime*, his inspiring documentary film about the odyssey to free Deborah Peagler, at the 2011 Sundance Film Festival, he immortalized Deborah's beautiful legacy, chalked up dozens of awards, and introduced my story to the world. The dynamic Sue Turley of ro*co films paired *Crime After Crime* with the Oprah Winfrey Network and introduced me to Beth Gebhard of Lightshop Media. Beth became the fairy godmother for this book; everyone should be blessed to have such a lovely and effervescent patron. Elise Bernhardt, Aviva Weintraub, Marion Dienstag, Andy Ingall, and the other magnificent people at the Foundation for Jewish Culture brought me to Lincoln Center, and Jane Friedman graciously hosted me. They introduced me to the incomparable Karen Gantz. Karen believed in me before she even met me and stood by me every step of the way as my extraordinary agent. The visionary Elisabeth Dyssegaard, editor in chief at Hyperion Books, believed in this book as much as I did, if not more. Elisabeth promised me that writing my story would be a rewarding experience, and she knew what she was talking about.

The Talmud says that when two intellects debate they sharpen each other like iron against iron. After a year of close collaboration and much debate with my tireless editor Matt Inman, I know my intellect is sharper, and I hope the same goes for Matt. The manuscript I first presented to Matt displayed a casual disregard for chronological order that perhaps only Kurt Vonnegut would have appreciated and equaled at least two books in length. With abounding patience, diligence, and expertise, Matt helped me shape my many childhood stories into the coherent narrative that now fills the pages of this book.

When I began putting my stories down on paper, I realized I was blessed (or cursed) with a trove of remarkably detailed memories from my very early years. Some of this can be credited to my better-than-average memory, but much of it is attributable to the fundamentally unforgettable nature of my childhood—a series of dramatic adventures stuffed into that high-resolution part of the brain where fight-or-flight moments are recorded. But even with all the detailed memories, much of the context was missing, particularly early on. Only my mother could fill in the gaps, and she readily agreed to consult with me on the book. Week after week I treated her to Sunday lunch and interviewed her about every detail of my childhood. The other Berkeley mothers in the lunchtime crowd looked on jealously. How come their grown sons weren't showing the same interest in them? I'm sure their jealousy would have turned to pity if they had known the purpose of our conversations was to splash my mother's every parenting decision across the pages of a book. Yet my brave mother came to lunch every week because she agreed that my story needed to be told. It takes considerable courage to bare your most intimate secrets for all the public to see. And it takes even greater courage to trust your son to do it for you. For over a year, my mother walked with me back through the strange saga of my childhood, and cast light onto the dark patches of my memory. She generously shared with me from her dream journals and diaries, and gave me photographs and artwork that helped to illuminate my past. This book would not have been possible without her invaluable assistance. Thanks also go to Uncle Tony for remembering a thousand little stories, and Crazy John and Erica for walking back with me through difficult terrain.

Geoffrey Chaucer wrote the first novels in the English language while simultaneously excelling in his day job at the Port of London. He was, no doubt, aided in the success of this double endeavor by his wonderful friends and colleagues at the Port. My Port people include: David Alexander the Great, Mary Richardson, Laurice Henry-Ross, Althea Roberts-Griffin, Christine Tam, and Pamela Kershaw. My intrepid readers were Noah Barish, Debbie Weinstein, Yoav Potash, Mary Richardson, Michael Wood, and Frank and Sasha Chordas. Officer James Alexander gave me peace of mind. My *havruta* and personal physician Mark Fenig lavishly hosted me on my trips back east, and he and Jessica Silver-Greenberg made me feel at home in New York. A number of brilliant people consulted with me on various aspects of the book, including its title and arrangement. These included Andrea Barton-Elson, Sarah Crow, Fabio Baum, Michael Kaye, Steve Chabon, and Joe Fendel. The Estimable Members of the Jewish Men's Rap Group provided invaluable nourishment for my soul throughout, and no doubt would have provided profound substantive contributions had various motions been seconded rather than sequestered in subcommittee for unlimited debate. The Members include Raphael Goldman, Devon Strolovitch (who provided extra linguistics advice and radio exposure), R' Joseph Schwartz, Jeffrey Israel, and Daniel Kennemer.

My greatest gratitude goes to my three delightful daughters, who sacrificed many many hours of Abba time so that he could revisit his own childhood. And to the Most High, I say *Yishtabach Shemo*!